*Employment problems
and policies in
developing countries*

The essays in this book reflect the experience of an
international group of economists who had the
opportunity of participating at first hand in the planning
process in Morocco. Their stay had been sponsored by
the Center for Research on Economic Development of
the University of Michigan, and spanned the years 1970
to 1973.
Although the case of Morocco has been chosen as a
typical example, the method of analysis of most papers
is sufficiently general to suit wider interests as well.
The approach is to view employment policy as an
integral part of general economic policy. The papers
cover the whole range of fiscal and monetary policy,
of trade policy and education policy. They offer
original suggestions for wage policy and industrial
protection. The final paper contains a thorough
evaluation of Labour mobilisation programmes.
The editor, Willy van Rijckeghem, served on a number
of advisory missions to developing nations, and is
the author of econometric models for Argentina,
Brazil and Puerto Rico, in previous collections of
essays, published in the sixties.

Employment problems
and policies in
developing countries

The case of Morocco

Edited by Willy van Rijckeghem

1976

Rotterdam University Press

188360

Preface

The essays in this book reflect the experience of an international group of economists who had the opportunity of participating at first hand in the planning process in Morocco. Their stay was sponsored by the Center for Research on Economic Development (CRED) of the University of Michigan, and spanned the years 1970 to 1973. Some time in 1973, after the work on the 1973–1977 development plan was finished, the idea was conceived of holding a conference at which Morocco's development problems could be analysed and discussed. The country's employment problem was then selected as a central and unifying theme. Several members of the group had invested a substantial amount of their time and effort in the draft of an employment programme and the formulation of a number of policy proposals.

Few countries suffer from such an acute employment problem as does Morocco at this moment. The growth rate of the economically active population is close to four per cent. per annum, a full point higher than the growth rate of population. This is a consequence of rising participation rates, especially for women, who had traditionally remained outside the labour market. Especially the urban areas, as elsewhere, have witnessed an excessive swelling of their labour force, probably at an annual rate of close to five per cent. At the same time, the absorptive capacity of the economy has been limited, and did not increase by more than two per cent. per annum. The consequences of a gap of this importance defy description: before the end of this decade, if no drastic measures are taken, open unemployment in Morocco may become as high as one million people, nearly a quarter of the labour force. This is aggravated by the fact that the traditional outlet for excess labour supply, emigration, has almost come to a full stop, as a consequence of the protective policies of the EEC-countries. It comes therefore as no surprise that the Moroccan planning authorities have selected the reduction of unemployment as one of their major objectives for this decade, together with the related targets of a more equitable income and land distribution, as well as a balanced regional development.

Although the case of Morocco has been chosen as a typical example, the analytic approach of most papers is sufficiently general to appeal to wider interests as well. This is especially true for the papers which treat employment policy as an integral part of general economic policy. The papers in Part I are primarily concerned with the impact of short-term economic policies: the paper by Wayne Snyder traces the impact of fiscal policy on effective demand and employment from 1952 to 1972; Van Rijckeghem proposes an analytic framework for estimating the effect of credit restrictions on short-term employment and output decisions in the non-agricultural sector; John D. Shilling describes the trade policies that were followed after independence and how they affected the implementation of the subsequent development plans. The papers in Part II cover the long-term, structural, policies which must be conceived if the employment problem is to be tackled in a more thorough way. The imaginative proposal by William P. Travis to promote industrial employment by conditional protection should appeal to both free-traders and infant-industry protectionists, and may well become a classic in the literature on the subject. The more controversial, but logically faultless proposal by Karsten Laursen to introduce a wage subsidy scheme, should even increase the attractiveness of the conditional protection proposal. His assumption of homogeneous labour is relaxed in the following paper in Part III, where George Psacharopoulos measures the earnings determinants in a mixed labour market, and comes out with a very strong case in favour of primary education. The book finishes with a thorough evaluation by Rajaona Andriamananjara of the Moroccan experience with a labour mobilisation programme during the sixties.

The recent years have witnessed a surge of interest in the issues related to employment in developing countries. To a large extent, this has been due to the impulse of the International Labour Office, which has sponsored a World Employment Programme, of which Mr. L. Emmerij, Chief of the Employment Planning and Promotion Department, has been the driving force. We were therefore very grateful that Mr. Emmerij not only agreed to deliver the introductory address, which is reprinted here, but participated actively in the discussions to which he brought his vast experience and insight. It may therefore seem appropriate to consider the proceedings of this conference as our modest contribution to the World Employment Programme.

The conference took place in Brussels on March 28th–30th, 1974, on the campus of the Free University of Brussels (VUB). The organising committee was composed of Mr. Jef Rens, Chairman of the Belgian Labour Council and of the Council for Development Aid, my colleague H. Glejser and myself. Financial support is gratefully acknowledged from NFWO, the National Fund for Scientific Research, and the University itself. The staff of the CEMS-research center, and particularly Mr. E. Vanderlinden, cheerfully assisted us in carrying out the numerous logistic tasks.

Les Rousses   *W.v.R.*

Contents

Abbreviations

BRPM = Bureau de Recherches et Participations Minières (Office for Research and Participation in Mining)

CCMF = Comité du Crédit et du Marché Financier (Credit and Capital Market Committee)

CEMS = Center for Econometrics and Management Science (Free University of Brussels)

CRED = Center for Research on Economic Development (University of Michigan, Ann Arbor)

CSPN = Conseil Supérieur du Plan et de la Promotion Nationale (Supreme Council of Planning and of Promotion Nationale)

DGPN = Délégation Générale à la Promotion Nationale (General Delegation to Promotion Nationale)

DH = (or MDH) Dirham

DPDR = Direction du Plan et du Développement Régional (Directorate for Planning and Regional Development)

DRS = Defense and Restoration of Soils

FAO = Food and Agricultural Organisation

GDP = Gross domestic product

ILO = International Labour Office (Organisation)

IMF = International Monetary Fund

IVS = International Voluntary Service

LDC = Less Developed Country

OCE = Office Central d'Exportation (Export Marketing Board)

OCP = Office Chérifien des Phosphates (National Phosphates Board)

OECD = Organisation for Economic Cooperation and Development

ORMVAH = Office Régional de Mise en Valeur Agricole du Haouz (Marrakech) (Regional Office for the Agricultural Development of the Haouz (Marrakesh))

ORMVAT = Office Régional de Mise en Valeur Agricole du Tafilalt (Ksar Es Souk) (Regional Office for the Agricultural Development of the Tafilalt (Ksar Es Souk))

PIB	=	Produit Intérieur Brut (Gross Domestic Product)
PN	=	Promotion Nationale
SCET	=	Société Centrale (Française) pour l'Equipement du Territoire ((French) Central Firm for the Outfitting of the (National) Territory)
SMAG	=	Salaire Minimum Agricole Garanti (Agricultural Minimum Wage)
SMIG	=	Salaire Minimum Industriel Garanti (Industrial Minimum Wage)
SRI	=	Stanford Research Institute
USAID	=	United States Agency for International Development
USPL 480	=	United States Public Law 480 (basic document for the U.S. surplus commodity disposal program)
WEP	=	World Employment Programme

Contributors

Rajaona Andriamananjara received his Ph. D. in Economics from the University of Michigan in 1971, after which he joined the Young Professionals' Program of the International Monetary Fund for one year. In January 1973 he was recalled by the Government of Madagascar to serve as technical adviser in the Directorate of Planning; in addition he is currently a member of the executive board of the Central Bank of the Malagasy Republic. He has also served on the Committee on Reform of the International Monetary System and Related Issues (Committee of Twenty), first as an adviser, then as a deputy.

Louis Emmerij was with the Directorate for Scientific Affairs, OECD, from 1963 to 1970. Since 1971 Head of the Employment and Development Department of the International Labour Organisation (ILO), World Employment Programme. Is the author and co-author of several books, most recently: *Can the School Build a New Social Order?* (Elsevier).

Karsten Laursen is Professor of Economics and Dean of the Faculty of Law, Economics, and Political Science at the University of Aarhus, Denmark. He has been economic adviser to the government of Colombia (1966–1968) as a member of the University of Harvard Development Advisory Service, and to the government of Morocco (1972–1973) as a member of the University of Michigan mission. He now participates in a research group on growth perspectives of the Danish economy. He has written books on monetary growth and development subjects, and articles on different problems of economic theory and policy.

George Psacharopoulos received his Ph. D. in Economics from the University of Chicago. After teaching at a number of American universities he joined in 1969 the London School of Economics where he is now a Lecturer in the Department of Economics. Combining teaching and research, he has served as a consultant to several international organisations. His main interest concentrates in the areas of macro-educational planning and the determinants of labour earnings. He has published numerous books and articles on educational subjects.

John D. Shilling received his Ph. D. in Economics from the Massachusetts Institute of Technology in 1971. Prior to completing his degree he worked in Ghana on a research project in trade and development sponsored by Williams College and taught Development Economics at Boston College. He then spent two years as an economic adviser to the Government of Morocco Planning Secretariat helping to prepare the 1973–1977 Economic Plan. In 1973 he joined the Comparative Analysis and Projections Division of the International Bank for Reconstruction and Development.

Wayne W. Snyder received his Ph. D. in Economics from Harvard University. For twenty years he has combined teaching, research and economic development advisory work which has taken him for extended periods of residence in Cyprus, France, Greece, Morocco, Turkey and Vietnam. From 1970 until 1972 he was Project Director for the University of Michigan's Economic Advisory Group to the Moroccan Planning Secretariat. Since 1972 he has been at Sangamon State University in Springfield, Illinois, where he is presently Chairman of the Department of Economics and Coordinator for International Education.

William P. Travis received his Ph. D. in Economics from Harvard University in 1961 and has taught international economics, economic history, economic development, and economic theory at Harvard University, MIT, Brandeis University, The Indian Institute of Management (Calcutta), The University of California (San Diego), the Institut de Statistiques et Economie Appliquées in Rabat, and, since January 1974, at Indiana University in Bloomington. He served for a year and a half as economic adviser to the Moroccan Planning Secretariat in Rabat, where he was engaged primarily in elaborating a proposal for a Moroccan commercial policy. His paper in this volume is an outgrowth of his work in Morocco. His other writings on commercial policy include *The Theory of Trade and Protection* (Harvard University Press, 1964) and several journal articles. He is currently working on methods for measuring prospectively the gains from trade and direct and indirect foreign investment.

Willy van Rijckeghem is Professor of Economics at the Free University of Brussels and Lecturer of Econometrics at the State University of Ghent, where he received his doctorate in 1961. He was Visiting Associate Professor at the University of North Carolina (Chapel Hill) and served on various advisory missions to developing countries, sponsored by American Universities. He has contributed to several collections of essays on economic development and policy, with econometric models for Argentina, Brazil and Puerto Rico. He was a member of the University of Michigan advisory group in 1972–1973.

Introduction: The world employment programme

L. Emmerij

1. WHY?

In many respects, the results of the first United Nations Development Decade (the 1960's) were disappointing. However, it remains a fact that the average rate of economic growth of the developing countries during that decade amounted to around 5 per cent. with several countries reaching the 7 to 8 per cent. mark. In spite of these very respectable rates of economic growth sustained over a relatively long period, it became 'suddenly' clear towards the end of the decade that the employment situation was deteriorating in the face of the growing number of people looking for productive income-earning opportunities. Simultaneously, the awareness grew of a worsening in income distribution trends and the consequent increase in the number of people living in absolute poverty. These interrelated observations also apply to those developing countries whose rate of economic growth was far above the average.

What had happened? How can this situation be explained? The economic and social development stiategy and approach which has been applied in the bulk of the developing countries since the end of the Second World War, and which is at the base of economic and social development planning and policies, can be traced back to the theoretical work of W. Arthur Lewis and Fei and Ranis [1]. In a nutshell, the approach inherent in this 'labour surplus model' amounts to the following. Within a country's economy two sectors can be distinguished: the modern sector and the traditional. The modern sector is supposed to be the engine of economic growth which will put into motion and move the entire convoy of economic and social development. The traditional sector delivers the cheap petrol for the engine in the form of labour which is present in abundant quantities. In this manner, unemployed and underemployed persons in the traditional sector move to the modern sector where they are all supposed to be fully and productively employed in the

1

rapidly expanding industrial and service sectors. Thus, the planners and political decision-makers should fully concentrate on the growth and expansion of the modern sector. An important assumption of this extremely simplified version of the labour surplus model is that wages and salaries in the modern sector remain constant in real terms as long as the supply of labour from the traditional sector remains abundant.

But how did this situation develop in reality? In actual fact, the modern sector developed into a highly capital-intensive (partly because wages and salaries did not remain constant there), high labour-productivity enclave concentrated in a few cities – an enclave of steel and glass where a handful of privileged people received incomes and salaries far above the country's average. In the meantime, the demographic horse continued its gallop, causing a population increase of $2\frac{1}{2}$ to $3\frac{1}{2}$ per cent. per year. At the same time, because of the bright lights and high salaries in the cities, the rural/urban migration towards the urban-based modern sector became more and more important – further stimulated by ill-planned educational policies and expansion.

In retrospect, we can now say that the modern sector, because of its capital-intensive character and its high labour productivity, could and did develop very fast, but created much less productive employment than was anticipated. Because of the rapid population increase, the educational explosion and the much slower growth of the traditional sector, under-employment in the rural areas was transformed into visible and open unemployment in the urban sector which, in turn, led to the creation and expansion of the 'urban informal sector', as it is termed [2].

This conventional development model was therefore based on the assumption that growth, with emphasis on the modern sector, was in itself *the* solution to development because, so the assumption went, the fruits of this growth would automatically and *within a short period of time*, spread to the less privileged sectors of the economy and to the poor segments of the population. This assumption has proved to be wrong. The economic growth based on this model concentrated on a few modern and capital-intensive branches of manufacturing and services which remained enclaves and which had a very small spread effect indeed. In this manner, it was possible to observe respectable growth indicators which, however, were hiding deterioration trends in the employment and income distribution situations.

In retrospect, it is amazing how long social scientists, civil servants and politicians considered all those facts as variations of the labour surplus model which could be accommodated in the existing theory with a small change here and there. It is amazing that more people did not realize at an earlier stage that the realistic solution would be an alternative development model focusing much more explicitly and *directly* on improving productivity and incomes in the low productivity sectors of the economy.

But what do we mean by the employment and income distribution problems? Although the notion of income distribution does not need further elaboration, it is worth clarifying what we mean by the employment problem. The employment problem, as we see it in the World Employment Programme, has three major aspects. The first is, of course, overt unemployment where income is zero. This is particularly dramatic but in reality, as a proportion of the overall employment problem, it is, quantitatively speaking, relatively small. The more so if we take into account the fact that, in terms of heads of family who fall into this category, the numbers become even smaller. In other words, and without minimizing the seriousness of overt unemployment, it is mainly a problem of dependence within the family. The most important aspect of the employment problem is the second, constituted of all those people who are not unemployed by any conventional criteria (on the contrary, they are often overemployed in terms of hours of work per day), but who only receive a poverty return for their labour. Here, therefore, we find all those people whose productivity is low, who are under-utilised and whose income falls below what has come to be called the poverty line. Finally, the third aspect might almost be called the psychological or frustration dimension of the employment problem. The most spectacular illustration of this aspect is the problem of the educated unemployed, i.e. people who could possibly find a job which, however, falls short of their aspirations and expectations through which they are led to believe they have an automatic right to a given status in terms of professional hierarchy linked to a given level of income.

The second, or poverty aspect is clearly the most important but this does not mean that the others are therefore unimportant. For young people to start their lives, whether they have had a certain number of years of education or not, with a frustrating round of job-seeking, can hardly be called a good beginning and may have important consequences on their subsequent actions. The low productivity and malutilisation of many people in the labour force are obvious es obstacl to a higher and better-spread economic growth.

In order to face the employment problem as just defined, and given its origin in what we have called the conventional model of economic growth, we must change this model of economic and social development. It is not possible to solve the employment problem effectively by just

3

tinkering with it. Much more drastic and radical action is required.

2. HOW?

The main objectives of the World Employment Programme can be
deduced immediately from the preceding discussion. At the most general
level they are:
  i. to reformulate economic and social development planning and policies,
     within a comprehensive development strategy, which can tackle much
     more effectively the problems of employment and income distribution
     as defined here; and
 ii. to assist countries in implementing the strategies or parts thereof.

These are extraordinarily ambitious objectives and people might wonder
what an international organisation – even if it works in conjunction with
the entire United Nations family as we obviously must do, given the
scope of the World Employment Programme – can possibly do in the face
of such a complex problem which has its roots in the entire economic and
social development fabric. The answer I would like to give to this important question is that we must set up means of action which, in their
ambition, are commensurate with the objectives, but we must be modest
in our expectations, because the political decision-making process obviously remains in the hands of national governments and not under the
control of international organisations.
  The employment problem, as defined, was totally new not only to the
International Labour Organisation but also to everybody else! In view
of its many dimensions, it has been necessary to design a variety of means
of action under the World Employment Programme in order to meet the
objectives. Four major and new means of action have thus been created:
  i. comprehensive employment strategy missions;
 ii. policy-orientated research programmes;
iii. country employment teams; and
 iv. regional employment teams.

The main purpose of what we call comprehensive employment strategy
missions has been to assist the governments of certain developing countries
in trying to define with more precision an 'employment-orientated
development strategy'. What does such a strategy look like? How does
it differ from the tried recipes, i.e. conventional development strategies?
Is the new strategy really significantly different from the conventional one,

4

and does it imply for the governments concerned a major break-away from policies pursued hitherto? These are some of the questions to which the first comprehensive employment strategy missions (to Colombia, Sri Lanka, Iran, Kenya and the Philippines) addressed themselves.

Clearly, these missions had to work in a fog owing to the many unknown relationships which exist when one tries to shift from the monarchy to the coalition, i.e. where a variety of priority objectives have to be met simultaneously instead of focusing entirely on, say, growth of GDP. Because of this fog the employment mission reports[3] have only been able to perceive the contours of an 'employment-orientated development strategy'. It is one of the major tasks of the action-orientated research component of the World Employment Programme to ensure that the fog is dissipated, and that all the details of the new construction come out in the sunlight.

The first four missions have been the subject of an evaluation that took place in March 1973, and in which the Chiefs of Mission, representatives of the countries concerned, consultants, and various International Agencies took part[4]. It was the participants' considered opinion that, as pilot operations, these four missions had served their main purpose with a measure of success in many ways exceeding expectations. It was stressed that the missions had been successful in bringing to light the comprehensive character of the problem, by placing the employment issues squarely in the context of overall economic and social development policy. By doing so, the missions have been able to contribute significantly to a clarification of how the coalition can hope to turn itself into a forceful political reality. The missions have also shown that fundamental re-orientations are indeed necessary in the approach to development problems of both governments and international organisations. Another important contribution of the missions has been to open up avenues for research and policy which are already attracting the attention of social scientists, policy-making authorities and a number of international agencies. The reformulation of development problems and strategies pioneered by the missions has dramatized the prevailing ignorance of many aspects of the development process, and the corresponding requirements for more adequate statistical and other information about employment, income distribution and the structure of socio-economic institutions in the developing countries.

As mentioned a while ago, the policy-orientated research component should ensure that the contours of the new development strategy come out in full detail. The specific objectives and content of this part of our work are described in a document which has received quite a lot of atten-

5

tion [5]. Here we concentrate on the major components of an employment-orientated development strategy such as choice of techniques, income distribution, demographic factors, education and training, international trade, urban employment problems including the informal sector, emergency employment schemes, i.e. policy measures and projects which have short-term implications for the employment and income distribution situation. Each of these areas is headed by a Project Manager in Geneva who works with a small hard-core group of people assisted by a Steering Group composed of between six and ten well-known persons in the profession, who have spent the better part of their lives thinking about that specific problem, although not necessarily in relation to the employment and income distribution aspects. The Steering Groups meet regularly, but their members are in continuous contact with their respective Project Managers. Conceptual and synthetic work is being undertaken by the Geneva staff and the members of the Steering Group. But the bulk of the work consists of concrete country-based case studies in developing countries undertaken mainly by local institutions and individuals, sometimes in collaboration with our country and regional teams, members of the Steering Group or the hard-core Geneva staff. Whenever possible, these country case studies are related to the employment missions, either in the form of follow-up activities in order to give more specific answers to problems which these missions were not able to clarify sufficiently, or as preparatory activities before such an employment mission visits a country. It follows that the main purpose of these research activities can be summarized as follows:

i. to arrive at more concrete and detailed policy recommendations in areas and in countries where the present knowledge and information bases are insufficient; and

ii. to use the building blocks and stepping stones (which the individual studies of the research programme are) to arrive at a complete and operational alternative development strategy which is employment-orientated.

One of the main criticisms levelled at the comprehensive employment strategy missions is that they are 'hit-and-run' exercises: a swarm of high-level and extremely knowledgeable persons descends upon a country for a relatively short period of time, investigates the various components of an employment-orientated development strategy in a great hurry, writes a first draft of a report and leaves the country again as suddenly as it came. This is, of course, an exaggerated picture, but it does make the point that these missions do not always have enough time to formulate their recommendations in the full knowledge of the political, institutional

6

and administrative constraints under which the local political decision-makers and planners are working.

It is, therefore, natural that the idea has arisen to design a means of action under the World Employment Programme which maximizes the advantages of the comprehensive employment strategy missions, while minimizing the disadvantages. The major advantage of the missions is clear: the possibility of attracting the best people in a given field precisely because they are only asked to come for a relatively short period of time; another advantage is that they combine a great number of people specialized in various fields, whose interaction during the period of the mission can have, and has had, a very constructive cumulative effect. The major disadvantage is also clear – the short duration of their stay in the country.

In the course of the evaluation meeting of the first four comprehensive employment strategy missions, it was therefore suggested that one of the new forms of co-operation which might usefully be developed could be 'inter-agency teams of typically perhaps about six people spending up to two years or longer in a country to help put into operation measures of employment policy: the personnel of such teams, and their specializations, might change from time to time, to allow wider coverage of problems. Such teams might or might not be linked with shorter, comprehensive employment missions, preparing the ground for them, following up their work or doing both'.

It might be useful to spell out the interpretation we have given to this idea of longer-term country employment teams. The basis of such a country team will be a hard-core group of four to six people, who would spend a minimum of two years in the country concerned. Provision will be made in the project formulation for supplementing the work of this hard-core group by shorter-term, highly specific expertise in order to work on particular problem areas which cannot be properly handled by the hard-core group. Such additional expertise would be phased sequentially over the duration of the project, or simultaneously. In the latter case, there would be a kind of comprehensive employment mission built into the longer-term programme of the hard-core group. Whatever the approach adopted, it will be clear that this formula would come close to combining the advantages of the employment missions with the advantages inherent in a longer-term technical assistance venture. The hard-core group would be in touch with the political and institutional realities of the country, could prepare the background material necessary for the shorter-term, high-level experts, and would thus enable these consultants to obtain a maximum output without losing sight of the peculiarities of the specific country situation.

7

In addition, such country teams can be used in assisting countries both with designing *and* with implementing employment-orientated development strategies and projects, thus combining elaboration and follow-up activities.

Finally, there are the regional employment teams for Latin America, Asia and Africa whose main role it is to participate in the design of all WEP activities in their respective regions and as much as possible in their implementation. In this way, they will gradually take on an overall regional co-ordinating function. This will also help them to develop specific regional expertise, constantly up-dated and enriched and instantly available for application at the country level. The regional teams will thus become regional 'centres of knowledge' on employment and income distribution problems and policies where the accumulated experience and expertise of the WEP in the various regions is stored, digested and made available through training activities, assistance in building up national machinery for employment planning and policy, and publications.

3. FIRST RESULTS

When we talk about the results so far obtained in our work under the World Employment Programme, we must distinguish between results in terms of *new insight* into the complex interrelationships between output, productivity, employment and income distribution on the one hand, and results in terms of *actual changes* in employment and income distribution problems in developing countries as a result of more appropriate development strategies being adopted on the other. Both dimensions are important simply because one cannot be achieved without the other unless we believe that we already have all the answers and that it is merely a question of getting the known facts politically implemented. Few people would hold such an extreme position and it is therefore important to start by giving a few examples of results obtained in terms of 'new insight'. And when referring to first results, whether it be from a technical or political point of view, we should not lose sight of the fact that the World Employment Programme started only five years ago and became operational some four years ago. It must be clearly understood that employment and income distribution problems cannot be set straight overnight, precisely because doing so implies changing not only a nut or a bolt here and there, but the general machinery of development.

The first insight we obtained was to define more clearly both the dimension and the characteristics of the employment problem. This has already been presented in Section 1 above and is now widely accepted. But this was not so only a few years ago when most observers would leave out the whole poverty aspect of the problem and concentrate on the open unemployment problem and certain aspects of underemployment. It is this emphasis on the poverty dimension which, through income distribution, links the employment problem to overall economic and social questions. It is this same emphasis which has led many economists now to the conclusion that the overall rate of economic growth as an indicator for development is inadequate and that different weights must be given to increases in incomes of different social groups.

A second form of insight was arrived at by putting forward a quantitative relationship between the income distribution in a country on the one hand, and the employment problem on the other – a relationship which was different from the usual one hypothesized in economic literature. This conventional relationship was still dominated by the assumption that people with higher incomes also saved more and that therefore a skewed income distribution would be a good thing for higher savings, thus more investment, and so benefit economic growth and employment. There was not enough emphasis on possible negative aspects of a very uneven income distribution on the employment problem. Indeed, the high incomes frequently have a bizarre habit of leaving the country, savings are often placed abroad, or large parts of the incomes are spent on imported goods and, if produced locally, on capital-intensive goods. Low incomes, on the other hand, are spent much more on locally-produced, labour-intensive goods. In this manner, the uneven income distributions we observe in many countries not only reflect the employment problem, but also *cause* it. This negative relationship has been underlined earlier but only in recent years have attempts been made to quantify the positive aspects of a given change in income distribution on the creation of productive employment opportunities. A very interesting situation is thus developing, where employment creation becomes one of the most effective means of obtaining a more even income distribution, which in turn will further stimulate employment creation. For once we have an upward-spiralling circle rather than the famous vicious one.

A third and, to my mind, very important form of insight which is basic to the alternative development approach emerging from our preoccupation with employment and income distribution, is the role to be played by the urban informal and rural traditional sectors. I have already made reference to the concept of the urban informal sector earlier in this Introduction, referring to the Kenya employment report. Basically this sector embraces activities that are characterised by:

9

i. ease of entry;
ii. reliance on indigenous preferences;
iii. family ownership of enterprises;
iv. small-scale of operation;
v. highly labour-intensive technology;
vi. skills acquired outside the formal school system; and
vii. unregulated and competitive markets.

The bulk of employment in the informal sector, far from being only marginally productive, is, potentially at least, economically efficient and profit-making, though small in scale and limited by simple technologies, little capital, and suffering from lack of links with the modern (formal) sector. There is considerable evidence of technical change in the urban informal sector, as well as of regular employment at incomes above the average level attainable in small-holder agriculture. In most cases one can observe strong discrimination against the informal sector activities through such means as unrealistically high standards and licensing systems. It is the emerging view that most indigenous enterprises are small because of the structure of the economy in which a number of policy measures favour the modern formal sector. Equally, or even more, important is the competitive advantage enjoyed by large enterprises, especially as a result of state measures reducing the cost of capital (duty-free imports of capital goods, low rates of interest) and restricting competition (high tariffs, quotas, and building, health and safety regulations). It is not always certain whether many large-scale firms would be competitive relatively to small enterprises if they were required to compete without state favours.

Thus, a positive attitude on the part of the government towards the promotion of the informal sector is advocated. The strategy which is recommended in this respect would embrace the following measures:
  i. reviewing trade and commercial licensing with a view to eliminating unnecessary licences;
  ii. intensifying technical research and development on products suitable for fabrication in the informal sector;
  iii. attempting to increase government purchases of products and services obtainable from the informal sector; and
  iv. using large firms to train sub-contractors in the informal sector.

An analogous emphasis in the emerging new development strategy is put on the traditional agricultural sector. In general, the main strategy advocated here is also based on progressive modernization from the bottom up. It is recognized that the role of the agricultural sector in the process of economic and social development has to be active rather than passive and dependent on the pull of the industrial sector as the leading dynamic sector, and that the emphasis within agriculture should be on the gradual development of the traditional small-scale, labour-intensive sub-sector.

Whilst the conventional development approach, based on the labour surplus model, favoured an indirect approach towards development via the modern sector, the emerging alternative approach favours a *direct* approach which, without of course neglecting the modern formal sector, puts an equal amount of its 'eggs' into the hitherto neglected and low-productivity sectors. Some critics maintain that such a development approach means perpetuating low incomes and poverty because of the very emphasis on the low-productivity sectors. Nothing could be further from the truth. Indeed, the choice is between, on the one hand, a strategy which favours disproportionately a small minority in the modern formal sector, while the majority of the population who cannot gain access to that sector eke out a precarious existence in the urban informal and rural traditional sectors, and, on the other hand, a strategy which, given this situation, attempts to raise directly the productivity and the incomes of people in those low-productivity sectors. It is the latter approach, therefore, which is the more progressive and the more equitable.

A fourth form of insight we have obtained in the course of our work is related to the link between education, training and employment. The strong emphasis on the quantitative link between the occupational structure and educational expansion cannot be considered the correct approach. The role and responsibility of education and training systems in employment and income distribution problems is not so much one of estimating the number of engineers or technicians required at a future date, but rather a question of structure and content of education. The formal educational system in most countries shows typical cannibalistic tendencies, in the sense that each level of education educates its products mainly for the next level, rather than for the world of work outside. Thus, the entire educational system is primarily geared to the minority climbing up to the top of the educational ladder, and not to the majority which drops out well before the end of the ladder is in sight. The aspirations and expectations stimulated and perpetuated in this manner cannot be remedied by a 'more of the same' approach, but only by changing the structure and content of education, linking it *qualitatively* to the immediate environment of the school in which the pupils and students have to spend the rest of their lives.

11

Another important question which is often forgotten by those who are obsessed by the planning of education and the expansion of secondary and higher education is: What happens to the 25 to 50 per cent. of the young people who either never go to school or who are very early drop-outs? This is one of the reasons why, in most developing countries, a re-allocation of resources is in order, in favour of basic education to cater more fully for the very young and to make sure that they get a minimum but complete educational base. In this connection it is also important to underline the importance of creating a link between formal and informal systems of education. Imaginative informal training centres must be set up which can pick up those who have fallen out of the educational boat or did not have a chance to get into it in the first place. There is much talk of an opposition between equity and efficiency: yet to re-allocate resources in favour of basic education and create second-chance informal institutions is both equitable and efficient.

It would be possible to continue this list of insight into and glimpses of emerging employment-orientated development strategies, for example in the area of choice of techniques, urban employment problems, etc., but the above examples are, I feel, sufficiently clear and representative for the purposes of this Introduction.

I now come to the implementation aspects of our work to date. But what criteria can and should we use to judge the political success or failure of a programme of this nature? Should it be the number of jobs created? The number of economic development plans which have in their objectives function employment and income distribution as the priority element? The intentions to which political decision-makers pay lip service? Or should we use the resource allocation patterns of governments as the main yardstick? I personally do not think that we can use, as the appropriate criterion, the number of jobs actually created in developing countries because this would suggest that the employment problem can be solved in no time by some kind of trick. The main criterion should therefore be a combination of the last three, and in particular the second and the fourth criteria, in as far as a development plan contains guidelines for resource allocations. One can judge a government's intentions not only according to the objectives to which they pay lip service, but more importantly according to where they put their resources. It is therefore important that one does not only look at the objectives of development plans proclaimed in the preambles, but also examines whether these intentions are translated in the main body of such plans into appropriate re-direction and re-orientation of investment and other resources. If this line of reasoning is acceptable, then the policy results to date are rather satisfactory, given the difficulties of the problem which, and this much has become clear in the preceding discussion, requires drastic and almost revolutionary changes in government policies.

In the first place it is significant that influential international organisations besides the ILO have changed their approach considerably in favour of the employment and income distribution problems. This is the case of the World Bank and the FAO, for example. Although it is more important to know what is happening at the level of individual governments rather than of international organisations, the influence of the latter should not be minimized.

With respect to government action, there is no doubt about the fact that, in recent years, an important landslide in the degree of consciousness and feeling of urgency of the employment problem has occurred in many quarters. For one thing, the subsequent chapters in this book illustrate an attempt, and a rather early one at that, to come to grips with the problem. With respect to our own experience, the examples of Kenya and the Philippines are important milestones where a wide ranging public debate has followed the submission of the Kenya and Philippine employment reports to the respective governments. In the case of Kenya, this resulted, in the first instance, in the publication by the Government of Kenya of a Sessional Paper on Employment (No. 10 of 1973), followed by the Third Economic Development Plan (1974–1978) which was published in early 1974. This Development Plan is an elaboration of the Government Sessional Paper and accepts, to a very large extent, the change in development strategy suggested by the Kenya employment report. This, according to the criterion we elaborated earlier, constitutes an important measure in order to judge a government's conviction to tackle the employment problem head-on.

The Philippine employment report was submitted much more recently, but many groups in the country, both from the private as well as from the public sector, were already discussing the pros and cons of the suggested approach in small but high-powered seminars among Philippinos. Again this list could be continued and it could also, of course, include less favourable remarks about impacts of other parts of our work. But I think that the main point is to underline the fact that more and more governments and interest groups are becoming convinced that present and current policies do not suffice with tackling the main problems of the last quarter of the century. There is a real chance, therefore, that for once very important changes in policies and strategies do not have to await a disaster.

13

4. FUTURE DIRECTIONS

I hope that at least one of the things that has become clear from the preceding pages is that we do not believe that the employment and income distribution problems, as defined, can be solved by superficial and partial changes, maintaining basically the same growth pattern of the past. On the contrary, we believe that these problems can only be effectively tackled by changing quite drastically the style and pattern of development along lines touched upon in the previous section. Although there is growing recognition that the more radical approach is the correct one, this is not yet universally accepted and there are still many individuals and quite a few governments who believe that the transition periods involved in the 'indirect approach' are, or can be, made acceptable in terms of duration and suffering.

The articles that are contained in this volume reflect to my mind a position which falls somewhere between the conventional approach and the more drastic emerging reappraisal of development policies advocated in this Introduction. This is small wonder, because the work on which these articles are based was undertaken quite some years ago and in this sense they must be considered as early efforts to make a government not only aware of the seriousness of the problem and its deep roots in the overall economic and social fabric, but also to start indicating alternative policy measures to deal with the problem. I am therefore grateful to the editor of this volume, Professor Dr. W. van Rijckeghem, for giving me this opportunity of putting the specific and early attempt made in Morocco in the wider context of our efforts under the ILO World Employment Programme.

A final remark. It is probably true to say that our efforts to date have mainly concentrated on the indispensable changes in *national* development policies. Although not neglected, we have not given, so far, equal attention to external factors influencing the national decision-making process. This will now be remedied very quickly in the light of the decision to convene a Tripartite World Conference on Employment, Income Distribution and the International Division of Labour – a decision taken by the ILO Governing Body in November 1974. The importance of an international framework conducive to the success of internal strategies cannot be exaggerated. Developments over the past decade have demonstrated time and again how even minor ripples in the industrialised centres of the international system grow into tidal movements when they reach the developing economies and swamp them in a manner which makes internal adjustments of little avail. More recently, the energy

14

crisis, global inflation, monetary instability and food shortages have demonstrated strikingly the interdependence of different parts of the world economy and the extreme vulnerability of the poorer developing countries to major changes in the international economic system. A favourable external environment is therefore crucial for the success of a national strategy focusing on fuller employment and equitable distribution of income. A dynamic process of industrialization, sustained by rapid expansion of labour-intensive manufactured exports, can make a major contribution to solving the employment problem. However, this presupposes a re-examination of present patterns of world production and trade, which might at the same time help to solve some of the more pressing problems confronting the industrialized countries, such as environmental pollution and inflation. The Conference, which will take place in June 1976, will concentrate on three topics:

i. a review of the effectiveness of internal measures taken by developing countries to improve the situation regarding employment and the distribution of income;

ii. alternative international divisions of labour, aimed at strengthening the internal measures taken by developing countries; and

iii. implications of changes in the international division of labour for advanced countries.

It is my sincere hope that with this World Conference we shall be able to turn our programme into a truly effective *world* employment programme.

REFERENCES

1. W. Arthur Lewis, 'Development with Unlimited Supplies of Labour', *The Manchester School*, May 1954; and John Fei and Gustav Ranis, *Development of the Labour Surplus Economy – Theory and Policy*, Homewood Illinois, 1964.
2. For a clear explanation of this concept, see *Employment, Incomes and Equality – A Strategy for Increasing Productive Employment in Kenya*, ILO, Geneva, 1972, Chapter 13. See also Louis Emmerij, 'A New Look at Some Strategies for Increasing Productive Employment in Africa', *International Labour Review*, September 1974.
3. See *Towards Full Employment: A Programme for Colombia Prepared by an Inter-Agency Team Organised by the International Labour Office*, ILO, Geneva, 1970; *Matching Employment Opportunities and Expectations: A Programme of Action for Ceylon*, ILO, Geneva, 1971; *Employment, Incomes and Equality: A Strategy for Increasing Productive Employment in Kenya*, ILO, Geneva, 1972; *Employment and Income Policies for Iran*, ILO, Geneva, 1973; and *Sharing in Development: A Programme of Employment, Equity and Growth for the Philippines*, ILO, Geneva, 1974.
4. See *Strategies for Employment Promotion*, ILO, Geneva, 1973.

5. See *Scope, Approach and Content of Research-Oriented Activities of the World Employment Programme*, ILO, Geneva, 1972. Since then a first progress report has been published: *World Employment Programme: A Progress Report on its Research-Oriented Activities*, Geneva, 1973.

Part I. General economic policies

1. The employment impact of fiscal policy

W. Snyder

The aim of this study is to measure the consequences of fiscal policies as they affected employment in Morocco during the two decades between 1952 and 1972. Admittedly, our understanding of the *exact* impact of particular budgetary actions, whether they concern expenditures or taxes, leaves much to be desired. And how to translate such measures into units of employment consequences is even less well understood. Progress, however, does not occur without venturing beyond the acknowledged paths. Whatever limitations this effort contains, hopefully they will not detract readers from the principal purpose which is to assess Morocco's budgetary policies with particular emphasis on their influence on employment – a manifestly critical objective among the country's development aims.

The analysis makes no pretense of being either exhaustive in its objectives or certain of the results; rather it should be viewed as a first attempt to quantify the consequences of budgetary policies in Morocco. Hopefully, future refinements and modifications will be undertaken with the end result that successive approximations will reveal more about this vital matter. The assumptions required and the qualifications offered are many, both as concerns the underlying economic theory and the data upon which the study is based. Every attempt has been made to make both elements as specific as possible so that the reader may decide what degree of credibility to assign to any part.

1.1. MEASURING THE IMPACT OF BUDGET CHANGES

In order to estimate the effect of budget changes on employment, it is first necessary to estimate their impact on domestic demand. The basic methodology is that developed by Hansen [1]. Although his model is small compared with the large econometric models which have been developed for some countries, and it was especially designed for use

19

among the so-called 'developed' countries, nevertheless it provides a useful basis of analysis for a developing country like Morocco, if one is careful to specify the assumptions required and to qualify the conclusions reached. The model assumes that private investment and exports are exogenously determined. It uses multipliers of various magnitudes to determine the impact of different kinds of budget changes, after allowing for leakages due to the estimated marginal propensities for private consumption, imports, indirect and direct taxes. Government expenditures distinguish between volume and price changes, the latter necessitated by the differentiation of direct from indirect taxes.

To determine the effect of the budget we must first estimate what would have occurred if there had been no change in the budget, i.e., if *all* expenditures and *all* revenues had remained constant from one period to the next. The difference between this estimate and the actual development can be attributed to a 'budget effect'. When government expenditures and revenues change, the effect occurs in a several stage process. First, there is the *direct* impact of the increased (or decreased) spending occasioned by the initial budget change. Subsequently, the initial change induces a series of *indirect* or 'multiplier' effects. The combination of all the direct and indirect effects is henceforth called 'total effects' or 'budgetary impact'; the two terms are used interchangeably.

The formula for the total of all the direct and indirect effects is based on a truncated version of the model which allows for all changes in central government revenue which are not credit transactions, and for all purchases of goods and services. Specifically,

$$
\text{Total Effects} = \frac{1}{1 - \alpha(1 - \mu)} \ (dC_g) + \frac{1}{1 - \alpha(1 - \mu)} \ (dI_g)
$$

$$
+ \frac{\alpha(1 - \mu)}{1 - \alpha(1 - \mu)} \ (C_g dP + I_g dP)
$$

$$
- \frac{1 - \mu}{1 - \alpha(1 - \mu)} \ (dT_i) - \frac{\alpha(1 - \mu)}{1 - \alpha(1 - \mu)} \ (dT_d).
$$

The above equation allows for the following factors:
  i. Changes in the *volume* of government purchases of current goods and services (dC_g) and investment expenditures (dI_g) are distinguished from their respective *price* changes $(C_g dP + I_g dP)$.
  ii. Changes in indirect taxes (dT_i).
  iii. Changes in direct taxes (dT_d).

iv. Leakages via the marginal propensity to consume (α) and via the marginal propensity to import (μ). The model contains no explicit corporate business sector; consequently α measures the total ratio between changes in personal consumption and changes in *total* private income minus only direct taxes. This implies the assumption of a constant relationship of business profits to income which is unaffected by changes in business income taxes. The validity of the assumptions which require α and μ to remain constant are discussed in an *Appendix*. As for business taxes, at most they are no larger than 1/10 the amount of total private investment. It hardly seems possible that annual variations could be a major factor determining the amount of private investment.

v. The weighing allows for changes in government expenditures ($dC_g + dI_g$) to have their full multiplier effects (i.e., direct plus indirect), while the other items have only indirect or second-round-and-after effects (e.g., increased wages to government employees or reduced taxes both raise private income, some of which is saved and some spent on imported goods, only after which does the change begin to affect domestic demand).

Two further aspects of the above equation for estimating the budgetary impact need to be discussed:

1. Neither tax nor price and wage changes are deflated. This is because the model assumes that prices, before indirect taxes, are exogenously determined and are only further influenced by discretionary changes in indirect taxes. This means that the estimated effects of budgetary changes only influence the *volume* of domestic demand, and do not spill over to cause either increased prices or imports (beyond the 'normal' propensity to import).

2. The weighing system implies that a unit of change in government purchases will have a greater effect than a unit change in taxes, and among the latter that the effects of a unit change in indirect taxes has a larger effect than a similar change in direct taxes. These results are well known from the literature about the 'balanced budget multiplier' and are generally consistent with the implicit multipliers of the 'big models'.

There remain, of course, many statistical problems which require explanation. Rather than pause here, however, the interested reader is referred to the Appendix where these are fully discussed. The multipliers for the various types of budget changes differ, and these and the leakage coefficients are given in Table 1.

Table 1. Leakage coefficients and multipliers

Leakage coefficients	
Marginal rate of consumption (α)	0.75
Marginal rate of imports (μ)	0.15
Multipliers for total effects	
Changes in the volume of government domestic purchases of current goods and services, and investment (dC_g and dI_g)	2.78
Changes in the value of government purchases due to wage-price changes ($C_g dP + I_g dP$)	1.78
Changes in total direct taxes (dT_d)	1.78
Changes in total indirect taxes (dT_i)	2.36

1.2. THE STABILIZING EFFECTS OF FISCAL POLICIES

Even without recourse to an attempt to quantify the role played by the government budget in the development of the Moroccan economy since 1952, in a *qualitative* way the general pattern is well known. During the years 1952–1954 the economy was expanding fairly rapidly but at a decreasing rate with the growth of uncertainty surrounding the events prior to independence. In fact, the years immediately preceding and following independence were characterized by slow growth, in part occasioned by restrictive budgetary policies. Concurrent with the introduction of national planning in 1960, the economy entered a new phase of expansion which in no small part was due to substantial annual increments to both the current and investment expenditures of the central government. This period of fairly rapid growth ended in 1964, and the following two years were influenced by special restrictive budgetary policies intended to 'cool-off' an over-heated economy. Unfortunately, 1966 was also an unusually poor agricultural year, and the GDP actually declined. But the next year, 1967, marked the beginning of a new expansionary phase which was particularly aided by the exceptionally good agricultural harvest of 1968. The years since 1968 have witnessed the most steady period of economic expansion in Morocco since independence.

We have made a number of qualifying remarks about the nature of the methods used to estimate the impact of budget changes and the data upon which they are based, but one further caveat is necessary before discussing the quantitative results. Agriculture has been and continues to remain the underlying basis for the Moroccan economy. Over one-half

22

of the working population is directly engaged in agriculture and this sector alone accounts for nearly one-third of GDP. However, the model described above is incapable of distinguishing the special effect that variations in agricultural output can have on the rest of the economy. More important, perhaps, the model does not allow for the possibility that budgetary effects affect demand within the agricultural sector in different ways and with less impact than they do demand in the rest of the economy. One approach would have been to have built a two-sector model capable of incorporating these differences. While this was not done, due to the absence of an adequate statistical basis for establishing empirically the necessary relationships, the paper in this volume by Professor van Rijckeghem does develop a two-sector model which shows how the agricultural sector can be explicitly incorporated to analyze the effects of monetary policy.

Nevertheless short of separating out agriculture as a special sector, some form of adjustment is necessary because agriculture has too large an influence to be simply incorporated without further modification. Annual variations in agricultural output are substantial and they can add or subtract as much as 5 percent to the growth rate, although the *average* contribution of agricultural output contributed only 0.8 percent to the rate of GDP growth between 1952 and 1972. Clearly, it would be inappropriate to compare the budget impact with *total* GDP because of the unstable nature of agricultural production. For these reasons, the following analysis uses *non-agricultural* GDP as the basis for comparison which reduces but does not entirely eliminate the erratic changes due primarily to fluctuations in agricultural output.

Adequately detailed budget and national accounts data exist from 1951 onwards which make it possible to estimate the budgetary impact for each year between 1952 and 1972. In order to compare the impact of one year with another, however, it was necessary to normalize them. This was done by expressing each year's impact as a percentage of the previous year's GDP. Estimates of the total effects are given in Table 2 which includes the principal components of the budget effects as well. The total effects are also illustrated graphically in the top portion of Fig. 1 (p. 26).

The budget impact has frequently been a very important factor in determining the short-term situation, and it has also affected the long-term rate of economic growth in a substantial way. As can be seen in either Table 2 or Figure 1, expansionary budgets amounted to about 7 percent in two years and in at least one year a dampening effect nearly as large occurred. As for the long-term budget impact, the average annual total effect was 1.7 percent of GDP. This means that the average growth rate

Table 2. Total effects of annual budget changes, 1952–1962 (expressed as

	1952	1953	1954	1955	1956	1957	1958	1959	1960	196
Total effects	11.8	4.5	−0.5	7.1	−3.2	−4.0	3.6	1.8	0.0	4
Current expenditures	2.9	3.8	3.0	5.5	2.1	1.1	4.3	0.7	2.1	2
Investment expenditures	8.2	1.4	−1.3	0.5	−2.6	−2.4	3.9	−0.7	−1.0	2
Wage and price changes	3.4	0.0	0.0	0.8	2.1	2.6	0.0	0.2	2.9	0
Indirect taxes	−1.9	0.0	−1.9	−0.3	−4.0	−5.0	−3.6	1.1	−3.5	−0
Direct taxes	−0.8	−0.7	−0.3	0.6	−0.8	−0.3	−1.0	0.5	−0.5	−0

Note: Column sums may not equal total effects due to rounding.

non-agricultural GDP which was 4.2 percent (measured in constant 1960 prices) would have been only about half as large without the generally expansionary effect of the budget.

This conclusion must be tempered by the cautionary comments made previously. The budget effects which were generally expansionary are overestimated for those years when, besides affecting the real demand for domestic output, the budget impact created additional pressure on prices and imports. While this is a recognized deficiency of the model, in fact there were only three years between 1952 and 1972 which clearly fall in this category. In 1952 the exceptionally large total effects of 11.8 percent occurred in a year of larger than normal price increases and as the effects were mostly due to the unusually large capital expenditures, much of the effects were offset by above normal imports – largely of capital goods. Again, in 1963 and 1964 the total effects occurred in years when both prices and imports increased abnormally, and hence the budget impact on real domestic demand must have been something less than the percentages indicated in Table 2. But outside of these years, it seems to be a reasonably good generalization that the Moroccan economy had sufficient unused capacity so that most of any expansionary impact from the budget directly affected real domestic demand rather than prices and imports.

Among the components of the overall budget impact, the average expansionary effect of annually increasing current expenditures (2.4 percent) was just exactly offset by the contractionary effect of increasing indirect taxes. However, because taken separately, increased investment spending (1.1 percent) and rising prices (1.2 percent) each outweighted the dampening effect of increased direct tax collections (−0.5 percent),

62	1963	1964	1965	1966	1967	1968	1969	1970	1971	1972	Ave.
.9	5.1	3.3	−4.8	−6.1	6.7	2.8	−3.0	−1.4	2.8	3.5	1.8
.4	4.1	1.8	−2.6	2.1	1.3	3.9	2.7	3.2	3.0	2.0	2.4
.9	2.1	−0.7	0.2	−2.1	7.6	2.3	0.4	0.7	0.2	1.1	1.1
.8	2.0	1.4	1.1	−0.4	−0.3	0.2	0.8	1.1	2.2	2.1	1.2
.6	−2.0	0.2	−0.4	−5.0	−1.5	−2.1	−6.6	−5.8	−2.3	−1.3	−2.4
.4	1.1	0.6	−3.1	−0.7	−0.4	−1.5	−0.3	−0.6	−0.3	−0.4	−0.5

the overall annual budget effect was substantial, as previously mentioned. The estimates of the total effects can be used to evaluate to what extent the budget did or did not help achieve short-term economic stabilization. We would argue that, *ceteris paribus*, a stable growth rate is desirable; we recognize, however, that merely dampening potential cyclical swings is not the only – perhaps not even the principal – criterion by which the impact of budget policies should be judged. The next section deals with the longer-term objective of achieving the highest possible rate of economic growth compatible with reasonable price stability and balance of payments equilibrium. But there were clearly some years between 1952 and 1972 when the government was particularly concerned with short-term stabilization.

The short-term stabilizing effect of budget changes cannot be compared with *actual* non-agricultural GDP, because actual GDP is itself influenced by budget policies. We can, however, construct a hypothetical series of GDP by subtracting from the actual GDP growth rate the total effect of budget changes for each year. This derived series is called the 'pure cycle', because it attempts to estimate what growth of non-agricultural GDP would have occurred in the absence of any change in the budget from one year to the next. The pure cycle still incorporates the effects of other government policies (e.g., local government budgets, social security, public enterprise investment and monetary policy) and autonomous factors (e.g., private investment and exports). Hence, the pure cycle is not so 'pure', but nevertheless it is a useful analytical device.

We shall define 'potential' short-term stabilization as the (absolute) difference between the pure cycle and the average non-agricultural GDP growth rate. Potential stabilization for the entire period is simply the

25

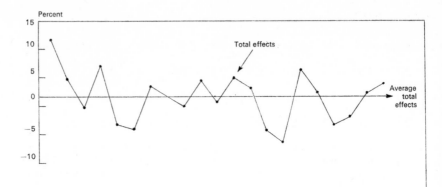

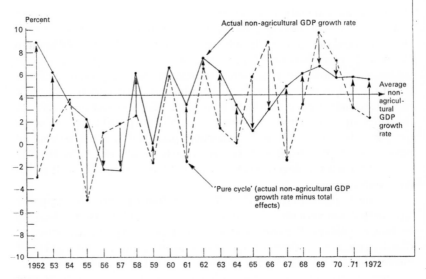

Figure 1

cumulated sum for the years from 1952 through 1972. We shall also define a budget effect to be stabilizing if its impact tended to reduce the difference between the pure cycle and the average GDP growth rate.*

* In cases where the budgetary impact is in the right direction but exceeds the amount necessary to reach the average growth rate, the impact is divided into two components: the part that was stabilizing, and the other which overshot and had destabilizing effects.

26

Figure 1 (bottom) shows the actual non-agricultural GDP growth rate (solid line), the pure cycle (dashed line), and the average non-agricultural GDP growth rate (4.2 percent). The arrows indicate the direction of the total effects of the budget changes, and they point from the pure cycle to the actual GDP; their magnitudes are identical with the data given in Table 2.

These definitions of the pure cycle and short-term stabilization are not without their conceptual complications. While on the one hand excluding the budgetary impact of the other government sectors (local government, social security and the public enterprises) may not cause any noticeable distortion because their impact cannot be very large, and on the other hand it is appropriate that the pure cycle should retain the influence of other autonomous factors, ignoring monetary policy does pose a certain ambiguity. Since the pure cycle includes the effects of monetary policy, it must be remembered that any estimation of the stabilizing effects of budget policies necessarily treats monetary policy as if it were determined exogenously. In fact, however, monetary policy is decided in conjuncture with fiscal policy; hence ideally the pure cycle should be defined to exclude it. If that were possible, one would then be able to distinguish separately between both kinds of economic policies: fiscal and monetary. But our knowledge about how these two kinds of policies interact is too limited to permit such a precise distinction. At best then the estimates of the impact of fiscal policies which are contained in this paper are but a partial interpretation of the impact of government policies in Morocco; again the reader is referred elsewhere in this volume to Professor van Rijckeghem's paper which discusses how monetary policy has affected the development of the Moroccan economy. The reader is cautioned that taken separately our conclusions about the stabilizing nature of government policies cannot be simply added together. That would only be valid if the pure cycle excluded the effects of both monetary and fiscal policies, and if we could measure separately their impact so as to exclude any interaction between them. Such sophistication, however, still escapes economic analysis, and for the present the best we can suggest is to accept our partial analyses recognizing the limitations that this requires.

This visual presentation of the budgetary impact in relation to the pure cycle illustrates several important characteristics of the effect of budgetary policies during the period 1952–1972. It clearly shows how the total effect was generally expansive, and how it helped maintain the actual GDP growth rate at a level considerably above what it would have been otherwise. It also shows the substantial effect that the budgetary impact had on altering and dampening cyclical fluctuations. More precisely, the extent to which they were a stabilizing (or destabilizing) factor can be measured as follows. The cumulated amount of potential stabilization was 73 percent (of a typical year's GDP). Total stabilizing effects, as defined above, amounted to 50 percent. These were, however, offset by 32 percent of destabilizing effects. Therefore, the *net* amount of short-term stabilization achieved was 18 percent. Or, in other words, the potential fluctuations of the non-agricultural GDP growth rate about its average were reduced by 25 percent during the period 1952–1972 (i.e., the 18 percent of net stabilizing effects divided by the 73 percent of the potential stabilization, both amounts cumulated and measured in terms of percent of GDP).

Moreover, it is remarkable to note that throughout the entire 20-year period with all the different economic and political climates that prevailed, there were only two years – 1956 and 1957 – when a fairly strong budgetary effect was clearly in the wrong direction, thus contributing to greater economic instability than would have otherwise prevailed. It should be recognized that these two years immediately preceded independence, and thus it is understandable that the French government attempted to reduce expenditures, particularly investment, while at the same time it increased taxes, especially indirect, in order to balance a budget which had been heavily in deficit the previous year when the former government had tried unsuccessfully to contain the independence movement.

As can be seen in Figure 1 there were several years when the *direction* of the budgetary impact was correct for achieving economic stability but the total effect was excessive and pushed the actual GDP beyond its long-term average growth rate (sometimes above, sometimes below). Even for these years, the amount of stabilizing effects were about half-again as large as the destabilizing effects, so that the *net* budgetary impact contributed to economic stability.

While not entering into a detailed description of each year's con-junctural situation, and how it was affected by budgetary policy, it is worth noting that the budget impact was one of the causes of the ac-knowledged overheating which occurred in the Moroccan economy between 1962 and 1964. Subsequently, it is equally clear that the budget was a strong instrument applied to cooling off the economy, and the budget exerted very large deflationary effects during 1965 and 1966 which were important in restoring economic equilibrium. What is perhaps even more remarkable is the extraordinary turn-around which occurred from the large contractionary impact in 1966 (-6.1 percent of the GDP) to the even larger expansionary effect exerted by the budget in 1967 ($+ 6.7$

28

percent). This combination considerably contributed to the reestablishment of a desirable development path.

Since 1967 the GDP growth rate has exceeded its long-term average but by itself this is not enough to imply a reoccurrence of the overheating which characterized the Moroccan economy between 1962 and 1964. It may well be that the substantial investments which were undertaken in recent years, private as well as public, are now showing their value in the form of a potentially higher rate of growth without the previous undesirable side effects; but only time will tell. It is also worth noting that there has been a strong underlying upward trend in the economy which began with the exceptional agricultural harvest of 1968 (see the pure cycle development in Figure 1). In light of this, the contractionary budget impact of 1969 seems to have been appropriate and helped maintain the economic expansion in a balanced position.

1.3. THE EMPLOYMENT IMPACT OF FISCAL POLICY

Since independence, the government of Morocco has attempted to stear the economy on a path of economic development designed to eventually eliminate unemployment. The 1960 census enumerated 11.6 million persons of whom 3.3 million or 28 % were in the labor force. Of these, 305 thousand or $9\frac{1}{2}$ % were classified as officially unemployed [3, p. 39]. Based on the recent 1971 census, the new 5-year development plan for 1973–1977 expresses the expectation that the population will reach 18.8 million by 1977 of whom about 5.2 million or 28 % will again be in the labor force. The plan aims to hold unemployment in 1977 to 350 thousand or 7 %. Thus, a major objective of the present as well as the past development strategy is to reduce open unemployment. In this final section we will attempt to measure the long-term impact of fiscal policy as it has affected employment in Morocco since independence.

In order to assess the employment impact, it is necessary to establish what were the long-term objectives. Some can be constructed from the explicit aims of the previous development plans. For example, Morocco's first development plan (1960–1964) set a 6.2 percent growth rate as the primary objective [5, p. 4]. The next plan (1965–1967) recognized the over-heating caused by the excessively ambitious previous plan and as a result set a modest 3.7 percent growth objective [7, p. 53]. The strategy of the last completed plan (1968–1972) was to aim for a somewhat faster pace of development, 4.3 percent on average, which it hoped could be accelerated to 5 percent by the end of the period [6, p. 48].

It would be possible to link these three plans together so as to create the implied employment objectives and compare them with the actual achievement. That, however, would be undesirable for at least one reason. The expansionary fiscal policy followed during the first 5-year plan (1960–1964) resulted in destabilizing the economy as witnessed by the depletion of Morocco's foreign exchange reserves and the creation of rapidly rising prices. Clearly, the 6.2 percent objective of the first 5-year plan was not compatible with balanced economic growth. If, however, the government had pursued a somewhat less expansionary budget policy it is entirely possible that it would not have been necessary to pursue the deflationary policies of the next development plan, notably in 1965 and 1966. Consequently, for the purpose of comparing actual budget policies with some reasonable 'potential' growth objective, we shall use a constant growth path of 5 percent from 1959 onwards. This is illustrated in Figure 2 and indicated as 'potential output'.

The fact that actual non-agricultural GDP exceeded potential growth during the early 1960's simply reflects the situation that the Moroccan economy was over-heated during those years. The deflationary policies of 1965 and 1966 were followed by generally expansionary budgets which by 1972 helped bring the economy back onto its 'potential' growth path.

In order to evaluate the overall impact of the budget, it is helpful to construct another series where actual GDP and the 'pure' cycle are expressed as percentage deviations from potential output, shown for convenience as a straight line in Figure 3. The vertical difference between actual GDP and the pure cycle for each year is equivalent to the estimated total effect of budget changes.* The arrows indicate the direction of the total effect and point from the pure cycle to the actual GDP.

As we did for evaluating short-term stabilization, here we will define potential stabilization as the absolute difference between the pure cycle and potential GDP. Budget effects are counted as stabilizing if they diminish the difference and destabilizing if they increase it. The total effects whose arrows in Figure 3 point towards potential GDP are counted as helping achieve economic stability and, generally, greater employment, and in those years when they point away the budget impact is counted as being destabilizing.

The accumulated amount of potential stabilization between 1959 and

---

* In Figure 3, the total effects of Table 2 have been deflated to 1960 constant prices and scaled down by 30% to make them comparable with non-agricultural GDP which is about 30% smaller than total GDP.

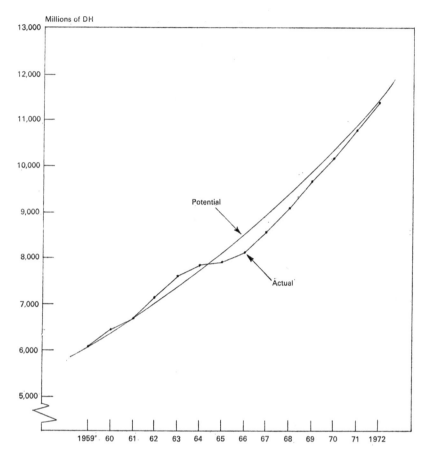

Figure 2. Non-agricultural GDP: constant 1960 prices

1972 was 38 percent (of a typical year's potential output). The sum of the net stabilizing effects was 8 percent which resulted from 23 percent of effects helping to stabilize demand at the economy's full potential less 15 percent of destabilizing effects. At face value the net stabilizing effects may appear to be relatively little, but similar evaluations covering comparable periods for several developed countries generally reveal no better performance [2, p. 932].

Over the entire planning period since independence, one of the most interesting questions pertaining to stabilization is to evaluate in terms of lost employment opportunities the cost of the restrictive fiscal policies

31

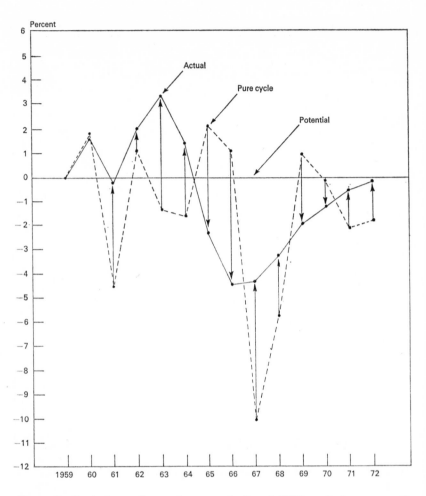

Figure 3. Deviations of actual non-agricultural GDP and the pure cycle from potential output

which were necessitated by the overly expansive development expenditures during the first 5-year plan (1960–1964). Or, expressed differently, if that over-heating had not occurred and if it had been possible to keep the Moroccan economy expanding at the 5 percent 'potential' growth rate, what increased employment might have resulted. During 1966 and 1967, actual non-agricultural GDP was 380 and 390 million DH (measured in constant 1960 prices) below potential output. The problem, then, becomes

32

one of translating this measure of inachieved output into some comparable unit of employment. While there is no generally acceptable method of making such a conversion, one approximation is to use the implied relationship between output and employment. For example, the explicit goals and projections contained in the present 5-year plan (1973–1977) imply that by 1977 output per man-year will be 5,300 DH (measured in constant 1973 prices) [4]. This output cannot, however, be used directly to measure the employment cost of the deflationary fiscal policies. It must first be adjusted by the implicit GDP deflator to constant 1960 prices (0.75) and further decreased by a rough estimate of the possible increased productivity which may occur between 1965/1966 and 1977 (10 percent). The result of these adjustments is to decrease the average output figure mentioned above to 3,600 DH per man-year (measured in constant 1960 prices). The 380 million DH output deficiency in 1966 can then be converted into 105 thousand man-years of lost employment opportunities. Thus, as many as 105 thousand persons may have been added in 1966/1967 to the unemployed which had previously amounted to 305 thousand, according to the 1960 census [3, p. 39]. In other words, unemployment may have increased by about one-third during 1966/1967, and this cost was only slowly compensated by increased demand which did not fully attain potential output until 1972.

Needless to say, at best this estimate is a very crude measure of the impact of fiscal policy on employment during a relatively short period, and the appraisal needs to be viewed in the larger context of the generally expansionary impact that budget policies had on Moroccan economic development. On the other hand, it is entirely possible that if 5 percent was an optimum growth rate in the early 1960's, by the end of that decade an even higher rate of growth may have been possible. To the extent that such a possibility is realistic, the calculations of the employment impact of fiscal policy are under-estimated for the years 1966/1967, and the amount of achieved stabilization would then be less than mentioned earlier.

Although the principal purpose of this analysis has been to quantify the impact of budget policies, before concluding it is possible to incorporate a few qualitative if not quantitative comments about monetary policy. One of the main conclusions of Professor van Rijckeghem's paper is that '... credit policy was probably too restrictive for about four years – 1965, 1966, 1969 and 1970 – out of the ten' (under review between 1962 and 1972). Since these years are precisely ones when the budget impact was excessively deflationary, we can safely conclude that both monetary and fiscal policies had a contracting influence on the economy which combined to depress demand below an optimum level. The only other period when both policies were excessive occurred during 1963 and 1964 when both fiscal and monetary policies were overly expansionary and together created the excessively high level of demand which existed then. While these experiences may be based on too few years to suggest any pattern in overall policy making by the Moroccan authorities, nevertheless the situation suggests that the government had some tendency towards policies of the 'stop/go' variety which became synonymous with those followed in the United Kingdom during the late 1950's and throughout the 1960's. That is, once a situation was recognized as being inherently below or above some level thought to be desirable, government policies – monetary and fiscal – were directed toward reversing the situation without any clear indication that the authorities were aware of the essentially short-run nature of the inbalance. An optimistic interpretation would be that the government learned from the unfortunate experiences of 1963/ 1964 and 1965/1966, and now more clearly understands the cumulative character of monetary and fiscal policies.

1.4. CONCLUSION

Briefly, this study has attempted to evaluate the impact of fiscal policy in Morocco from both the short-term stabilization perspective and from the implied employment cost of deviating from the economy's full 'potential'.

The conclusions must be considered provisional to the extent that some of the budget impact which has all been counted as affecting real domestic demand must have been partially dissipated on some occasions by rising prices and larger than normal imports. Another limitation is that the measures of the budget impact neglect any effect of monetary policy although some qualitative remarks about the appropriateness of the latter have been included.

If the time reference is the entire twenty-year period between 1952 and 1972, our estimates suggest that potential fluctuations in the growth rate of non-agricultural GDP were reduced by 25 percent through the stabilizing effects of budget policies. If, however, we use as the basis of comparison a 5 percent growth in potential output since the beginning of development planning in 1960, after 1964 actual demand was kept substantially below this norm by explicit deflationary policies and these may have increased unemployment in 1965/1966 by as much as one-third.

APPENDIX. A NOTE ON THE STATISTICAL METHODS

The national accounts data are those published by the Secrétariat d'Etat chargé du Plan. Government expenditures and revenues refer to only those of the central government and are those published in the *Annuaire Statistique du Maroc* and in the various *Situation Economique du Maroc*. The data, of course, leave much to be desired both as regards the details with which they are available, and the degree to which homogeneity has been maintained throughout the period covered. One known deficiency is that the budgetary data refer to exercise years up to 1964 and only afterwards are they on a calendar year cash-flow basis as required for purposes of such an economic analysis. Direct taxes are the total of revenue collected in Chapter 1 of the General Budget, as published in the *Annuaire Statistique du Maroc*, while indirect taxes include besides those enumerated in Chapter 3 of the General Budget, the other types of revenue which are conventionally termed 'indirect taxes' *net* of subsidies (as published in the National Income accounts submitted to the United Nations).

The equation used to estimate the total effects of budget changes uses multipliers which depend on two leakage coefficients; these and the multipliers were given in Table 1. The expenditure multipliers may seem large, but it should be noted that they refer to budget effects excluding tax leakages which are accounted for by explicitly including dT_i and dT_d (scaled by their appropriate multipliers, too). The corresponding multipliers which include tax leakage coefficients (instead of dT_i and dT_d) are substantially lower; for example, the multiplier for changes in the volume of government purchases in Morocco is 2.78 *without* tax leakages but only 2.25 *after* allowing for normal tax increases. While the multipliers cannot be accepted as being exact or applicable for every budget change, they are, nevertheless, sufficiently representative to indicate relative orders of magnitude among the various types of budgetary changes.

The equation requires the assumption that the marginal propensities to consume and import have remained stable throughout the period, and have not been subjected to any substantial influence from government policy, otherwise it would be questionable at the very least to use them as exogenously determined parameters. These propositions require discussion in some detail, as does the other implicit Keynesian assumption that there have generally been enough idle resources, namely labor and capital, so that budgetary effects influence the *volume* of domestic demand rather than tending to increase prices or imports beyond the norms allowed for in the model.

The marginal propensity to consume is estimated to be 0.75. If this coefficient seems small, it must be remembered that it is the ratio between changes in personal consumption and changes in total private income (GDP at factor cost) less net direct taxes and transfers. Because a complete series for social security contributions and benefits does not exist, and government interest payments to individuals too do not exist, extrapolations for these were based on the Economic Tables for 1958 and 1965, contained in the first five-year plan [5]. The relationship between personal consumption and net private income for the period 1952–1969 implies a *marginal* rate of consumption which is *less* than the *average* rate, a normal occurrence which has been observed for other countries. For Morocco, however, it appears somewhat surprising because due to the departure of many thousand families with income levels several times the average income, one might anticipate a rising trend in the marginal rate of consumption. In fact, since 1965 there does seem to be some support for such a hypothesis, but the period is too short to predict that a new trend has indeed been set, and a uniform rate has been retained for the analysis. If, however, a new trend is indeed underway, this will have definite and detrimental effects on the potential savings, and consequently on the mobilization of the domestic resources which are necessary to achieve Morocco's development objectives. Understandably, the year-to-year changes in consumption did not remain totally stable relative to private income, particularly during the years of and immediately following poor agriculture harvests as occurred in 1955, 1959, 1961 and 1966, but nevertheless the assumption of a constant marginal propensity to consume does not appear to do violence to the facts.

The marginal propensity to import is estimated to be 0.15, based on a free-hand linear approximation of the general trend between imports and the GDP, both measured in current prices. For theoretical reasons, the coefficient should be based on the volume relationships between imports and the GDP. Such a series established within the concepts of the system of national accounts does not, however, exist for Morocco, and the relation is based on current prices which themselves are only available for the years after 1957. In so far as domestic prices have tended to rise more rapidly than the prices paid for Moroccan imports, the estimated marginal propensity to import is undervalued, and evidence suggests that this is indeed the case. For example, the implicit GDP deflator for Morocco increased about 5½ percent annually between 1957 and 1967 whereas the export prices of commodities from France (the principal furnisher of Moroccan imports) grew at a rate of less than 3 percent annually during the same period.

Unlike most countries, the *marginal* propensity to import is less than the *average* rate. One reason for this unusual relationship may be because throughout the period covered (1958–1969) many thousand families with relatively high propensities to import left Morocco, and their departure tended to reduce the marginal propensity to import below what it would have otherwise been. Another factor, and one that may be even more important, is that imports have been regulated – sometimes with considerable restrictions – throughout the period studied. Thus, to speak of a 'propensity to import' under these conditions may not do justice to the actual situation. Hence, the marginal propensity to import should not be thought of as a strictly exogenously determined parameter, but rather the combination of private behavior and government regulation.

One further assumption must be discussed. The model for estimating the effects of budgetary changes assumes that they influence only the *volume* of domestic demand and not prices or imports beyond the 'normal' propensity to import. We have already said that imports were generally regulated so that any excess demand was unable to result in excessively high imports, although the year 1960 is certainly an exception. As for prices, Morocco has not had any sustained periods of inflation, but neither have price increases been less than elsewhere on the average. The year 1952 was an exceptional situation because the implicit GDP price deflator increased 14 percent, and consequently the budgetary effects undoubtedly did contribute to rising prices as well as to the volume of domestic demand. To a lesser degree this was probably true also for the years 1956, 1957 and 1960 when the same price index increased about 8 or 9 percent. Certainly for these years, and especially for 1952, the interpretations which are given to the impact of the budgetary effects can only be accepted with qualified reservations. Nevertheless, even if all the years from 1952 through 1969 are included, the average annual increase in the implicit GDP deflator was only 3.5 percent which was not excessive when compared with the experience of European countries; and if the four exceptional years mentioned previously are excluded, the average is no more than 1.5 percent annually which suggests a very low level of inflationary pressure because wage-drift and the changing structure of the Moroccan economy are together sufficient to explain this low average increase.

36

REFERENCES

1. Bent Hansen assisted by Wayne Snyder, *Fiscal Policy in Seven Countries, 1955–65*, OECD, Paris, 1969.
2. Wayne W. Snyder, 'Measuring Economic Stabilization', *American Economic Review*, 60, December 1970, pp. 924–933.
3. Service Central des Statistiques, *Annuaire Statistique du Maroc 1961*, Rabat, 1961.
4. Government of Morocco, *Morocco on the Move: Economic and Social Development, 1973–77*, Rabat, 1973.
5. Ministère de l'Economie Nationale et des Finances, *Plan Quinquennal 1960–64*, Rabat, 1960.
6. Ministère des Affaires Economiques, du Plan et de la Formation des Cadres, *Plan Quinquennal 1968–72*, Volume I, Rabat, 1968.
7. Economic Co-ordination and Planning Division, *Three-Year Plan 1965–67*, Rabat, 1965.

2. The employment cost of credit restrictions

W. van Rijckeghem

It is a widely accepted view in Morocco that, on several occasions during the last decade, restrictive credit policies have severely limited the growth of output and employment. It has been stated repeatedly in a number of confidential reports by international agencies, including the ILO, and has finally surfaced in the introduction of the new development plan for the period 1973–1977:

'il convient de noter que la politique suivie en matière de crédit a été, en dernière analyse, trop restrictive; certes, les mesures d'encadrement avaient leurs raisons d'être, mais on peut craindre qu'elles n'aient privilégié la stabilité monétaire au détriment de la croissance économique...' [1, p. 16].

What is less clear is the *process* through which credit restrictions affect output and employment. No simple model exists similar to that used by Professors Hansen and Snyder to measure the impact of fiscal policy. We are treading uncertain ground, and our results are bound to be tentative.

The limited objectives of this paper are threefold:

– to present a simple theoretical framework from which we can derive a reduced-form relationship between employment and output on the one hand, and credit policies on the other;
– to present an econometric estimate of the parameters involved;
– to describe the policy instruments used to control credit expansion.

2.1. A MODEL FOR ANALYZING THE EFFECT OF CREDIT RESTRICTIONS

Our starting point is a *demand-for-credit-function*, which relates bank credits to the private sector to the output value of that sector:

$$B = \kappa \, PY \, R^\rho \tag{i}$$

where

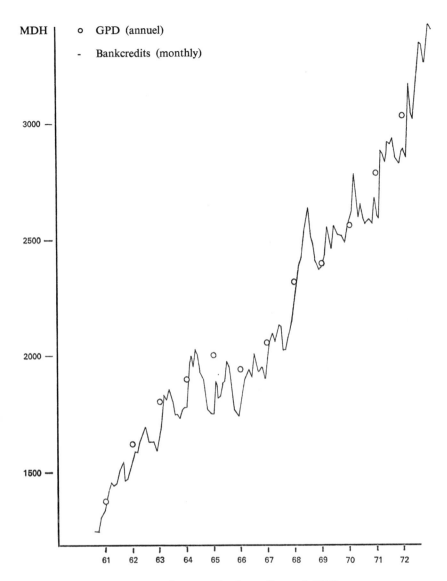

MDH | o GPD (annuel)
| - Bankcredits (monthly)

Figure 1. Comparative evolution of bank credits and GDP

39

B = bank credits
PY = private GDP at current prices
R = rate of interest.

The existence of such a function for Morocco is suggested by the remarkably stable empirical relationship between loans outstanding to the private sector ('crédits à l'économie') and the level of private gross domestic product at current prices ('production intérieure brute'). Not only is there a parallel trend between the two series, but also an almost perfect coincidence between the deviations from the trend. This is strengthened by the fact that the interest rate has remained unchanged throughout the period under consideration.* As a consequence, the proportion between B and PY has been practically constant, which is illustrated by Figure 1. In this diagram we have superimposed the series of annual GDP on the monthly credit series, after multiplication of the former by the constant factor 0.17. The resulting numbers are represented by large dots on the diagram.

Why relate demand for credit to output, rather than to fixed capital formation, or the asset structure of the enterprise sector? The reason is that, in Morocco, the quasi-totality of bank credits represents short-term commercial loans. For instance, at the end of 1970, short-term credit represented 94 % of total credit to the private sector [2, p. 32]. Such commercial loans are tied to the level of economic activity rather than to medium- or long-term financing of capital expenditures. They supply working capital to advance wages and other costs for work in progress, just as long-term loans are used to finance fixed capital [3, p. 1128]. In practice, it will be difficult to avoid some short-term loans being used for long-term purposes through repeated re-financing, but in a situation of tight credit, such practices would leave short-term needs even more unsatisfied.

Our second corner-stone is an aggregate production function, e.g. of the Cobb-Douglas type:

$$Y = AL^\alpha K^\beta e^{\gamma t} \qquad 0 < \alpha, \beta < 1$$
$$\alpha + \beta = 1 \qquad\qquad \text{(ii)}$$

---

* Ever since the establishment of the Central Bank in November 1951, changes in interest rates have not been used as an instrument of monetary policy, and the basic discount rate has remained unchanged at 3.5 per cent. Interest rates charged by deposit money banks in their lending operations are regulated by the Minister of Finance in consultation with a Credit and Capital Market Committee (CCMF).

40

where
$Y =$ private GDP at constant prices
$L =$ labour input
$K =$ fixed capital input.

No econometric estimates of the parameters are available, but if we accept the equality condition between real wages and marginal productivity, they can be obtained indirectly:

$$\frac{W}{P} = \alpha \frac{Y}{L} \text{ or } \alpha = \frac{WL}{PY} \tag{iii}$$

where
$W =$ wage level
$P =$ price level.

Using the factor shares given by Laursen in this volume, we can estimate α at $1/3$ and β at $2/3$.

Before solving the model, it is as well to translate the three equations into relative changes, indicated by lower-case symbols:

$$b = p + y + r \tag{i}'$$
$$y = \alpha l + \beta k + \gamma \tag{ii}'$$
$$w = p + y - l \tag{iii}'$$

This three-equation model contains seven variables, which means that we are left with four degrees of freedom. If we accept that $r = 0$ (a constant interest rate), which is historically correct, the degrees of freedom are reduced to three. Since we wish to study the impact of credit restrictions, it seems logical to consider b as exogenous, thus using up an additional degree of freedom. The institutional set-up of wage determination through minimum wage setting in Morocco also leads us to include w among the exogenous variables. Finally, if we concern ourselves mainly with the short term, it is convenient to consider as exogenous the growth rate of capital accumulation as well. We then wind up with the following classification of variables:

Endogenous variables	Exogenous variables
l employment	b credit
y output	w wages
p prices	k capital
	r interest rate ($r = 0$)

Solving the model under these assumptions, we obtain:

$$l = b - w \qquad \text{(a)}$$

$$y = (\beta k + \gamma) + \alpha(b - w) \qquad \text{(b)}$$

$$p = -(\beta k + \gamma) + (1 - \alpha)b + \alpha w \qquad \text{(c)}$$

For our purposes, equations (a) and (b) are of immediate interest, since they allow us to establish directly the effect of credit restrictions on output and employment. Equation (a) shows that employment will fall if bank credits fail to compensate the increase in nominal wages. Output will also be affected, but to a lesser extent, depending on the value of the coefficient α. The basic trend in output growth is represented by the term between brackets, $\beta k + \gamma$, and fluctuations around this trend by the term $\alpha(b - w)$.*

We shall now try to test this proposition.

2.2. AN ECONOMETRIC ESTIMATE OF A TWO-SECTOR VERSION OF THE MODEL

Any model for an underdeveloped country, and particularly for Morocco, that did not take into account a two-sector division of the economy, would be extremely unrealistic. As far as the analysis of the impact of credit restrictions is concerned, there is an additional reason for distinguishing between agriculture and the rest of the economy. The reason is that whenever in Morocco the monetary authorities decided to apply credit restrictions to the economy, agriculture was always exempted from these restrictions (cf. Section 2.3, on the instruments of credit control). Consequently the burden of adjustment fell entirely on the rest of the private sector, since it had to depend on whatever credit was left after agricultural needs were satisfied.

The equations for the two-sector model are straightforward and are here immediately expressed in terms of relative changes.

$$b_a = p_a + \bar{y}_a \qquad \text{demand for credit in agriculture} \qquad \text{(i)}$$

$$b_r = p_r + y_r \qquad \text{demand for credit in the remaining sector} \qquad \text{(ii)}$$

$$y_r = \alpha l_r + \beta \bar{k}_r + \gamma \qquad \text{production function for the remaining sector} \qquad \text{(iii)}$$

---

* An equation similar to (b) was established econometrically in our earlier paper on Argentina[4]. More recently, a model has been derived along the same line of thought by M. Selowsky for Chile [5].

42

$$\bar{w}_r = p_r + y_r - l_r \qquad \text{marginal productivity condition} \qquad \text{(iv)}$$

$$\bar{b} = \lambda b_a + (1 - \lambda) b_r \qquad \text{credit allocation between the two sectors} \qquad \text{(v)}$$

$$p_a - p_r = -\varepsilon(\bar{y}_a - y_r) \qquad \text{relative price function} \qquad \text{(vi)}$$

The variables that are considered as exogenous in the short run are now indicated by a bar over the corresponding symbols. They are:

$\bar{y}_a$: the growth rate of agricultural output
$\bar{k}_r$: the growth rate of physical capital stock in the remaining sector
$\bar{w}_r$: the growth rate of nominal wages in the remaining sector
$\bar{b}$: the overall growth rate of bank credit to the private sector.

Equations (i) and (ii) are the demand-for-credit functions of the two main sectors of the economy. Equation (iii) is the production function for the non-agricultural sector. Equation (iv) follows from the marginal productivity condition for the rest sector.

Equation (v) is a definitional equation which describes the allocation of bank credit between the two sectors. Finally, equation (vi) determines relative prices of agricultural to other goods in function of the relative availability of these goods. In years of good agricultural crops, the relative price of these products will fall, and vice-versa.

The most efficient way to solve this model is to start from (v) and to substitute equations (i) and (ii). This yields:

$$\bar{b} = \lambda(p_a - p_r) + \lambda(\bar{y}_a - y_r) + p_r + y_r$$

which allows us to use equation (vi), and so to arrive at:

$$\bar{b} = \lambda(1 - \varepsilon)(\bar{y}_a - y_r) + y_r + p_r$$

We then replace p_r by its expression which follows from (iv):

$$\bar{b} = \lambda(1 - \varepsilon)(\bar{y}_a - y_r) + \bar{w}_r + l_r$$

y_r is then replaced by (iii), which yields:

$$\bar{b} = \lambda(1 - \varepsilon)(\bar{y}_a - \beta \bar{k}_r - \gamma) + [1 - \alpha\lambda(1 - \varepsilon)] l_r + \bar{w}_r$$

This allows us to derive the reduced-form equation for employment in the remaining (i.e. non-agricultural) sector:

$$l_r = \frac{1}{1 - \alpha\lambda(1-\varepsilon)} \, (\bar{b} - \bar{w}_r) \; - \; \frac{\lambda(1-\varepsilon)}{1 - \alpha\lambda(1-\varepsilon)} \, \bar{y}_a +$$

$$\frac{\lambda(1-\varepsilon)}{1 - \alpha\lambda(1-\varepsilon)} (\beta\bar{k}_r + \gamma)$$

The equation is similar to that of the simple model, apart from the term involving agricultural output and the trend term. These additional terms disappear, however, if $\varepsilon = 1$, i.e. when relative prices move exactly opposite to relative outputs.

When $\varepsilon < 1$, the claim on credit made by increases in agricultural output reduces the possibility of employment expansion in the rest of the economy. Note that $\bar{b}$ represents the overall growth rate of bank credit to the private sector, and not just b_r, or credit to the remaining sector.* The negative effect of $\bar{y}_a$ has therefore to be seen as offsetting the positive influence of $(\bar{b} - \bar{w}_r)$.

Unfortunately, it is impossible to test this employment equation directly, since no employment series exists for the non-agricultural sector, nor for the agricultural sector, for that matter. The only hard facts on employment are those contained in the results of the 1960 and 1971 censuses, which reflect an increase in employment in the private sector of less than 2 per cent. per annum (see Table 1).

Table 1. Growth of employment, 1960–1971

	1960	1971	Annual growth
	(in thousands)		rate
Agriculture	1,845	1,990	0.7%
Remaining sector	905	1,385	3.9%
Total, private sector	2,750	3,375	1.9%
Total, public sector	200	255	2.2%
Total	2,950	3,630	1.9%

On an *average*, the increase in employment opportunities in the non-agricultural sector appears to have been substantial. This does not exclude the possibility that during a number of years restrictive credit

---

* This differs from our Argentina-model, where $(b_r - w_r)$ was used as an explanatory variable, and where as a consequence y_a was likely to have a positive effect on employment and output.

policies limited the expansion of employment that would otherwise have taken place.

This proposition can be tested indirectly, by means of the reduced-form equation for output, which is obtained after substituting the reduced-form equation for employment into the production function (iii):

$$y_r = - \frac{\alpha \lambda (1 - \varepsilon)}{1 - \alpha \lambda (1 - \varepsilon)} \bar{y}_a + \frac{\alpha}{1 - \alpha \lambda (1 - \varepsilon)} (\bar{b} - \bar{w}_r) + \frac{\beta \bar{k}_r + \gamma}{1 - \alpha \lambda (1 - \varepsilon)}$$

Alternatively, it is also possible to derive a reduced-form equation for total output, using as definitional equation:

$$y = \mu \bar{y}_a + (1 - \mu) y_r$$

$$= \frac{\mu - \alpha \lambda (1 - \varepsilon)}{1 - \alpha \lambda (1 - \varepsilon)} \bar{y}_a + \frac{\alpha (1 - \mu)}{1 - \alpha \lambda (1 - \varepsilon)} (\bar{b} - \bar{w}_r) + \frac{(1 - \mu)(\beta \bar{k}_r + \gamma)}{1 - \alpha \lambda (1 - \varepsilon)}$$

One further complication which arises when we attempt to test these output equations is that for Morocco no wage series exists for the private sector. All we know is that minimum wages were not raised until the end of 1971. On that occasion, the agricultural minimum wage (SMAG) was increased by 30 per cent., and the industrial minimum wage (SMIG) by 12 to 31 per cent., according to the geographical area. We have, therefore, tested our equations for the period 1962–1971 only, for which $\bar{w}_r$ was probably close to zero, and can be dropped from our specification. These were the results:

$$y_r = 2.54 + 0.001\ \bar{y}_a + 0.24\ \bar{b}$$
$$ (0.058) (0.15)$$

$R^2 = 0.43$
$\bar{R}^2 = 0.27$
$DW = 1.28$
$COL = 0.71$

$$y = 1.77 + 0.32\ \bar{y}_a + 0.14\ \bar{b}$$
$$ (0.04) (0.10)$$

$R^2 = 0.96$
$\bar{R}^2 = 0.95$
$DW = 1.39$
$COL = 0.71$

The coefficient of $\bar{y}_a$ in the second estimating equation corresponds exactly to the a priori value of μ, which has been practically constant over the period: the share of agriculture in total GDP was 32 % in 1962 and 31 % in 1972. This implies that the value of the relative price elasticity ε is approximately equal to unity. In this case, the coefficient of $\bar{y}_a$ in the first estimating equation should be zero, which is also borne out by the

45

regression result. If $\varepsilon = 1$, the coefficient of $(\bar{b} - \bar{w}_r)$ in the reduced-form equations becomes α and $\alpha(1 - \mu)$ respectively. If $\alpha = 1/3$ as the factor shares indicate, the coefficients should be 0.33 and 0.22 respectively. The estimated coefficients are somewhat lower, viz. 0.24 and 0.14. Of course, when our hypothesis $\bar{w}_r = 0$ is not fulfilled, the coefficient of $\bar{b}$ will laways be biased downwards.* This may explain the discrepancies with the theoretical values.

The relatively low R^2 obtained for the output function of the non-agricultural sector indicates that there are other important factors determining fluctuations of the growth rate in this sector. We must keep in mind that our model only describes the supply side of the economy, and that the demand side is at least equally important in determining variations in the growth rate, especially for the remaining sector. This therefore leaves sufficient room for the operation of fiscal policy measures, as estimated by Professor Snyder in the previous chapter.

2.3. INSTRUMENTS OF CREDIT CONTROL

In controlling the overall value of credit extended by the deposit money banks, the central bank has made use of various monetary instruments. It has relied on:

a. individual rediscount ceilings on deposit money banks and other specialized credit institutions;

b. minimum reserve requirements;

c. different ratios related to the liabilities of the deposit money banks;

d. from February 1969 to June 1972 quantitative limitations on bank lending, by limiting the overall rate of short-term credit expansion to the private sector ('encadrement du crédit');

---

* Assume $\varepsilon = 1$. If we estimate the equation

$$y_r = (\beta \bar{k}_r + \gamma) + \alpha \bar{b} + (u - \alpha \bar{w}_r)$$

instead of

$$y_r = (\beta \bar{k}_r + \gamma) + \alpha(\bar{b} - \bar{w}_r) + u$$

we find:

$$a = \frac{m(\bar{b}y_r)}{s_{\bar{b}}^2} = \frac{m\bar{b}[(\beta \bar{k}_r + \gamma) + \alpha(\bar{b} - \bar{w}_r) + u]}{s_{\bar{b}}^2}$$

the probability limit of which is

$$\text{plim } a = \frac{\alpha \sigma_{\bar{b}}^2 - \alpha \mu \bar{b} \bar{w}_r}{\sigma_{\bar{b}}^2} = \alpha \left(1 - \rho_{bw_r} \cdot \frac{\sigma w_r}{\sigma_b} \right)$$

For $\rho > 0$ plim a will always be smaller than α.

46

e. changes in interest rates have so far not been used as an instrument of monetary policy, and the basic discount rate has remained unchanged at 3.5 per cent. since the Bank was founded.

Since 1965 Morocco has undertaken a series of stabilization programmes, supported by six consecutive stand-by arrangements with the IMF, designed to contain the rate of domestic credit expansion within limits consistent with the objective of restoring and strengthening Morocco's external position.

Table 2. Foreign reserves, in MDH

December 1961	1,008	December 1967	448
1962	911	1968	312
1963	694	1969	417
1964	380	1970	598
1965	611	1971	958
1966	548	1972	1,301

In 1964 foreign reserves fell dramatically as a consequence of a poor agricultural harvest, and a huge outflow of private capital. A fall in overall output was avoided by stepping up bank credits to the private sector (+ 7.2 %). The rate of inflation was moderate (+ 4.2 %).

In 1965, agricultural output picked up again, but, as bank credits did not match the increase in costs, manufacturing output fell, and the overall growth rate of the economy remained very modest (+ 2.3 %). Imports fell slightly and foreign reserves were restored to the 1963-level.

The first IMF-stand-by credit was accorded in September 1965. In December, money supply suddenly jumped by 185 MDH, which was more than the total increase for the first eleven months. Bank credits to the private sector accounted for 86 MDH of the December increase. This so alarmed the monetary authorities that on February 11th, 1966, it was decided to create a special 'monetary reserve' account, where all credit institutions had to deposit the equivalent of the amount of the increase in deposits. This in effect introduced a 100 per cent. marginal redeposit rate with the central bank. In addition, rediscount ceilings were set for credits to the private sector as well as for government paper. It was also decided to reform the institutional framework of credit control at a later stage [6, p. 34]. The new measures were extremely effective: outstanding loans declined for five consecutive months. In the meantime, preliminary crop forecasts indicated a substantial drop in agricultural output, which was to reduce demand for credit later in the year. The economy was

47

therefore negatively affected by the joint impact of credit restrictions and a poor harvest. It is important to note that the decision to limit credit was taken *before* the information regarding agricultural output became available. The overall output of the private sector fell by 2.2 per cent. that year. On November 29th, 1966, the marginal monetary reserve ratio was reduced to 25 per cent., and made applicable only to demand deposits. Consequently, credits shot up again in December, to finish at a slightly higher level than the year before (+ 1.9 %).

Direct controls

From February 1969 to June 1972, quantitative limitations were introduced on bank lending by limiting the overall rate of short-term credit expansion to the private sector ('encadrement du crédit'). The credit measures taken in 1969 were inspired, with some justification, by the rapid credit expansion (+ 14 %) during the preceding year, and the historically low level of foreign reserves (see Table 1). The 1968 agricultural bumper crop (+ 30 %) and the expansion of the rest of the economy (+ 5 %) had considerably overheated the economy, although the effect on the price level was not noticeable until the following year.

The credit reform of 1967 was apparently insufficient to cope with such a situation, since it did not allow the use of the interest rate as a credit allocating mechanism.

In February 1969, it was therefore decided to introduce a limit to the permissible growth rate of bank credits. First, it was specified that, for each individual credit institution, outstanding loans at the end of April should not exceed the level reached at the end of September of the previous year. Then, at the beginning of July, a permissible growth rate of 5 per cent. was established, for the period from September 1968 at December 1969, and for all credits excluding those for financing cereal crops. The actual overall growth rate of credits between those two data was 3.7 per cent., well within the permissible limits. Nevertheless, if we calculate the average monthly growth rate for 1969 over 1968, we arrive at an annual growth rate of 7.7 per cent., which is twice as high.

The reason is that in 1968 credit had only started to expand rapidly during the second half of the year, under the pressure of crop financing. By choosing September 1968 as a bench-mark, the monetary authorities still left room for high growth rates with respect to the earlier months of that year (see Table 3).

As a result, the growth rate of the non-agricultural sector did not suffer too much from the credit restrictions (+ 5.1 per cent.), and the

48

Table 3. Bank credits to the private sector, 1968 and 1969 (in MDH)

	1968		1969	Relative change
January	2028		2524	(+ 25.1%)
February	2033		2477	(+ 21.8%)
March	2058	(—2.8%)	2414	(+ 17.3%)
April	2124	⌐———→	2367	(+ 11.4%)
May	2169		2381	(+ 9.8%)
June	2272		2421	(+ 6.6%)
July	2358		2555	(+ 8.4%)
August	2405		2520	(+ 4.8%)
September	2434⌐		2462	(+ 1.2%)
October	2528		2569	(+ 1.6%)
November	2590		2549	(− 1.6%)
December	2629 └—————→		2523	(− 4.0%)
		(+3.7%)		
Average	2302		2480	(+ 7.7%)

overall setback for the economy was not as great as it had been in 1966.

The same policy was pursued until June 1972. During this period, the growth of credit was very restrained (+ 4.8 % in 1970 and 5.5 % in 9171).

Agricultural production recovered from its 1968 fall, and growth of the remaining sector was moderate. Foreign reserves recovered spectacularly, and at the CCMF-meeting of July 1972, it was decided that the quantitative limitations on credit were no longer necessary, and a return to more classical instruments was recommended [7].

2.4. CONCLUSION

In the course of the past decade, credit policy was probably too restrictive in about four years out of ten (1965, 1966, 1969 and 1970). This undoubtedly resulted in under-utilization of available manpower and real growth of the economy below its potential. The exact impact of these restrictions in terms of man-years lost is impossible to estimate, because we do not possess all the relevant information to implement our econometric equations (e.g. that concerning nominal wages). Nevertheless, as far as the future is concerned, our model supplies a rule-of-thumb for credit policy, which is that *bank credits to the private sector should be allowed to expand at a rate which exceeds that of nominal wages by at least four per cent.* (the latter being the desired growth rate of employment). This, of course, is only a necessary, and not a sufficient condition for employment growth. The measure must be supplemented by appropriate fiscal, and

49

other policies on the demand side, and by structural policies on the supply side.

[In a comment, P. Coenraets, of the Belgian Central Bank, and a former adviser to the Moroccan Central Bank, during the period of credit controls 1969–1970, elaborates on the difficulties of monetary management in a country with a large public deficit. The only check on money supply is through restriction of credit to the private sector. He doubts that a deliberate expansion of bank credit could create employment. He also points out the difficulties of identifying the demand-for-credit function during a period of credit restrictions.]

Appendix. Statistical series

	y	y_r	y_a	$\bar{b}$	p
1962	12.3	6.5	27.0	15.2	5.1
1963	5.5	5.0	6.6	9.2	5.6
1964	0.6	2.0	−2.3	8.8	4.2
1965	2.3	0.9	5.4	−1.4	3.5
1966	−2.3	2.3	−11.8	1.1	−1.1
1967	6.7	5.1	10.4	8.5	−0.6
1968	12.7	5.3	29.6	14.0	0.2
1969	0.4	5.1	− 8.3	7.7	3.1
1970	5.1	6.6	1.9	4.8	1.2
1971	5.1	4.6	6.2	5.5	4.1
1972	4.6	5.1	3.5	4.6	3.8

Source: *National Accounts* and *Statistical Yearbook*.

REFERENCES

1. Secrétariat d'Etat au Plan, *Plan de Développement Economique et Social 1973–1977*, Volume I.
2. Banque du Maroc, 'Le Système Bancaire Marocain', *Etudes et Statistiques*, July 1971.
3. P. Davidson and S. Weintraub, 'Money as Cause and Effect', *The Economic Journal*, Vol. 83, No. 332, December 1973, pp. 1117–1132.
4. G. Maynard and W. van Rijckeghem, 'Stabilization Policy in an Inflationary Economy: The Case of Argentina', in G. Papanek (ed.), *Development Policy: Theory and Practice*, Cambridge, Mass., 1968, pp. 207–235.
5. M. Selowsky, 'Cost of Price Stabilization Policies in a Strongly Inflationary Economy', *Quarterly Journal of Economics*, 1973, pp. 44–59.
6. Banque du Maroc, 'Rapport Présenté à Sa Majesté le Roi' (Exercice), 1966.
7. 'L'Encadrement du Crédit Remplacé par une Technique plus Simple', *La Vie Economique*, 23 June 1972.

3. Effects of trade policy on economic development and employment

J. D. Shilling

Morocco's planning authorities have viewed and to a large extent continue to view the foreign trade sector primarily in terms of finding the means (foreign exchange) necessary to cover the import demand generated in the other producing sectors and among consumers.

'Foreign trade represents about 40% of our [Morocco's] Gross Domestic Product: which is to say it is of vital importance for our economic development, and by means of our exports we cover, at least partially, our imports of all kinds, particularly of capital equipment ...
But in any case our commercial balance remains structurally in deficit due to the needs of our development. This is a necessity that must be accepted on condition that the country impose on itself an iron discipline in the selection of imports and give preference to capital equipment over non-indispensable consumer goods' [1, pp. 543–544].

However, this concern about foreign trade is primarily oriented along commercial lines: the problem of matching the country's purchases with its ability to pay. Little direct or detailed attention is paid to the composition of trade other than the general and now almost axiomatic preference for capital over consumer goods. In effect, the Moroccans tend to treat foreign trade as an extension of the domestic commercial sector where the limitations are foreign exchange availabilities, duties, and quotas rather than credit availabilities, taxes, and allocation controls. Proper government activity is then centered on conception, promulgation, and enforcement of regulations concerning these commercial problems. Questions of 'optimal' (in terms of their own objectives) allocation of foreign exchange reserves are of only secondary importance. The distribution of import quotas is the only policy of direct allocational impact, but even here the distribution is based more on commercial criteria than on analytic judgements of the efficiency of such allocations.

This treatment of foreign trade as an extension of the commercial sector stems primarily from long association with the French. Under the Protectorate, most of the trading was carried on by French firms and

51

restrictions on their trade were minimal. Since independence the situation has changed more rapidly than the analytic techniques used, to the detriment of Moroccan planning efforts. Attempts to adapt Moroccan foreign trade policy to the needs of development since independence have been less than systematic. There has been little attempt to integrate the foreign trade sector into overall economic analysis beyond trying roughly to balance imports and exports through tariffs and quotas. Trade policies have been applied in a rather *ad hoc* manner in response to specific balance of payments crises and to the needs of protection for domestic industry rather than as part of a coordinated plan to influence the industrial development or to maximize growth or employment. Even though the 1968–1972 Plan outlined a theoretical procedure for evaluating the foreign exchange impact of new investment projects (p. 318, vol. II), this procedure was not applied to any of the proposed investment projects in the Plan and no consistent import estimates were made. As a result, specific trade policies have on occasion led to unexpected results, often inconsistent with the stated goals of growth and maximum employment.

Given the lack of an overall and consistently developed trade policy in Morocco, it is not possible to provide a consistent analysis of 'The Moroccan Trade Policy'. To the extent possible, trade policy will be treated as a whole, remembering that this is in large part an artificial construct for the sake of this presentation. It will frequently be necessary to analyze individual policies to show whether they were consistent or not with achieving the stated goals, particularly those of growth and employment.

In discussing critically the effects of certain sets of policies, one must first set forth some criteria by which the effectiveness can be judged. In a field with as much uncertainty and as few quantifiable standards as economic development, this is not at all simple. There are so many intangibles and unknowns that lack of, for instance, adequate (however that is defined) growth or employment can hardly be regarded as sufficient evidence of a policy's ineffectiveness in this field. Simple performance is not a good guide since a policy may not produce the expected results for reasons totally unrelated to the policy itself. The analytically rigorous frequently suggest hypothetical norms as standards. In the field of trade policy, the case of 'free trade' is thus usually proposed as the standard for judging different trade policies. This seems to me an inappropriate criterion. The assumptions of free trade are not satisfied in LDC's, and they are not going to be satisfied under any conceivable set of circumstances that the policy-maker will face. He is condemned to operate in a world of second, third, or worse, best where the norm of 'free trade' is of little use. Likewise comparing the hypothetical results of a free trade policy to those of an actual policy are of little use since the divergences are likely to be so great for any practical policy that the comparison is of little value.

Instead I will apply a dual criterion of suitability. By this I mean to judge policies on their analytic ability to achieve their stated goals and then by the practical effectiveness of the policies in achieving the goals. An example of the first part would be to analyze the effectiveness of Morocco's capital subsidy ('primes d'équipement') system. Analytically one could conclude that this would tend to increase the capital intensiveness of investment and increase the return to the owners of capital, thus working against the goals of more equitable income distribution and expanded employment. The overall effects on production would be indeterminate depending on capital-output ratios of the projects. Thus one could judge such a policy is not effective or suitable on analytic grounds alone.

An example of the second part would be to study the wheat improvement program and related extension work. The policy itself was well conceived and in principle capable of achieving large increases in wheat productivity and thus production by the introduction of new, improved grains. However, administrative problems relating to the timely delivery of necessary materials (seeds, fertilizers) and to the placement of sufficient Moroccan extension officers in the field (lack of staff, vehicles, etc.) prevented the program from achieving its goals. Thus one could say that the policy was not effective or suitable in the sense that with the existing or foreseeable bureaucracy it could not be implemented. This is a reflection of the ability of the administration to implement a particular policy, although related judgments about the quality of administration should be tempered by consideration of the many problems that are beyond the control and foresight of the administration.

Admittedly this dual criterion is not absolute in any sense and might well be criticised for its own judgmental nature. But it does provide a useful approach for judging policy in a practical sense as well as a basis of discussion about the effectiveness of various policies when considered opinions differ about their effectiveness.

In the rest of this paper I will try systematically to present Moroccan trade policy and analyse its effectiveness. The first section will present the Moroccan planning goals and discuss their consistency. That will be followed by a section tracing the important developments in the foreign trade sector since independence and describing the specific policies used.

The next section will deal with effects of the specific policies on industry, growth, and employment. The final section considers the new directions in trade policy indicated in the 1973–1977 Five Year Plan and recent trade developments.

3.1. POLICY GOALS AND THEIR CONSISTENCY

The overall goals of the Moroccan planning effort are typical of LDC's and quite commendable in general. Drawing from the various planning documents and other statements of intent, the primary goals relevant to trade policy can be listed as follows:
1. rapid growth of GDP;
2. increased employment and better distribution of income;
3. freedom from dependence on foreign trade;
4. balance of payments equilibrium;
5. changing composition of imports toward capital and intermediate goods (import substitution);
6. promotion of exports (primarily traditional ones till the current Plan);
7. diversification of markets;
8. stemming capital outflows;
9. providing for the economy the best trading terms possible.

This list is synthetic in that no such clear listing is produced in the Plan documents, nor are the goals formulated in precisely these terms. However, it is a fair representation of the variously stated objectives of the Moroccan development efforts insofar as they concern the foreign trade sector. There is no specific analysis of these goals in terms that adequately relate trade policy action to their achievement. Some qualitative relations are made, but no general model, either implicit or explicit is used to provide any quantitative relation. Even the qualitative relations are often insufficiently analyzed and incorrect.

This is not to depreciate the validity of these goals nor the good faith with which they are presented. Rather it underlines the analytical difficulty in judging the effectiveness of the policies implemented without the benefit of a framework relating the policies to the goals they seek to achieve. In general, except for goals directly concerning foreign trade (e.g. numbers 3, 6, 7, 8), the foreign trade implications of the other goals are often ignored. I believe that this is in large part due to the conceptualization of foreign trade as essentially a commercial activity rather than a problem of allocation of scarce resources (imports or foreign exchange generally).

Indirect effects such as increased import requirements for import substitution industries are rarely even considered in discussions of these goals. The lack of a general model to relate the policies to the achievement of the goals often leads to difficulty in policy formulation and to the promulgation of occasionally unsuitable policies.

Before going on to a discussion of specific policies, these goals deserve some commentary. The first two of growth and increased employment and income distribution have become the standard aims of development planning, the latter fairly recently. Morocco's first Five Year Plan (1960–1964) projected a 6.2 % rate of growth and the subsequent Three Year Plan a more modest 3.5 %. The actual growth rate of GDP during the period 1960–1967 was about 3 % per year. The second Five Year Plan (1968–1972) achieved a rate of growth of 5.6 %. The current Five Year Plan (1973–1977) projects a more ambitious 7.5 %, a rate which proved over-optimistic for 1973, but will probably be realized for the period as a whole due to the trebling of phosphate prices in the end of 1973.

Quantitative estimates of the employment and income distribution goals is harder to come by. The 1968–1972 Plan projected the creation of 485,000 new jobs with an achievement of about 400,000. However the reduction of unemployment was seriously underestimated: 115,000 projected unemployed versus 350,000 actual. Census figures indicated a relative decline in the income shares of the poorest segments of the population during the last Plan and the current Plan aims at least to stop this decline. The employment goal of 800,000 new jobs in the 1973–1977 Plan appears optimistic. Heretofore, the trade impact of these goals has not been analyzed, and imports and exports were projected independently of the sectoral growth and employment projection[2]. It is likely that policies of low tariffs on capital imports and capital subsidies have not helped employment expansion.

The third goal of reduced dependence on trade is largely rhetorical and rather poorly defined, though frequently mentioned in discussions of trade policy. Taken literally and pushed to the extreme, it would imply a move toward autarchy – a state which even large and well developed countries cannot reasonably hope to achieve. More frequently it is taken to mean increased ability to produce domestically goods that were previously imported, and thus it becomes kind of a code word for import substitution programs. But even at this level the goal is subject to a fundamental fallacy for a country as small as Morocco. Given the relatively large optimal plant sizes in most industries and the diversified input needs of most modern industry, it is doubtful any amount of import substitution would free Morocco from dependence on imported

55

inputs or the necessity of importing a relatively large number of finished goods in exchange for those goods Morocco can efficiently specialize in producing.

In fact the evidence of a large number of countries from Japan and Singapore to the Benelux countries shows that as smaller countries develop, they become increasingly dependent on trade, while at the same time they are increasingly able to benefit from the gains due to specialization in trade. The most meaningful interpretation of this goal is increased freedom from *constraints* imposed by balance of payments deficits and increased ability of the economy to pursue its domestic goals without undue concern over foreign exchange constraints. This is a legitimate goal. However, under close scrutiny, it tends to imply more emphasis on export promotion than on import substitution, as the Moroccans are slowly coming to realize. Unfortunately, unless stated clearly in this latter form, pursuit of this goal often leads to trade-reducing policies such as excessive import substitution.

Thus far the goal of balance of payments equilibrium has been conceived of by the Moroccans in a rather narrow framework of increasing foreign reserves and/or maintaining the current account deficit within the limits that can be financed. Little attention is paid to the relation of the deficit to the overall growth process and thus automatic policy response has been to restrain expenditures, primarily imports, whenever a problem arose. Although more attention is now being paid to increasing receipts, the Moroccans have not yet begun treating foreign exchange as a scarce resource to be allocated for the maximization of their other goals, as for example comparing the net foreign exchange impact of alternative import substitution and export promotion projects.

The goal of import substitution has been a primary factor in the industrialization policy of Morocco to date. Although rarely explicitly stated or developed, it has consistently characterized investment projects approved or undertaken by the state and has led to an appropriate protection policy. Where large-scale avowed import substitution projects have been carried out in Morocco emphasis has primarily been on the direct reduction of imports (e.g. sugar) or on domestic value added as an indicator of import reduction (vehicles). Some attention has been paid to the physical capital import costs, which usually appear to be out-weighted by the imports replaced. The intermediate material and foreign capital financing costs have not been included in any Moroccan study I have seen, although their weight often seriously reduces or eliminates any import savings of import substitution projects.

On the other hand, the goal of promotion of exports has been – until recently – limited to traditional agricultural and mineral products. These promotions were heavily favored by the large producing and exporting organizations with important vested interests in the traditional products (OCE for agriculture; OCP for phosphates; and BRPM for other minerals), and often continued in the face of unfavorable world demand conditions, as with citrus. Nowhere to my knowledge were calculations made to determine the relative value of resources directed into these sectors in terms of earning foreign exchange, improving growth or employment, etc. The planning authorities have not yet been able to exert enough control over these decisions to make economic analysis of their relative value to the economy as a whole.

The goal of diversifying markets presents a ticklish problem for the Moroccans. Primarily aimed at reducing traditional heavy dependence on the French market, real diversification may prove to be costly and difficult to achieve in the face of the expanding EEC. Before and immediately following independence, the French market had been particularly lucrative for Morocco due to special agreements, some of which were maintained after France joined the EEC. However, over time the value of this special status has diminished. The share of France in total trade of Morocco has fallen from more than 41 % of imports to less than 35 % from 1966 to 1970, and from 45 % to 40 % for exports[3]. Some further decline seems probable after 1973 as the effects of Moroccanization take hold, but it is doubtful any very sharp decline will occur. Trade with the rest of the EEC is increasing as a result of the Accord of Association signed in 1969.

A large part of the decline in imports from France was due to the shift of cereal purchases to North America, so the overall dependence on France for other products has hardly diminished. With the new agreements of association under negotiation and the expansion of the EEC, it is unlikely that Morocco will be able to diversify a large part of its trade away from Europe. Its main directions of diversification have been toward Africa and the Socialist Bloc countries. The former diversification is beginning to show signs of success with imports from Africa rising to 5.8 % of the total in 1972 and exports to 6.3%, with Algeria accounting for a large part of the trade[4]. The expansion of trade with the Socialist Bloc through barter agreements was less successful. Morocco often had difficulty finding desirable products in the list eligible for barter and service was frequently unsatisfactory. As a result Morocco accumulated a credit on these agreements of some 130 million dirhams over the period 1966–1971. About 100 million dirhams of these credits were discounted to other countries to cover Morocco's trading deficits there[5].

The objective of stemming capital flows is primarily aimed at slowing the repatriation of French-owned capital accumulated prior to independence and for which Morocco is understandably reluctant to use up its foreign exchange. This has resulted in the accretion of a large number of controls on capital movement and investment. As often as not, these have also staunched legitimate capital flows and have created a great deal of uncertainty among potential investors. While it is easy to sympathize with the aim of this goal, it is quite likely that its pursuit has seriously retarded the achievement of other more fundamental goals and employment by clouding the investment picture.

3.2. DEVELOPMENTS IN THE TRADE SECTOR AND DESCRIPTION OF TRADE POLICIES

Developments in the trade sector, particularly balance of payments problems have exerted important influences on trade policies. Given the conservative orientation of Moroccan authorities, payments difficulties have quickly led to import restraints. While such restraints may have been necessary under the circumstances, it is probable that better analysis and planning could have mitigated the problems and avoided the need for such stringent and *ad hoc* reactions.

To illustrate the developments in the trade sector, the trade flows disaggregated by end-use category since 1956 are shown in Table 1, along with the figures for gross interior production (gross domestic product less government wages and salaries) and gross national product. The trade patterns can be divided into roughly four periods of alternating restraint and expansion which reflect both domestic developments and the overall balance of payments constraint faced by the economy.

The period from 1956 to 1959 was one of constraint, or more properly restraint. It was a time of uncertainty and consolidation after independence. Total imports did not grow during this period as imports of capital equipment and consumption goods fell below historically expected levels. This was due to the departure of large numbers of French after independence and to the ensuing uncertainty over the investment prospects of the country. In addition the newly independent government increased tariffs. No longer a French protectorate, Morocco felt the need to push toward current account equilibrium, which was essentially achieved by 1959. Exports increased normally during this period which assured the balance on the current account. Their growth was concentrated in the traditional agricultural and mining sectors, which still benefited from some advantages on the French market. The production and marketing structures of these sectors were largely unaffected by independence although control of many of the major organizations was nominally passed from French to Moroccan hands.

By 1960 the economy was prepared to undertake more ambitious economic activity and launched the first Five Year Economic Development Plan (1960–1964) with a target rate of growth of 6.3 %. This was quite expansionist in terms of previous growth rates and entailed a sharp increase in investment. Imports took off rapidly in 1960, led by capital equipment and consumption goods. Agricultural imports also increased as the farming sector was unable to keep up with domestic food consumption demands and Morocco became a net importer of cereal grains for the first time in recent history. Exports of agricultural and mineral products continued to grow but their increase fell short of the growth in imports and a current account deficit again opened. Reserves were depleted so that by 1964, Morocco faced a severe foreign exchange crisis (see also Table 2 of the previous chapter, p. 47). The high level of investment during this Plan created more domestic demand than could be satisfied by increased production or paid for with increased exports and Morocco quickly reached its foreign exchange constraint.

1965 saw the imposition of severe trade restrictions in the form of import quotas covering the majority of imports and the restraint of domestic credit expansion. Import growth slowed, most markedly in terms of consumption goods, although it did not stop entirely as had happened in the first period of constraint. Investment was maintained and imports of investment goods even increased toward the end of the period in 1967–1968. Agricultural imports peaked in 1967 and began to decline in 1968 as the effects of that year's exceptionally good harvests began to be felt. In the application of the trade controls, the Moroccans made serious efforts to be selective in order to allow planned investment to be undertaken and to be sure existing plants had the raw materials to operate. This allocation was in terms of satisfying the needs of the existing industrial structure however, and was not designed to optimize the use of foreign exchange by allocating imports to more efficient users. Investment goods imports were not generally subject to quota controls, though a large part of planned investment was controlled directly or indirectly.

Exports during this period essentially stagnated: agricultural exports grew slowly and mineral exports actually declined. Agricultural exports suffered from both marketing and production problems while mineral production declined due to the depletion of existing mines and/or

59

Table 1. Foreign trade, 1956-1972 (millions of current dirhams)

	1956		1957		1958		1959		1960		1961		1962	
	Val.	%	Val.	%	Val.	%	Val.	%	Val.	%	Val.	%	Val.	%
IMPORTS														
Total:	1607		1491		1669		1456		2087		2257		2193	
Food, Beverages, Tobacco	396	24.6	412	27.6	411	24.6	327	22.5	445	21.3	561	24.9	528	2
Energic	102	6.3	128	8.6	131	7.8	126	8.7	153	7.3	158	7.0	86	
Primary products, animal & vegetable	103	6.4	114	7.6	134	8.0	107	7.9	186	8.9	208	9.2	220	
Primary products, mineral	5	0.3	7	0.4	10	0.6	9	0.6	12	0.6	12	0.5	15	
Intermediate goods	241	15.0	217	14.6	298	17.9	260	17.9	374	17.9	394	17.5	400	
Capital equipment, agricultural	16	1.0	18	1.2	36	2.2	19	1.3	16	0.8	10	0.4	20	
Capital equipment, industrial	209	13.0	156	10.5	213	12.8	167	11.5	265	12.3	300	13.3	275	
Consumption goods	483	30.0	390	26.2	419	25.1	409	28.1	567	27.2	594	26.3	597	2
Gold			6		16		26		67		20		7	
EXPORTS														
Total:	1190		1179		1450		1444		1793		1731		1763	
Food, Beverages, Tobacco	572	48.1	449	38.1	664	45.8	646	44.7	822	45.8	748	43.2	817	4
Energic	18	1.5	20	1.7	18	1.2	18	1.2	16	0.9	16	0.9	14	
Primary products, animal & vegetable	103	8.7	148	12.6	122	8.4	113	7.8	149	8.3	135	7.8	133	
Primary products, mineral	277	31.7	438	37.2	510	35.2	522	36.1	647	36.1	673	38.9	638	3
Intermediate goods	77	6.5	78	6.6	84	5.8	87	6.0	96	5.4	88	5.1	93	
Capital equipment, agricultural	–		–		–		–		–		–		–	
Capital equipment, industrial	7	0.5	11	0.9	8	0.6	7	0.5	7	0.4	7	0.4	11	
Consumption goods	34	2.9	33	2.8	44	3.0	40	2.8	54	3.0	64	3.7	56	
Balance, as % of exports (–) = surplus	417	35.0	312	26.5	219	15.1	12	0.8	294	16.4	526	30.4	430	2
Gross interior production	641		652		739		724		820		808		954	
Gross national product	749		764		851		831		926		911		1069	

production limitations. In spite of the import controls imposed, the stagnation of exports led in an increasing commercial account deficit during the period 1965–1968. Fortunately, workers' remittance and tourist receipts began to increase significantly during this period and it was possible to reconstitute reserves from the low 1964 level. Increased capital flows also helped avoid further balance of payments difficulties.

The fourth period, one of expansion, began in 1969 and continues through the present. This corresponds roughly to the Second Five Year Plan (1968–1972), the most successful Plan so far, and its continuation with the Third Five Year Plan (1973–1977). The Second Plan was late in preparation and had little effect on 1968. Investment and industrial

1963		1964		1965		1966		1967		1968		1969		1970		1971		1972	
l.	%	Val.	%	Val.	%	Val.	%	Val.	%	Val.	%	Val.	%	Val.	%	Val.	%	Val.	%
43		2328		2291		2418		2620		2790		2844		3471		3533		3577	
55	20.7	636	27.3	688	30.0	660	27.3	723	27.6	619	22.2	452	15.9	583	16.8	701	19.8	625	17.5
10	3.6	137	5.9	119	5.6	117	4.8	127	4.8	166	5.9	165	5.8	189	5.5	236	6.7	255	7.1
19	11.1	243	10.4	301	13.1	294	12.2	269	10.3	327	11.7	292	10.3	387	11.2	417	11.8	410	11.5
7	0.8	19	0.8	22	1.0	24	1.0	22	0.8	36	1.3	51	1.8	40	1.1	49	1.4	58	1.6
57	20.4	454	19.5	448	19.6	516	21.3	550	21.0	616	22.1	731	25.7	864	24.9	790	22.4	945	26.4
27	1.2	20	0.9	24	1.0	27	1.1	23	0.9	51	1.8	54	1.9	43	1.2	152	1.5	40	1.1
43	15.3	324	13.9	329	14.4	358	14.8	506	19.3	537	19.2	610	21.4	791	22.8	737	20.9	670	18.7
98	26.7	480	20.6	348	15.2	416	17.2	397	15.2	433	15.5	483	17.0	567	16.3	545	15.4	561	15.7
7		14		10		6		4		5		7		6		5		12	
43		2186		2176		2168		2146		2278		2455		2470		2526		2963	
13	48.5	1074	49.1	1050	48.3	1052	48.5	1662	49.5	1168	51.3	1185	48.3	1249	50.6	1206	47.7	1384	46.9
15	0.7	16	0.7	13	0.6	7	0.3	11	0.5	16	0.7	0	0,3	9	0.4	9	0.4	6	0.2
10	7.3	145	6.6	140	6.4	174	8.0	141	6.6	134	5.9	238	9.7	166	6.7	153	6.1	259	8.8
17	31.3	812	37.1	848	39.0	778	35.9	754	35.1	738	32.4	768	31.3	784	31.8	762	30.2	877	29.7
17	4.0	72	3.3	94	4.3	110	5.1	122	5.7	156	6.8	144	5.9	136	5.5	188	7.4	188	6.4
–	–	–	–	–	–	–	–	–	–	–	–	–	–	–	–	–	–	-3	0.1
9	0.5	10	0.5	6	0.3	5	0.2	2	0.1	8	0.4	3	0.1	13	0.5	40	1.6	27	0.9
51	2.6	64	2.9	52	2.4	44	2.0	55	2.6	57	2.5	109	4.4	112	4.5	167	6.6	207	7.0
10	15.4	142	6.5	115	5.3	250	11.5	474	22.1	512	22.5	389	15.8	1001	40.5	1007	39.9	624	21.1
13		1115		1180		1141		1210		1366		1414		1504		1642		1781	
10		1262		1325		1288		1371		1536		1611		1715		1888			

production both increased markedly after 1968, as did the corresponding imports of capital and intermediate goods. Total imports did not increase so rapidly because the record harvest of 1968 greatly reduced the need for food imports in 1969. Beginning in 1967, the import quota system was liberalized slowly and imports of consumption goods began to reflect this by 1970. Exports grew at moderate rates through 1971, due primarily to agricultural exports. In 1972 however, mineral exports surged and the growth in consumer goods exports began to make itself felt, giving total exports a sharp boost. The juxtaposition of low agricultural imports in 1969 and rapid expansion of imports of industrial goods in 1970 led to a surprisingly large increase in the deficit in 1970 and caused a great deal

61

of concern over the possibility of another foreign exchange crisis. The continued high level of invisible receipts, however, stayed the imposition of further controls. Growth and investment slowed considerably in 1971 and early 1972 due to domestic political uncertainty. Imports remained roughly constant as exports began to grow once again.

The overall impression drawn from this brief history of trade flows serves to reinforce the conclusion that the application of trade policy is viewed primarily in commercial terms. To the extent that the foreign exchange position permitted, imports were made available to domestic users on easy terms. When the foreign exchange position was tight, imports were restrained, first with high tariffs and later with the addition of quotas. To the extent that attempts were made to allocate restricted imports, they were in terms of supplying existing users as equitably as possible (supplying 'old customers') or in response to an industrial policy that did not explicitly take foreign exchange considerations into account, as for example with the uniformly low duties on imported new capital equipment. Foreign exchange availability was largely viewed as an exogenous constraint on the execution of projects requiring it. No effort was made to determine the indirect or total foreign exchange impact of various projects and to choose among them at least partially on this basis.

The specific trade policies used include high protective tariffs and quotas on imports, special tariff rebates on approved capital equipment imports, special tariff derogation schemes for imports used in exports, and bilateral and multilateral trade agreements directing trade with certain countries. In addition a number of export promotion schemes such as a free trade zone at Tangiers and tax holidays for selected industries have been passed. Besides these more strictly trade oriented policies, a number of industrial and agricultural policies and important direct and indirect effects on trade. These include the capital subsidy in the investment code and the agricultural self-sufficiency programs. In spite of the relatively clear statement of most of these investment promotion policies and of their benefits, the prevading feeling among those investors who would potentially profit and thus improve the trading position of Morocco has been one of uncertainty, both as to whether the stated or implied benefits would actually be extended and as to whether once extended in principle, they would be received in practice[6]. Inasmuch as this uncertainty resulted from government actions, whether coordinated to this end or not, it must also be viewed as a *de facto* policy, and it, more than any specific policy, dominated many activities relating to the foreign trade sector.

The tariff and quota policies should be discussed together since they were designed to complement each other. Tariffs generally have been raised progressively from their relatively low level under the protectorate and follow the typical pattern of LDC's: low on capital goods, somewhat higher on intermediate goods, and quite high on most final consumption goods. In principle this also implies a relatively high level of effective protection for Morocco's industry, which produces primarily finished goods. No detailed study of effective protection has yet been done on Morocco, but some preliminary studies have given estimates of potential effective protection on the order of two or three hundred percent in some industries. It is doubtful that this potential has been fully exploited in most cases. With few exceptions, however, high tariffs have been adjusted to provide needed protection as perceived by Moroccan industry. Detailed examination of the structure of protection shows a high correlation between high tariffs and/or quotas and the existence of Moroccan producers.

Quantitative controls on trade in Morocco have existed since independence. In the first years after independence, Morocco signed a number of bilateral trading agreements with its trading partners, in part to diversify its trade away from France and in part to assure its supplies and markets while maintaining equilibrium on the current account. The administrative problems and delays that resulted from attempting to direct the trade flows so closely proved too time-consuming and costly to the economy and in 1967 a program of 'liberalization' was introduced. This freed all trade except that with the Socialist Bloc from the constraints of the bilateral trade agreements. Overall quantitative controls were maintained however in terms of the import lists.

All goods were classified into categories A, B, or C. Those in A could be imported freely without prior authorization, those on B required prior authorization and for a number of them specific volume limits were imposed on total imports each year, and those on C could not be imported at all. Initially, more than two-thirds of total imports fell under list B, with the rest coming under A: presumably no goods on list C were imported. Since 1967 more goods have been shifted from list B to A, so that those on B accounted for about 40% of imports in 1972. The Moroccan authorities claim that this liberalization has not been responsible for the upsurge of imports in the 1970's since the liberalized products did not show sharp increases. This position is supported by detailed studies done by the Ministry of Commerce. This argument also leads one to discount the amount of actual decontrol which has resulted from the policy of liberalization. It indicates that the quantitative controls were probably not binding on those products.

63

The Moroccan authorities argue that the use of the quota system in conjunction with tariffs is less disruptive to the economy than use of tariffs alone to restrict imports. Setting tariffs sufficiently high to achieve the desired reduction of imports may entail too high a domestic price, they say, so a quota is applied with a relatively low tariff to keep prices down. The quota is set at approximately the difference between expected domestic production and domestic demand. Thus in principle demand is satisfied, domestic prices kept within reason, and local production protected. Since the prices of most manufactured items that would be affected by this system were administered at either the ex-factory or wholesale level, rather than determined by market forces and since there are no adequate data on commercial mark-ups, it is not possible to say whether this policy worked as planned, except for commodities such as cereals and sugar whose marketing and price are directly controlled by government boards.

On the whole, imported items command significantly higher prices than their domestic counterparts, but to what extent this was due to quality differences or to 'snob' appeal is not possible to tell. The use of quotas does give the domestic producer a near absolute monopoly over that part of the domestic market he can supply. With external competition thus quantitatively limited, there is little incentive to improve either quality or price, especially since quotas were set to complement domestic production and not to provide it with limited competition. The allocation of quotas has favored the large and well-established users or importers and has thus acted as an impediment to small operators who depend on imports on list B.

Unfortunately the data do not permit quantitative estimates of the restrictions imposed by the quotas. However, a pair of studies of the distribution of protection by tariff category completed during my stay in Morocco do reveal the extent to which the Moroccan system of tariffs and quotas is highly protective of Moroccan industry[7]. These studies examined the level of tariffs in relation to the levels of trade and of domestic production. The Moroccan tariff nomenclature is based on the Brussels Tariff Nomenclature, and the studies were done at the 4 digit level or finer for some industrial sectors.

The first study dealt with agricultural products and food processing industries, chapters 1–24 of the nomenclature. These chapters contained 178 4-digit subchapters and an initial survey showed that 71 of these subchapters were on the list C, 38 on B, and 69 on A. Of those on list A, 41 had tariffs greater than 50 %[8], leaving only 28 subchapters open to relatively free trade, and little trade was carried on in about half of these categories. In another 4 subchapters with large amounts of imports, trade can hardly be called free even though the products are on the list A and have low duties. These products, sugar, tea, and raw and processed tobacco, can be traded only by government boards so the amounts imported are also under government control. Particularly in the case of sugar, less expensive foreign imports have been reduced in favor of more expensive local production.

Of the 36 specific products imported in quantities greater than 1 million dirhams in 1971, 13 were on the list B and 23 on A. Of those 23, 17 carried tariffs less than 50 %, but these included a large number of products deemed necessary for Morocco such as breeding stock, day-old chicks, unprocessed coffee, tea, cocoa and other non-competitive imports. The only case of liberal importation of potentially competitive imports is the case of butter and concentrated milk. Morocco has taken advantage of low European prices to satisfy cheaply large domestic demands for these products to the disadvantage of the Moroccan dairy industry. Interestingly enough this controvenes another policy which is aimed at encouraging the dairy industry through other import controls such as placing fresh milk imports on the list C. Thus deprived of a market for important joint products, the Moroccan dairy industry has not been able to achieve the expected results in spite of its ostensible protection[9].

Among the 40 exported products whose value exceeded 1 million dirhams in 1971, 16 were on list C, 7 on B, and 17 on A, of which 8 had high tariffs leaving only 9 without important protection. Only citrus among these nine accounted for an important volume of exports. The rationale for the large protections of fresh-food exports is to protect Moroccan producers from seasonal dumping by other major exporters, but given the relatively long Moroccan season for most of these products and its relatively good competitive position, such protection is largely superfluous. On the other hand the high protection of the food processing industry seems to be aimed at guaranteeing high prices on the local market to these industries which also export significant quantities.

In general the agricultural sector seems grossly over-protected in terms of its export potential and of the significant price implications of this protection for basic consumer goods. The protections of such major products as cereal grains, sugar, and food processing are the result of domestic agricultural policies to increase rural incomes and to increase the production of these crops as an import substitution measure. There has not been any attempt by the Moroccans to analyse the indirect effect of these policies on the foreign exchange situation. A study done by Professor van Rijckeghem casts doubt on the net foreign exchange savings of the sugar production program, especially if alternate uses of the land are considered[10].

The study of industrial sector protection followed the same lines as that of agriculture, covering chapters 25–99 of the tariff nomenclature. These chapters included 916 4-digit subchapters, 69 of which were on list C, 151 on B and 696 on A, and of these 696, 596 had tariffs of less than 50 %. Apparently the industrial sector is much less protected than agriculture. However it must be remembered that these categories contain a large number of mineral products and capital or intermediate goods without domestic competition and for which low protection is consistent with Morocco's import substitution policy. Imports in excess of 1 million dirhams in 1971 were recorded in 281 of these subchapters, 211 on list A, 68 on B and surprisingly enough, 2 on C. 60 subchapters had exports larger than 1 million dirhams, 23 on list A, 24 on B and 13 on C. Again with the exception of export products with little potential domestic market, the exports industries received a great deal of protection.

Given the great diversity of products in the industrial chapters and the Moroccan policy of low duties on capital and intermediate goods, the study was narrowed to the 104 domestic industrial sectors identified by Moroccans. Since these are associated with tariff nomenclature sub-chapters it was possible to determine the levels of protection by industrial sector reasonably accurately. 92 of the 104 sectors thus identified produced tradable goods, the others being local services such as auto repair. Of these 92 sectors, 61 were protected by being on list C or B; of the 31 remaining, 16 had high duties leaving 15 relatively unprotected. Four of these latter had exports of more than 1 million dirhams in 1971 (refractory products, pulp, essential oils and animal gut). With the exception of motor bikes and large metal containers, the other relatively unprotected industries enjoyed special status either by virtue of large natural protection (bottled gas for home use), local markets (printing), special supplier relationships (tin cans for the canning industry or springs for auto assembly), or state assured markets (aluminium pipes for irrigation projects). With the exception of the four export industries noted above, no major Moroccan industry is without significant protection in one form or another. And historically this protection has been extended as new industries develop.

Other than the general guidelines of high protection on finished goods which compete with Moroccan industry and low protection on capital goods, Moroccan tariff and quota policy has been elaborated on an *ad hoc*, case-by-case basis. No attempt has yet been made to determine the effects of the tariff structure on industrial structure or on growth and

66

development. So far the Moroccans have been willing to use tariff and quota policy to encourage and maintain existing industries and to attract interested foreign investors with the offer of a protected market, but not to encourage efficiency in general or to explicitly influence existing industry to achieve goals of more rapid growth or expanded employment.

Within the tariff and quota structure, a number of specific derogations have been used to encourage certain kinds of investment. Until recently, these derogations have been on a case-by-case approval basis rather than automatic. First is the rebate of duty on capital imports on those investments approved by the Investment Commission. Given the already low level of duties on capital, these rebates were rarely crucial to the investment decision, although they did serve to lower the relative cost of capital. More important derogations were the export promotion schemes of 'drawback' and temporary import. The former allowed a rebate of tariffs paid on imports that were included in exported products for approved industries. This included rebates on duties paid on steel used in making the tin cans for exported processed food, and cloth used in exports of ready-to-wear clothes and the like. Rebates are given only on the physically identifiable products re-exported and not on scraps and wastes generated in the production process.

Temporary imports allowed certain goods into the country for processing and immediate re-export. In general this facility was limited to certain bonded manufacturers and to the duty-free zone at Tangiers. This latter is an attempt to create a Hong Kong-like free trade zone for export manufacturing industries using inexpensive Moroccan labor and producing solely for export. To date it has not been successful. Through 1972, these schemes have involved a great deal of administrative intervention and delay, and their benefits have thus far been deemed marginal by most potential or actual beneficiaries. The current 1973–1977 Plan aims to ease their application and expand their use.

As noted above, the administration of trade policy has constituted a form of covert or indirect policy. The ease and promptness with which import applications are processed or goods cleared through customs can greatly influence the effective level of protection of the stated policies. Delays and impediments have been frequent in this area although it is impossible to quantify either the extent to which this has slowed trade or the extent that it was deliberate. The effects are, of course, uneven. Generally the small scale importer has faced greater difficulty than the larger one.

The purpose of Morocco's various trade agreements has been to both expand and diversify exports while assuring the economy of sources for necessary imports within the perceived balance of payments constraint. The costs of trying to allocate such a large part of trade turned out to be too great, particularly with the convertible currency countries where the whole burden of allocation fell on the Moroccans. By 1967 most of the trade agreements were abandoned in favor of the generalized quota system described above. There remained the bilateral barter agreements with the Socialist Bloc countries and several mutually concessionary trade agreements with certain African and Arab trading partners. In 1969, Morocco signed an Agreement of Association with the EEC which generalized many of Morocco's tariff concessions on the French market to the EEC, but at the expense of others.

A detailed study of the barter agreements with the Socialist countries casts some doubts on their value to Morocco. As mentioned above, Morocco has been a net creditor on the total of these agreements, which account for about 15 % of its trade. To a certain extent, these agreements assure supplies of necessary imports such as sugar (Poland, Cuba), tea (China), oil (Russia) while providing supplementary outlets for its traditional exports of citrus and phosphates. Where these constituted new markets rather than diversion from convertible currency markets, Morocco benefitted. It is not possible to tell how much, however, since relative price comparisons are not available on the barter part of the trade, nor has it been determined whether Moroccan resources could have been better used expanding other productions. With one exception these agreements have not provided markets for Morocco's industrial exports and thus are of limited value for future growth. The exception is the agreement to supply China with Berliet trucks assembled in Morocco. This gave an important boost to Morocco's nascent vehicle industry, particularly local parts suppliers. On the whole these agreements have not worked in Morocco's favor from an economic standpoint.

Mutually concessionary pacts have been concluded with Algeria, Saudi Arabia, Senegal and Tunisia. These agreements lower or eliminate entry restrictions on certain products exported by each country into the other on a bilateral basis. The pact with Algeria has been by far the most beneficial to Morocco, permitting large-scale exports of Moroccan textiles to Algeria. In return Algeria exported primarily oil to Morocco. In principle the agreements with Algeria and Tunisia are to provide the basis for a Maghrebian common market in the near future. However, the differences in political and economic structure among the three countries seem to preclude any rapid movement along those lines.

The Agreement of Association with the EEC granted Morocco significant import duty reductions or exemptions for a large number of manufactured products in the European market. In return Morocco had to lower some of its import duties and guarantee that specified amounts or shares of trade in certain goods categories would be purchased from the EEC. Morocco chose to generalize the tariff reductions; however with the system of quota restrictions and the set of goods this measure applied to, its effect on overall trade was minuscule. Also, since EEC participation in Moroccan trade already exceeded the quotas of the agreement no readjustment of trade was necessary. Significantly, Morocco did not receive concessions on its major agricultural exports and lost some special rights on the French market. Since raw materials were already duty-free in the EEC, the benefits to Morocco's mineral exports were also limited. In fact during the first three years of the agreement, there was no significant change in the pattern of Moroccan trade with the EEC countries [3]. Some manufactured exports, particularly rugs did begin to expand significantly after 1972.

The association agreement is to be revised after five years and negotiations began in 1972 to that end. The Moroccans wanted more concessions for agricultural exports and increased levels of financial and technical aid from the Community. The EEC on its side was pushing toward a Mediterranean free trade zone and wanted gradually to establish bilateral free trade agreements with all its Mediterranean trading partners, who would also be free to extend free trade among themselves[11]. The Moroccan authorities feel, justifiably, that the association agreement has not yet been of any great benefit to Morocco, but that it is necessary to preserve their present position. The recent world economic crisis has probably delayed any expansion of the trade agreement.

The Moroccan government retained direct control over most of the trade in primary products and processed foodstuffs by means of various marketing boards. Imports of the major food products such as wheat, sugar, tea and tobacco were all conducted by marketing boards. Almost all agricultural exports were handled by the Export Marketing Board (Office Central d'Exportation, OCE). These boards were established to replace large private and primarily foreign owned trading concerns and to assure that Morocco would benefit from these exchanges by means of economies of scale and concentrated buying and selling power. In the case of the importing boards, they operated primarily to protect and encourage domestic productions by importing only enough to fill the domestic deficit while maintaining prices at levels high enough for domestic producers. These boards were used primarily to implement domestic agricultural policy by protecting domestic producers from the world market, maintaining government controlled prices, and at the same time importing

69

sufficient commodities to make up for domestic deficits.

The OCE was organized not only to consolidate handling and marketing of agricultural exports, but also to help organize production to meet the needs of the external markets by introducing new product varieties, growing techniques, and crop cycle timing. By thus consolidating the collection, packing, shipping and marketing of fresh produce and the marketing of processed foods, it was hoped that the Moroccan production could be made more responsive to market conditions and more efficient. The success of the OCE thus far has been mixed. By requiring nearly all agricultural exports to pass through the OCE, which collected a small fee, a number of established export producers were discouraged. They felt they could have marketed their own products more profitably themselves and resented paying a fee to the OCE. In these cases the OCE was relatively less efficient and probably lost some exports. The OCE also lacked sufficient authority over many of the small producers and was not able to control production as much as it would have liked, or to increase the volume significantly. In fact the volume of tomato exports in 1970 was significantly lower than the level in 1960, before the inception of the OCE[12]. On the other hand, the OCE did manage to change the variety mix of tomatoes, peppers and citrus toward higher priced types and to increase export earnings per unit faster than the general price increase. In the current Plan, the OCE is trying to correct some of the problems that slowed exports of certain products and to encourage production of more profitable varieties.

The National Phosphates Board (Office Chérifien des Phosphates, OCP) mines and markets Morocco's phosphates and is run as a semi-autonomous business operation. Other than the employment it generates and the revenues it turns over to the government, it has little effect on the rest of the economy and is essentially an enclave operation. It is allowed to follow its own investment and promotion policies. In the new Plan, it is planning to branch out into some industrial processing of phosphates, although again primarily for export.

In addition to these policies and institutions directly affecting trade, a number of internal industrial and agricultural policies have had rather important effects on the foreign trade sector. The large-scale dam building and irrigation projects imposed heavy burdens on the import bill. Since the dam building activity greatly exceeded the equipment of the perimeters to be irrigated, the realization of gains from improved production in irrigated sectors was delayed. This had the double impact on the trade balance of increasing materials imports without corresponding reductions in agricultural imports or increases in exports. Thus there was less foreign exchange available for other investment programs. Better coordi-

70

nation of these programs would have led to more efficient use of available foreign exchange.

The industrial incentive program was based on tariff derogations on capital and intermediate goods, tax concessions, and capital subsidies ('primes d'équipement'). The net effect of all of these benefits was to reduce the relative price of capital with respect to wages and to encourage the use of relatively capital intensive techniques in new investment and in expansions. Since investment in used capital did not benefit from these provisions, there was further incentive toward the use of highly automated techniques. As a result, there was an investment of more than $ 15,000 per new job created in industry during the 1968–1972 Plan. Only 30,000 new jobs were created by a total industrial investment of nearly $ 400 million [13, p. 370].

3.3. EFFECTS OF TRADE POLICIES ON GROWTH AND EMPLOYMENT

To simplify the discussion of the effectiveness of these trade policies, I will group them into three categories: the protective and/or restrictive policies of tariffs and quotas, the trade control and development policies embodied in the various trade agreements, and the export promotion and marketing policies. I will discuss their effectiveness primarily in terms of their ability to achieve the goals of growth and industrialization, and of maximizing employment. Even so it is not possible to make quantitative estimates of the effects of these policies with respect to these goals. Sufficient data do not exist and there is too much overlap between the trade policies and other policies to isolate entirely the effects of either. This analysis will be in terms of the dual criteria of suitability suggested in the introduction: the theoretical and the practical suitability of the policy to achieve the intended goals. It should be noted that the criteria apply only to the suitability of policies attempted. It provides an answer to the question, 'Is a particular policy effective in reaching a certain goal and how effective?' It does not provide an answer to the question, 'What is the best policy to achieve a given goal?' either on a theoretical or practical level. Strictly, determination of the 'best' policy would require a far more elaborate optimizing model than now exists; and non-rigorously, 'best' is a very subjective concept.

As shown above, the trade-restrictive policies were largely related to protecting domestic industry in an import substitution strategy of industrialization and development. Without reiterating in detail the many theoretical criticisms of import substitution currently in the literature, I will summarize the important theoretical shortcomings of this strategy

71

as they apply to Morocco. The protection of the local market is supposed to supply sufficient incentive to entrepreneurs to invest and develop the protected industries, and after a reasonable time to become efficient enough to export, thus outliving the need for protection. At the same time, dependence on imports should be reduced as formerly imported goods are produced locally, or at least with a significant local value-added component. Since production of finished goods is generally considered easier and markets for them already exist, tariff structures are usually developed to have high duty rates on the finished goods and lower rates on intermediate and capital goods which are not to be produced locally. It has since been shown that this tariff structure implies even higher rates of effective protection for the finished goods industries. Protection is envisaged as a short to medium-term tool to bring about rapid increases in industrial production and of employment in the modern sector. Once industrialization is well under way, it should be able to continue without further protection.

Unfortunately the optimistic achievements predicted for import substitution policies were frequently not realized, and the general lack of success of this strategy in the 1960's provoked more critical analyses of its theoretical underpinnings. Serious doubt has been cast on even the theoretical suitability of this policy to achieve long-run goals of sustained growth and employment expansion in the modern sector, particularly for smaller countries. Without sufficiently large domestic markets, the protection will encourage installation of less than optimally sized plants that are aimed solely at the domestic market and unable to compete on world markets – even after a reasonable working-in period. And if the domestic market is quite small, this may even lead to a large amount of excess capacity if the minimum plant size is considerably larger than the domestic market. In either case an important vested interest is created to continue protection and preserve what industry there is. Unless considerable backward integration is possible in the substitution industries, this policy will not free a country from excessive dependence on imports as it must continue to import capital and certain intermediate goods. In fact the economy may become even more dependent on trade as the viability of whole domestic industries depends on certain imports and the incompressible minimum of 'necessary' imports grows rather than shrinks. Since the profitability of these import substitution industries depends on the growth of domestic sales, it often becomes necessary to allow domestic consumption to expand in order to provide adequate domestic markets, thus reducing current savings and the possibility of later growth.

Import substitution industries are admittedly high-cost (at least initially) and the increase in money incomes registered may not be reflected in comparable increases in real income. Thus apparent short and middle-term growth of income and employment may be the precursor of longer run stagnation as the economy becomes saddled with relatively inefficient and high-cost import substitution industries. At this point it would also become more difficult to reduce protection since that might well entail the failure of the protected industries and a major set-back to industrial development. In many cases the size of operation justified by the relatively small protected local market is inadequate to survive without protection.

In light of these recent reflections about import substitution as a strategy for development, it can no longer be considered generally suitable on a theoretical basis without considerable modification. It may provide short-run spurts of growth, but is unlikely to lead to long-run sustainable growth. This analysis however benefits from a great deal of hind-sight and is not meant to be critical of Moroccan planners who were acting on the best available theory when Morocco began its strategy of import substitution.

In practice, Morocco has run into most of the pitfalls now associated with import substitution. Much of its industry is running well below capacity[14] and seems to be high-cost, although the whole price structure is so distorted that it is hard to determine to what extent.

A number of industries have been established with a guaranteed monopoly of the local market and have adjusted their plant size to fit. An example is General Tire which was assured a local monopoly and built a factory just the size of the local market. Later investigation has shown that Morocco is not inherently a high-cost place to produce tires and a larger sized plant could have been built which could have produced more tires at lower unit cost and exported the surplus, had not the local market been so readily guaranteed[15]. In fact, Good Year has subsequently been granted the right to build a plant so both firms will have to export to survive, although both will be operating relatively small sized plants. There is no indication that the Moroccans are going to liberalize tire imports.

The Moroccans instituted the system of quotas to supplement tariffs in order to achieve protection without the associated sharp rise in prices. It is not clear what effect this had on prices, but it did serve to further reduce the amount of potential competition faced by local producers who were guaranteed that share of the market they could fulfil. This has probably preserved the share of the market for local producers and thus assured some industrialization and employment in the short run, but will

73

increase the difficulty of facing any competition in the future.

There are also cases where the import substitution policy has led to increased imports of those goods in the form of intermediate goods in order to allow that industry to operate profitably. The auto assembly sector is perhaps the best example of this. The auto assembly industry has existed in Morocco since 1962 and until 1968 it had operated at a level of about 5,000 units a year, which was well below the one-shift capacity of 10–12,000 units. Given the existing tariff structure, demand was then about 7,000 units a year, the difference being made up of imports, primarily 'prestige' cars and types not assembled locally. The 1968–1972 Plan projected needs over that period to be 12,000 units a year, that is, full one-shift capacity production. In 1967, the import expenditure on cars, both assembled and knocked down (CKD) for local assembly was about 60 million dirhams with another 30 million spent for spare parts. In the course of the Plan, production was increased to about 20,000 units to lower unit costs and the selling prices of locally assembled cars were lowered to little more than the landed price of comparable imports in order to sell the increased production. Duties on imported assembled cars went up while cars in CKD state came in duty-free to the local assembly plant. Total imports of cars, primarily in knocked down form, shot up to about 100 million dirhams in 1972, and of parts to 75 million[16].

Although it is difficult to say what the real 'needs' of Morocco are in terms of new cars, it does seem a reasonable judgment that maintaining the price of locally assembled cars at about the world level is low for a country in Morocco's situation. It did allow rapid expansion of the assembly industry, but with domestic value added at most 20 % and employment of about 900, it is not clear that this expansion was worth the additional 85 million dirhams of imports entailed. In this case, the expansion of one ostensible import substitution industry was carried out in such a way as to greatly increase imports without considerably enhancing the industry's long-run viability. It is still heavily dependent on imports and now has a vested interest in maintaining a high level of production and thus of imports. No attempt was made to measure the foreign exchange impact of this expansion, nor any of other presented in the 1968–1972 Plan.

In light of these and other cases, one would have to conclude that the policy of protection and import substitution followed by Morocco has led to some industrialization and creation of employment, but much of the increase seems to be in industries of doubtful long-run viability. Continued growth will have to be based on other sectors. The drawbacks are to be found largely in the policy itself rather than its application. However, in

Morocco there was little systematic analysis in the application of the policy and few attempts to optimize the use of foreign exchange in relation to the strategy of industrialization by import substitution. The only estimates of the balance of payments impact of various import substitution projects were the level of reduction of competing (final) imports and the foreign exchange component of the initial investment. Neither the intermediate goods imports for operations nor the carrying charges on the capital were included in the evaluation of the projects as presented in the Plan. Consistent and coherent application of the stated policy were lacking and it is thus likely that Morocco's recent growth has been lower than it might have been.

Morocco's trading agreements were primarily aimed at assuring stability and finding new markets for its traditional exports, and only secondarily at securing markets for new exports. There is little theoretical basis for evaluating trade agreements other than a general theoretical preference for having trade as free as possible. However, in a world which is far from that ideal, there is wide scope for profiting from trade agreements. By nature such agreements are commercial documents, but a total set of trade agreements can have a great effect on the rate of industrialization and the form that it takes. To the extent that such agreements commit a country to certain levels of exports, the productive structure must be adapted to those commitments, and to the extent they open or expand potential markets, new production incentives are created. Depending on their specific nature, such agreements can be greatly beneficial to expanding trade, or they can have a restraining effect.

Morocco has experienced both results from its trading agreements. Although intended to diversify and secure markets, the early bilateral trading agreements were generally stultifying. The administrative problems involved in trying to balance and direct trade bilaterally with many countries and in a multitude of goods was more than Morocco's bureaucracy could handle without severe delays and may often ending up buying in high priced markets. Dropping the majority of these agreements greatly benefitted Morocco's trade.

The bilateral trade agreements with the Socialist Bloc are still in force, though they suffer many of the same problems. They are somewhat easier to administer since the range of products is smaller and the trade is often linked to aid programs. It is also arguable that these agreements do open new markets for Moroccan goods whereas the agreements with the European countries clearly did not. However merely opening new markets for traditional export is not sufficient to give these trade agreements good marks. In addition to the net creditor position Morocco maintained, the relative prices were not always favorable, especially for manufactured products. One reason why the agreements were in surplus was that it was difficult to sell the Soviet Bloc machinery on the Moroccan market. There were many complaints about the quality and service in addition to a general prejudice in favor of Western goods. At best it can be argued that these agreements allowed Morocco to continue emphasis on its traditional exports longer than reliance on Western markets would have allowed. But this is not a clear gain as the resources directed toward expanding traditional exports might have been better directed toward the development of new manufactured exports as is now being done. The question was never asked.

Morocco's mutually concessionary and association agreements have worked out much better. The former opened potential markets in neighboring African states and the latter in Europe. In practice, the agreement with Algeria has been the most beneficial so far, allowing the Moroccan textile industry to expand its exports rapidly in that direction and giving that industry a timely boost. The agreement with the EEC also opened the possibility for manufactured exports (Morocco's traditional exports were not particularly affected by the agreement), but into a much more competitive market. Rugs are the only product so far that has significantly benefitted and they are really more an artisanal product.

In terms of practical effectiveness, Morocco has eliminated most of the early problems and mistakes with its trade agreements and is now in the position of trying to reach the more favorable agreements with its trading partners. By its very commercial nature, the trade agreements policy is more consistent with the Moroccan view of foreign trade as primarily a commercial activity, and has been more carefully developed and improved over time. Many of the current limitations in the agreements are more due to Morocco's relatively weak bargaining position rather than a lack of skill in bargaining.

The export promotion and marketing policies have thus far been the least successful, and it is in this area that Morocco is directing most of its attention in the current Plan. With the consolidation of marketing of agricultural products under the auspices of the OCE and with the control of phosphate production and sales, and sales of other minerals in the hands of public boards, more than 80 % of Morocco's exports are under the direct control of the government. Thus the export promotion schemes directly concern a small segment of the export market dealing with manufactured goods even though most discussion is in terms of expanding all exports. In principle consolidation of export sales through marketing

76

boards should improve the country's terms of trade in these goods by making it possible to meet large buyers with single seller, to promote sales in general, to establish trade mark identification, to assure the quality and uniformity of the product, and to conduct the necessary research and development to adapt commodities to the demands of the world market. In effect this argument relies on the assumption that the economies and other advantages of scale outweigh the added costs and inconveniences of creating a government bureaucracy. In a trading world dominated by oligopolies of various sorts, such an argument for scale in marketing carries some weight even when the production does not require a large-scale operation as in the case of many agricultural products. However the argument for replacing large private marketing organizations with an even larger public one is less forceful on economic grounds, though there may be important political justifications. Theoretically, there is no strong argument for or against the suitability of such marketing boards; their value depends on the efficiency of their operation.

Morocco established the OCE in 1964 to allow the state to benefit from the profits of exporting Morocco's agricultural products, to establish the quality of the Moroccan label and to maintain high standards, to adapt Morocco's products to world demand, and to help develop domestic production. In practice, the OCE did not achieve the intended results. It is true that agricultural exports increased since the OCE was created, but this was largely due to secular price increases. Where existing marketing networks existed, the OCE merely added another handling cost along the line. It did succeed in opening some new markets, but other than those governed by bilateral trade agreements; it is hard to show that such expansions would not have taken place in any case given the developments of other major suppliers and the growth of these markets. The OCE has not been able to increase the volume of production of traditional crops significantly above historical trends and in some cases the volumes are lower than before the OCE was created (e.g. tomatoes). The OCE has succeeded in introducing new high value crops which will probably provide the basis for future growth of agricultural exports. However, it has not yet been successful in introducing new techniques of production or inducing the farmers to adopt them on a large scale. This is in part a problem of the limits of its authority over producers. Cooperation with the Ministry of Agriculture has been limited. The OCE is currently trying to extend its authority, but such a change is still subject to the workings of the internal politics between the two organizations.

Overall the OCE has succeeded in directing the trading profits of agricultural commodities to the state, but it has been a relatively costly operation. Its successes in establishing the Moroccan trade-mark and quality standards have not been matched in increasing export volumes or lowering handling costs. Any judgment about its suitability is thus necessarily mixed: it is expanding exports, but neither as widely nor as profitably as could reasonably be expected. And by not significantly increasing the volume of production, it contributed little to increase employment either.

The consolidation of phosphate production and sales in the OCP dates from before independence. It has developed into an efficient enterprise that allows the state to profit from its monopoly. With its powerful foreign exchange earning position, the OCP is allowed to elaborate and execute its own program with little interference from the government planning authority. It has accepted the goals of expanding output and exports and pursued its investment policy accordingly. Although successful in expanding production and exports, there was little attempt to analyse the implications of the investment programs in terms of anything other than its contributions to exports. As a result, the investments were highly capital intensive, resulting in relatively larger burden on imports and capital servicing with a relatively small increase in employment[17]. This outcome underscores the importance of coordinating export goals with employment and foreign exchange use goals to increase the benefits from the export promotion program. Thus while the export expansion of the OCP was clearly suitable for the production and export goal, the particular program of investment followed was not well suited to the goals of employment creation or foreign exchange economy.

With regard to export incentive programs for other, primarily manufacturing products, the theoretical analysis is less well developed than that for import substitution. Basically such incentives work to provide direct or indirect subsidies to export industries by means of concessionary interest rates, special access to foreign exchange, duty-free access to imported capital and material, tax breaks and certain other privileges. These incentives are supposed to aid the exporter meet the higher costs of local production or of entering world markets while allowing him to pay world market prices on his imported inputs. In general export promotion is superior to import substitution as a strategy of industrialization. It avoids the problems of limited market size and thus limited plant size while providing incentives for efficient operation. It also allows developing countries to benefit from the gains of trade far more than does import substitution. However, export promotion is not free from potential problems. The subsidy element can be excessive and promote the development of inefficient export industries which have vested interests in continuing the subsidy program. By allowing exporters access to duty-free imports, backward linkages may be discouraged and parallel enclave-like export industries may develop without leading to an integrated industrial development. These dangers can be avoided by appropriate policy however, so these export promotion schemes appear to be suitable on a theoretical basis.

The attempts at promoting manufactured exports through various incentives schemes have as yet had little identifiable effect, largely due to lack of implementation. The 1968–1972 Plan outlined a number of measures to be adopted to promote industrial exports as well as the creation of a special commission to study the problem. The Plan proposed the following general measures:
a. strengthening of commercial relations;
b. increased mineral and petroleum prospecting;
c. fiscal advantages for exports;
d. simplification of export procedures;
e. improvement of the system of temporary admission (of imports) [1, p. 554].

No specific policies were outlined in the Plan to implement these general suggestions. While some progress could be cited in each area, there was little overall impact on exports that could be measured: some administrative procedures were eased, some export taxes were reduced or eliminated, and some commercial relations were improved, but there was no concerted set of actions to encourage new exports.

The Interministerial Commission on Exports proposed in the 1968–1972 Plan issued a special report in 1971 suggesting the following major export promotion incentives:
a. subsidies and tax exemptions for exports;
b. improving tariff policies favoring exports (drawback and temporary importation);
c. export insurance;
d. preferential interest rates for exports.

Plus the accompanying measures:
e. sending commercial counsellors to major trading partners;
f. simplifying administrative procedures;
g. creating a Foreign Trade Information Center;
h. instituting an exporter's card;
i. instituting an Export Council;
j. creating an interministerial liaison committee[18].

79

There have been continuing efforts to improve application of customs policies although this is still a subject of complaint among exporters. A program of tax exemptions for exports was announced along with the 1973–1977 Plan in mid-1973. It granted 50-100 % exemptions from the IBP (income tax) for periods of 5-10 years depending on the industry location, and level of exports. This applies to extensions as well as new installations and includes additional duty-free import facilities. The 1973–1977 Plan also echoes points e, f, g and h from the Interministerial Committee's report [19, p. 378]. It remains to be seen whether these proposals will be implemented.

The overall effectiveness of all the export promotion measures is hard to quantify. Exports are an important engine of growth for Morocco both in terms of generating domestic incomes and demand and in terms of earning the foreign exchange necessary for continued industrial growth. And export industries are major employers in both the rural and urban areas of Morocco. However, with the exception of the very recent upswing in manufactured exports, Morocco's exports have followed a relatively slow (3.7 %) traditional growth pattern dominated more by climate variations and the world phosphates market than by any export policies. Even the expansion in industrial exports (carpets, textiles, assembled trucks, phosphate fertilizer) is primarily due to developments outside the range of export promotion measures. To date then, one would have to conclude that the export promotion policies have had little direct effect on exports, and thus on growth or employment. There is the strong expectation that the new policies will have a more pronounced effect, but that depends a great deal on the overall industrial policies and general investment climate.

Viewed as a whole, the foreign trade policy package has been much more effective in restricting trade, particularly imports, than in expanding it in the field of exports. In the short and middle term, the restrictive import policies have led to more rapid industrialization and increases of industrial employment. This growth however was at the price of higher domestic costs, inefficient production, and relatively large capital use per job created. If Morocco lowers its trade barriers, it is doubtful that all of these industries will survive and the short-run gains would turn into larger run losses. Even with comparatively high level of protection, Morocco's growth rates have only been mediocre.

Morocco's recent trade agreements have managed to find new markets for its exports and thus provide a fillip to its export industries, although direct trade promotion policies have not yet been very effective. A great deal of hope is being placed on these in the near future as Morocco is shifting its trade policy emphasis from one of protection and import substitution to an expansive policy of export promotion. There is even discussion in the 1973–1977 Plan of linking future protection in the domestic market to some obligation to export, though the details of this scheme have not yet been determined by the Moroccans.

The effectiveness of trade policy has been hampered by the lack of a coherent view of the position of trade in a developing economy. Specific policies have been implemented primarily to effect results in other sectors without regard to their relation to the rest of the economy. Trade policy developed piecemeal to protect certain industries, to reduce the balance of payments deficit, to open politically interesting markets, to nationalize exporting activities, to promote certain exports, and so forth. No attempt was made to evaluate the effect of trade policy as a whole on growth and development, to estimate the trade-off between restricting imports and promoting exports or even between restricting different imports, to evaluate the benefits from bilateral trade agreements as opposed to changing the export mix away from traditional exports, etc.

Morocco's trade policy has not been entirely suitable for achieving its goals of growth, employment creation, or relative independence from balance of payments constraints either on a theoretical or practical level. On occasion the implementation of specific policies or the conjunction of trade and industrial policies has actually been detrimental to the achievement of those goals. The various defects were due to inadequate analysis of policies and their effects (on both theoretical and practical levels), inadequate execution, and lack of a coherent approach to the foreign trade sector. This lack of a coherent view of the trade sector is probably the most important underlying factor in explaining the general ineffectiveness of Moroccan trade policy. It is a conceptual problem that will have to be overcome before planning and trade policy can become effective.

3.4. NEW DIRECTIONS IN TRADE POLICY

Developments in Morocco's trade policy during the next five years will be dominated by three major factors: the effects of raw materials price changes, the success of its export promotion program, and the extent to which the EEC begins implementing its Mediterranean Free Trade Zone.

The first factor is essentially a question of the relative effects of petroleum import prices on the one hand and phosphate export prices on the other. At the end of 1973, Morocco posted a threefold increase in the export price of phosphate rock, and at about the same time the price of petroleum imports more than doubled. Given the fact that phosphates account for about 25 % of Morocco's exports and petroleum for only about 7 % of its imports (in pre-1973 prices), the immediate effect of these changes is a considerable improvement on the current account balance. Preliminary analysis indicates that this development will relieve Morocco of major balance of payments problems during the 1973–1977 Plan if these changes are not reversed. This analysis is based on somewhat more modest assumptions about investment and growth goals than those presented in the 1973–1977 Plan. These assumptions take account of the setback in growth realized in 1973 and project that the Plan's average target growth rates will only be achieved by the end of the Plan period.

The stability of the rise in phosphates prices depends a great deal on the reactions of the other major suppliers. The sharp price increase reflects the reaction to the withdrawal of the u.s. as a major exporter. Morocco has subsequently raised prices another 50 % as supply remains short. The ocp has planned a nearly 50 % increase in output over the Plan period, a number of other heretofore marginal or submarginal producer countries will find the new price quite profitable and will probably increase production. Spain is just beginning to exploit large reserves in the Spanish Sahara. It is likely that prices will ease somewhat over the term of the Plan as supply increases, but remain much higher than they have heretofore. Analysis of the effects of the increased earnings from the price rise, other than on the balance of payments is more difficult since these earnings accrue first to the ocp, and it is not possible to determine how they will be used. The government will receive increased revenues from taxes and earnings and this will help finance the government investment budget.

The second effect, export promotion depends on the success of Morocco's new export incentives in particular and its overall investment climate in general. It is not possible to be more than very cautiously optimistic about the immediate effects of these policies, particularly those aimed at attracting direct foreign investment. Furthermore, if the oil crisis does precipitate a general world recession and slowdown in trade among the developed countries, it will be all the more difficult for Morocco to increase its manufactured exports in the face of generally declining markets in the developed countries. Its association status with the EEC may alleviate this problem to some extent, but not entirely. The high phosphate prices and the large planned investments in projects to process phosphates into more finished products ('valorisation') will delay temporarily the necessity to expand other industrial export and will allow

Morocco to depend on traditional exports somewhat longer than would otherwise have been the case. But it cannot afford to reduce its emphasis on developing industrial exports.

The third factor affecting trade policy is the actions of the EEC in the Mediterranean area. Prior to the oil crisis, the EEC had grandiose plans to turn the Mediterranean countries into a large free trade zone, which would naturally have been dominated by the industrial might of the Six cum Nine. If such a plan had been implemented within the 12 to 17 year time horizon projected, it would have had severe consequences on the viability of a large number of Morocco's industries. It is doubtful that many of them could have survived such free competition with European manufacturers. And this would have led to a major restructuring of Moroccan industry. As such a free trade zone developed, Morocco would have had rapidly to readjust its trade policy away from a protectionist one and to concentrate on a relatively few industries which could be competitive without protection. Although this will probably entail some severe, if localized, dislocations in Moroccan industry, it is my view that this is a desirable direction for Moroccan trade policy to follow in terms of its long-run effect on growth, real income, and employment. Given the recent events in oil prices and the predicted slowdown in growth in Europe, it is unlikely that the EEC will push the free trade zone rapidly, thus postponing pressure for Morocco to adjust its industrial structure. But at the same time, it is unlikely that the EEC will be prepared to grant significant new concessions in the revised association agreements with Morocco or other associated countries.

Viewed together, it seems that these factors work in Morocco's favor in the near term. Simultaneously it will receive increased resources from its traditional exports at a time when they are needed to finance important new export-oriented industry, and it seems to be granted additional time to develop these industries and implement revisions in its trade policy before pressure from an expanded EEC free trade zone forces it to reduce its protective policies. However, to take advantage of these factors, trade policy and analysis will have to be more imaginative than has been the case in the past.

REFERENCES

1. 1968–1972 Five Year Plan, Division de la Coordination Economique et du Plan, Rabat, 1968 (my translation).
2. Data taken from introductory volumes of the 1968–1972 and 1973–1977 Five Year Plans, DPDR, Rabat, 1973.

3. J. Shilling, 'Analyse et Prévisions du Commerce Extérieur par Zone Monétaire et Région', Working paper DPDR, Rabat, March 17, 1972.
4. *Revue Bimensuelle de la Banque Marocaine du Commerce Extérieur*, No. 15, May 15, 1973.
5. J. Shilling, 'Analyse Chiffrée des Résultats des Accords de Clearing', Working paper DPDR, August 28, 1972.
6. For example the fish canneries complained of a two year delay in receipt of 'draw back' payments on canning steel used in canned fish exports. The delay hampered their operations and increased costs.
7. J. Shilling, 'Protection dans le Secteur Agricole', and 'Note sur la Protection Industrielle au Maroc', Working papers DPDR, October 26 and December 11, 1972.
8. This understates the amount of tax collected at the boarder since several administrative taxes are added as well, increasing the actual level by about 25% or more.
9. S. Wellisz, 'Rapport sur les Agro-Industries', Working paper DPDR, Rabat, October 1972.
10. From discussions by the author with Professor Van Rijckeghem in Morocco.
11. J. Shilling, 'Remarques sur la Proposition de la CEE de Créer une Zone de Libre Echange Méditerranéenne', and 'Résumé des Documents Concernant la Politique de la CEE envers le Maghreb et Commentaire', Working papers DPDR, October 1972 and April 1973.
12. Office des Changes, *Statistiques du Commerce Extérieur*, Rabat, 1960, 1970.
13. DPDR, 1973–1977 Five Year Plan, Vol. II, 'Développement Sectoriel, Industrie', Rabat, 1973.
14. Industry-wide average was reported to be about 60% capacity utilization by the 1971 Industrial Survey.
15. Based on investigation in Morocco by Professor Travis. See also chapter 4 of the present volume.
16. Figures derived from the 1968–1972 Five Year Plan; Direction de l'Industrie, *Situation des Industries de Transformation en 1970*, January 1972, and Secrétariat d'Etat au Plan, au Développement Régional et à la Formation des Cadres, *Statistiques Rétrospectives 1967–1972*, Rabat, 1973.
17. There were investments in excess of 629 million dirhams carried out by the OCP during the 1968–1972 Plan with negligible increases in employment; see 1973–1977 Five Year Plan, Vol. II, p. 338.
18. From the 'Rapport de la Commission Interministérielle Chargée d'Etudier les Mesures à Mettre en Oeuvre pour une Politique de Promotion des Exportations', Prime Ministry, Rabat, January 1971, pp. 3–10.
19. 1973–1977 Five Year Plan, Vol. II, Chapter 8, 'Industrie'.

Part II. Sectoral problems and policies

4. Conditional protection and industrial employment

W. P. Travis*

Morocco, like many other countries, faces the problem not only of eliminating unemployment but of transferring a large proportion even of its currently employed workforce from agriculture to other sectors of the economy. This double necessity exacerbates the unemployment problem inasmuch as new employment must eventually be found for practically the whole labor force and not just the twenty percent or so said to be currently out of work.

The reason that workers must be transferred from agricultural to other employments is not that Moroccan agriculture is backward relative to the other sectors, but rather that current Moroccan agricultural employment is large relative to *world* employment in modern agriculture. The Moroccan agricultural workforce is in fact twice as large as that of the United States which, despite a domestic population fifteen times as numerous as Morocco's, nonetheless exports about a third of its total food output. If Moroccan farm workers were to achieve American productivity standards, Moroccan food *exports* would have to be about twice as large as current American food *production*, and therefore enormously greater than American exports. Obviously world food prices would then deteriorate. This means that Moroccan agricultural productivity would have to be *substantially greater* than U.S. productivity in order for Morocco, through 'agriculturalization' alone, to attain the U.S. level of income. It is unnecessary to point out that Moroccan land and rainfall may be unable to support such a high level of production, even with the best modern techniques and equipment.

The total Moroccan workforce is relatively small, by contrast, to the world workforce employed in modern industrial, commercial, and other non-agricultural activities. It is equal, roughly, to the workforce of the greater Paris area; adding the output of such a region to current world

---

* Mr. Zine El Abidine Oualhadj has aided me immensely in the formulation of the arguments of the paper.

output would have negligible effect on world prices. That is, the world market can easily absorb a fully industrialized, but not an exclusively agriculturalized Morocco.

Indeed, by the time that Morocco acquires a modern industrial economy, Morocco itself will be rich enough to absorb most of its products. This evident truth may lead one to feel that Morocco has only to aim its industrialization from the outset at its own home market, protected by prohibitive import duties and quotas if necessary. This strategy would fail because the present domestic market would be unable to absorb enough of most products to operate at full capacity plants of efficient size. Industry needs world markets not when it is mature, but at the outset, when the home market for its products is absent. The Moroccan Five Year Plan for 1973–1977 recognizes the resulting need to promote exports of manufactures and envisages specific programs and commercial policies for such promotion.

This paper discusses a general commercial policy developed and discussed at the DPDR[1] for accelerating the development of indigenous (as opposed to foreign direct investment) manufactured exports. Such a policy, it should be emphasized, does not run counter to a policy of simultaneously encouraging foreign investment in manufacturing in Morocco; indeed it is specifically designed to operate alongside such a policy. Direct foreign investment in manufacturing for export can provide much of the labor training, knowledge of world markets, and managerial experience that Moroccan firms will require.

The proposed commercial policy can best be stated by putting it somewhat paradoxically: protect only *export* (not *import competing*) industries. That is, the protection of the domestic market for a given product should be accorded only on condition (hence the name *conditional protection* for this commercial policy) that its Moroccan exports equal a stated percentage of Moroccan production plus imports of the product in question. Moroccan production and exports would be defined according to the Moroccanization codes, and would not include therefore the activities of any foreign enterprises in Morocco producing (for world markets) the same products. Any local sales of products of foreign enterprises, operating on Moroccan soil would be treated as imports for purposes of defining Moroccan apparent consumption and would also be subject to customs duties on behalf of any conditionally-protected Moroccan products competing for the same markets.

Conditional protection may offend pure free-traders. On the other hand, because it requires export performance, ardent protectionists too may fear it. Obviously such a policy, having no natural friends among established doctrines, requires solid arguments in its favor. It is possible, I believe, to root conditional protection firmly in the context of received, modern, international trade theory.

According to that theory (as expounded by Eli F. Heckscher, Bertil Ohlin[2], Abba P. Lerner[3], Paul A. Samuelson[4], and many other writers), a relatively small country (Morocco) and a relatively large country (the EEC) can equalize their factor wages (notably the wage rate and the real rate of return on capital) provided that they share a common technology in at least as many products as there are factors primary to both countries. It does not matter if country A (Morocco) lacks entirely the technology to produce most efficiently a wide range of products, provided only that it freely imports those products. What is important is that Morocco operates only those industries for which its technology is equal to that of its trading partner. If this condition is met, then the factor-price equalization theorem (for the case of many products and a few factors, cf. Samuelson[4] and W.P. Travis[5]) ensures that Moroccan wages will equal European wages, which are currently about ten times as high. This effect alone would suffice to raise Moroccan per capita income to many times its present level.

One might feel that the large gain in income would be due largely to the acquisition of the superior technology and not to trade. This is not true. Europe, in the aggregate, is only about three and one half times as efficient as Morocco. Through acquiring European technology alone (no trade) Morocco could hope therefore only to triple its per capita income, whereas equalizing Moroccan and European wage rates would yield a much larger total gain. To triple income through technological transfer alone would require, moreover, that Morocco acquire the technology of practically the whole gamut of European industries, rather than that of only a few export industries. Given the substantial costs and uncertainties of transfering or duplicating technology, it is obvious that using trade to specialize and thus to minimize the necessary amount of such transfer promises by far the higher net gains.

This leaves the practical problem of which industries, out of the several thousand that exist, to encourage in Morocco. It is easy enough, but misleading, to enumerate their desirable characteristics: labor intensiveness not only in production but in marketing, ease of technological transfer and duplication, compatibility with the present or most easily achievable skill composition of the Moroccan labor force, stability of long-term export prospects, immunity to competition from Tunisia, Greece, and other low-wage countries also associated with the EEC, etc., etc. Of these only labor intensiveness (at least on the production side) is fairly easy to identify, but they are all more or less irrelevant.

This is because ability to borrow overseas for Moroccan industrialization renders quite unimportant the exact selection of industries for export. Only the importance of a *small* selection remains. Overcoming capital intensiveness or any other entry barrier, including the threat of other similarly-situated countries, is a matter of open foreign credit lines. Given the scarcity of Moroccan capital that credit must come from Europe, America, Japan, and the oil-exporting countries. The best way to establish international credit is, of course, to demonstrate general export performance and thereby the country's ability to repay loans in hard currency.

Conditional protection obliges enterprises producing protected products to export. By exporting they will acquire a name overseas and thus an overture to foreign banks. Any generalization of conditional protection to new products implies an extension of exports, and thus additional hard-currency earnings. Each industry's *own* exports will guarantee, without any drain on the national payment balance, its ability to repay its expansion loans. The government has only to set, or if necessary to adjust, the tariffs and export quotas of protected products in order to assure any desired balance of payments. Higher tariffs would imply a larger export obligation.

The *fact* of protection meanwhile will attract both domestic and foreign investors into a given industry. It is well known that public agencies often can obtain loans at relatively low rates of interest because of their ability to tax, if necessary, to service the loans. Conditional protection operates on a related principle: Moroccan industrialists can cite the protection of their domestic market as a safeguard for investments made in their enterprises.

This is a substantial point. Exports of manufactures established without any protection or subsidy are subject to certain risks, just like any other undertaking. Whatever those risks may be, conditional protection, by guaranteeing Moroccan enterprises a protected home market, obviously reduces them. If exports are established by means of a direct subsidy, on the other hand, the foreign and domestic investors must fear the remission of the subsidy along with the ordinary risks of business. If the enterprises cannot, after a reasonable trial period, export, then Morocco has no more interest in protecting the industry (such protection would frustrate the operation of the factor-price equalization theorem, which alone guarantees the increase in Moroccan real wages) than would foreign investors (who require payment in their own currencies of interest and principal) to continue financing it.

One might feel that the continuance of protection on successfully exported products, while it would soften borrowing terms, nonetheless would exert a lasting and undesirable burden on domestic consumers of the products. That burden however will automatically disappear through the competition of exporting firms. The world (or even just the EEC) market for most products can accommodate many Moroccan firms all operating at efficient scale although the strictly Moroccan market for most products cannot do so. Once firms begin to realize even small profits on their export sales, their protected Moroccan markets will necessarily be positively lucrative. Expansion in overseas markets will be lucrative too, since those markets cannot be easily saturated. Presumably, once an industry begins to make profits on export sales, its own interests will drive it to export regardless of the export quota justifying conditional protection of the home market. When this stage is reached, the industry will become very attractive to new entrants. Both the export quota and the import duty will become redundant and therefore free of any distortionary impact.

The new entrants at first need only to consider the domestic market, since under conditional protection no particular firm needs to export. The only condition is that exports bear a stated relationship to Moroccan consumption of the *product*. Once exports are successfully established, *domestic* competition will supervene to protect the consumer. The tariff will become *nugatory*. Its only function then will be to act as a cushion for the industry against fluctuations and as a counter in bargaining for tariff concessions from partner countries.

It is still true, of course, that the development of export potential in given products will be subsidized, in effect, by Moroccan consumers of those same products. All alternatives to such subsidization place more or less of the burden on those who do not consume the product, and notably on the general taxpayer. Obviously it is not clear that the alternative subsidies are better on grounds of distributive justice. Some may be economically more efficient inasmuch as consumers will reduce their demands for protected products. On the other hand, it may be desirable to associate consumers with export promotion so that producers will know as soon as possible how well their products are received. Such 'feedback' from foreign markets may well come too late. Let domestic consumers know that they are subsidizing exports, through the tariff, and let their price and quality complaints be heeded! In this respect conditional protection is a practical application of Stefan Burenstam Linder's famous assertion that a country can hope to export *only* those products for which it has a domestic market[6].

Customers of most products, all those which are not exported, will, in the meantime, enjoy duty-free privileges under conditional protection. To the extent that conditional protection enables the country to establish solidly a few viable and dynamic export industries, the typical Moroccan customer will end up paying lower total duties than under any system of generalized tariffs, notably one aiming at import substitution as opposed to export promotion.

4.2. FREE-TRADERS' OBJECTIONS TO CONDITIONAL PROTECTION

Under the assumptions (costless information, constant returns to scale, and no externalities) according to which free trade is optimal conditional protection is tantamount to free trade. Since only exports can be protected, all tariffs as well as all export quotas will be redundant and consumers will pay world prices. The only cost of maintaining conditional protection in such a world would be the cost of publishing the unconsulted duties and export quotas. All other purist objections to conditional protection can be dismissed forthwith.

Most free traders, however, accept certain so called 'infant-industry' arguments for temporary protection under stated exceptions to the assumptions justifying unqualified free trade. If simple or unconditional protection under infant-industry conditions meets free-traders' objections and brings about better and possibly optimal resource allocation, then of course conditional protection is an unnecessary refinement. Robert E. Baldwin[7], on the other hand, dismisses all three of the classic infant-industry arguments for temporary protection and thereby raises the question of whether, even under the circumstances thought to justify tariffs, any customs protection, including conditional protection, is warranted. Perhaps the best way for us to proceed, therefore, is to review Baldwin's arguments against tariffs to see if they confute not only classic infant-industry arguments for protection, but the case for conditional protection as well.

According to the first infant-industry argument, the acquisition of technology is costly to, but not appropriable by the individual firm. The pioneer firms in the new industry need customs protection to meet foreign competition because, once they have caught up with foreign techniques, other domestic firms will adopt, at little or no cost, the techniques perfected by the pioneers.

James E. Meade asserts that this argument requires more than just initially higher domestic than foreign costs if those costs are purely internal to the firm. Meade argues that firms can borrow on the basis of their long-term, and not just their short-term prospects: investors will excuse initial losses if later gains are sufficiently certain and large. They therefore need no tariff protection[8].

Meade's argument, which Baldwin[7, p. 298] accepts, is asymmetrical. It postulates foresighted and efficient capital markets and institutions in countries lacking production knowledge that is already well known overseas. Indeed, in view of the importance of industrial self-financing in any industrial country, one might question whether the capital markets in the so-called developed countries have the acumen that Meade and Baldwin assume those in underdeveloped countries to possess.

In any event, capital markets are not a repository of technology specific to firms and cannot therefore be counted upon, no matter how perfectly they match investors with entrepreneurs, to eliminate the risk and uncertainty inherent in transfering, adopting, or creating new technology.

Baldwin[7, p. 297] attacks Meade's belief that the technological *externality* argument can justify temporary protection. According to Baldwin, the fact that technology is costly to acquire by the first producer but not by his imitators will remain whether or not the tariff is imposed, and the tariff therefore will not induce innovation.

Baldwin could have attacked the externalities argument directly. There is no general reason why the first producer should find it costly to imitate a foreign producer while the second producer finds it costless to imitate *him*. In fact both acts of imitation will cost resources and will take time. This means that the first comer will not only have a longer time to amortize a given investment in research and imitation, but will be able to reap higher extraordinary profits during the time it takes for domestic competitors to appear.

What then is the role of the tariff? Simply to provide the first comer the occasion to make extraordinary profits for financing his later expansion.

The first argument for infant-industry protection therefore boils down to the fixed costs of starting up an industry in a country that lacks either percipient or trustworthy capital markets (cf. Sodersten [9, pp. 375–378]), or rich entrepreneurs, each one capable both of conceiving *and* financing projects. This argument is valid on its own terms, but the protection it justifies will work only if it is made conditional, as we shall see at the end of this section.

The second infant-industry argument for tariff protection is probably the best known: costs associated with on-the-job training cannot be recouped by the training firm. Baldwin[7, p. 301] correctly points out that, whenever their training renders their services more valuable to other firms, workers will be obliged to finance it themselves by accepting apprentice wages in their first job.

The Moroccan labor market is probably already flexible enough to accommodate this way of forming certain types of human capital. The problem is, of course, the income distribution: most young workers and their families lack the means to finance on-the-job training just as they lack the means to finance secondary and higher education. Baldwin feels, again, that the capital market will finance workers' early training.

The training does not constitute any collateral for securing the loan, however, and the worker would not need the loan if he had other collateral. Given the moral hazard involved, the capital market will not lend money to young and impecunious workers even in Morocco, where their average age would be about fifteen years. In the United States 30-year old medical students cannot finance their studies through the banks. The legal and practical difficulties of attaching future earnings are too great.

Baldwin may be correct, nonetheless, in asserting that the protective tariff will not help matters if the workers cannot finance their own apprenticeships. He believes that domestic competition, at any given level of the tariff, among firms will force each one to pay marginal productivity wage rates so that early firms cannot recoup training costs by underpaying workers once they are trained. All that the tariff can do, he states (p. 301) is to raise the product's price high enough so that production is profitable without training workers, and this merely creates an inefficient industry.

This sound argument is met, however, by making protection conditional: the inefficient industry will be unable to export and thus to qualify for protection.

Obviously a method other than the tariff is necessary to finance worker training in new but nonetheless competitive (easy-entry) industries. Firms might be paid, from general tax revenues, a subsidy for training workers. Such a subsidy would be proportional to labor turnover (the number of *new* workers engaged per year or other conventional time period) rather than to steady-state employment. The expenses would eventually be recouped through the higher taxes paid by the better qualified workers.

The third argument for temporary or infant-industry protection Baldwin attributes (p. 302) to A. Kafka[10], although it is difficult to

94

distinguish it in principle from the first argument. Suppose that a potential entrant to a new industry could borrow funds from investors if he provided them, at his own expense of course, a detailed technical analysis of his undertaking. The investor however would thereby make both his intentions and his secrets known to the financial community, which might leak them to rivals. This problem arose in Morocco in the context of the official Investment Commission which, it was said, would not only leak information to certain quarters but would further protect them by refusing or delaying resources to the parties submitting the original proposals.

Obviously there is an intrinsic risk of losing one's secrets if one has to borrow money. This is undoubtedly the reason that new enterprises in industrial countries are typically financed within closed circles or else at exorbitant interest rates. Baldwin concedes (p. 303) that under these circumstances a temporary duty may draw more resources than otherwise into socially useful pursuits.

Baldwin retorts, however, that investors will not learn from their earning experience that they are overestimating risks in new protected industries: they may simply attribute those favorable earnings to the tariff and keep on overestimating risks to new enterprises. Conditional protection overcomes this objection because investors will be able objectively to assess performance in terms of exports.

Baldwin's own recommendation, in lieu of temporary duties, for promoting new industry is a subsidy to the initial entrants into an industry for discovering better productive techniques (pp. 298 and 304). This position is unassailable in principle, but, I submit, unworkable in practice. This is because new productive and marketing knowledge cannot really be assessed independently of market performance. To pay the subsidy on knowledge creation, the government would have to wait to see which firms made profits in the marketplace and *then* reward them. If there were any scientific way to identify a priori the productive and marketing knowledge that Morocco needs, one would not need to subsidize its acquisition.

Rather the problem is much more complicated, sociologically as well as economically. A Moroccan worker may return one day from a factory in France or Belgium with an idea relevant to implanting a new industry in Morocco. He will know more about his scheme than any government or bank official, but he may well be unable and unwilling to reach them directly. Other people meanwhile may have other or similar ideas for Moroccan production of the same product. There is no general reason to induce them all to come together or to channel their projects through a common agency. Let the Government instead grant a stated duty as of a given date, subject to a stated export quota for that product. Anyone who thinks that he can produce profitably for export in the long run will have an incentive to enter the industry; anyone who knows or cares too little about the product to develop its profitable exportation would be well advised to stay out. Meanwhile, anyone interested in producing the product could petition the Government to establish its conditional protection. The Government might well publish such petitions in order to inform the business community of the extent of interest in given products, and act upon them when they become sufficiently numerous.

Leaving now Baldwin's exceedingly useful summary of the infant-industry question, we conclude this section with a powerful but little noted argument against unconditional import duties *even though they might meet the objections listed above*. The infant-industry argument for protection is implicitly a partial equilibrium argument: it takes no account of the fact that protection of a given industry draws resources away from less protected industries, including potential export industries. Infant industry protection alone cannot therefore be counted upon to find the country's best pattern of specialization. It risks instead to close down the type of foreign trade potentially capable of equalizing Moroccan and European wages.

This new argument against infant-industry protection (which, in a different context, has been given by me elsewhere, cf. Travis[5]) uses the following notation and assumptions. Let the set $F(y_i)$ ($i = 1, \ldots, n$) represent all the alternative factor-service input combinations, the vectors $f = (f_{1i}, \ldots, f_{ri})$, each of which is capable, under Morocco's technology, of producing an amount of the ith product worth just \$$y$ at *world* (or EEC) prices. Assume that the set $tF(y_i)$ (where t is any positive scalar) produces \$$ty$ worth of product i and, for the sake of simplicity, that the only primary factors are labor and capital. The argument will generalize to any number, r, of primary factors, so long as products are even more numerous.

Next, take the convex hull of the n sets $F(y_i)$. Its boundary is, in effect, Morocco's *isoquant* for producing (through foreign trade) a real income evaluated at \$$y$ at world prices. A whole family, determined by varying the scalar t, of such isoquants exists. Morocco's highest attainable income, given its present technology, is determined by the highest real-income isoquant [the boundary of the convex hull of the n sets $tF(y_i)$ for some t] that contains its factor-service input vector $f = (f_1, f_2)$ (where labor is the first and capital the second primary factor).

The isoquant we have just constructed, under the constant returns assumption, consists of a certain number of straight-line segments in the two-dimensional space measuring factor-service inputs. A subset of the n factor-service input sets (each one corresponding to the amount of a single product that is worth $\$ty$) will touch the isoquant. The production of all other products will be uneconomical regardless of the exact vector $f = (f_1, f_2)$ of factor-service inputs.

That vector will however determine, among the above subset of efficient industries those which *efficiently employ* the factor-service input vector $f = (f_1, f_2)$. The slope of the real-income isoquant where it contains the vector f determines, furthermore, Morocco's relative (and therefore, because $\$ty$ is known, absolute) factor prices.

In the special case in which Morocco and its trading partner know the same technology for producing all goods, the real-income isoquant will contain a single straight-line segment to which all n sets $tF(y_i)$ will be tangent. If the vector f lies in this segment, Morocco can with equal allocative efficiency produce some amount of each of any number up to n of the n products: the exact specialization pattern will be *indeterminate* (cf. Samuelson[4] and Travis[5]). The infant-industry context assumes away technological parity of course, but in particular situations more than two sets $F(y_i)$ nonetheless may be tangent to the real-income isoquant in the same straight-line segment through f, so that specialization is indeterminate.

Next, we stipulate, in the spirit of the infant-industry argument, that some of the sets $F(y_i)$ *not* touching the real-income isoquant of level $\$ty$ would nonetheless turn out eventually to be technically efficient if Morocco ran the industries in question during their necessary breaking-in periods. The acquisition of the technology involved would provide Morocco with a new $\$ty$ convex hull of which the original convex hull necessarily would be a *proper* subset. The scalar t could now be adjusted upward until the highest $\$ty$ isoquant containing f was found. This would correspond to Morocco's highest attainable income given not only its *new* technology, but its full realization of the gains from trade. Once again, the slope of the real-income isoquant where it contains f would indicate Morocco's relative factor earnings.

We must however consider the determination of factor earnings and national income during the breaking-in period. The tariff on, say, product h (one of the n products) gives rise to a factor input set, $F(y_h{}^*)$ of which the original (world-price) set $F(y_h)$ is a proper subset, that is, it shifts downward that set by an amount exactly proportional to the tariff. As before, we obtain a new real-income convex hull of which the original (tariff-free) convex hull is a proper subset.

The new, tariff-constrained, real-income isoquant corresponds to a *lower* level of real income, however. This is because of the input set $F(y_h)$ which, by hypothesis, does not touch the isoquant defined for world prices of all products, but which appears in the tariff-constrained isoquant. Not only has real income been reduced, but in general relative factor prices will have been altered as well. The change in relative factor prices means that *all but one* of the industries which Morocco formerly operated (including even export industries) will shut down. This is because the input vector f will lie in the straight-line segment of the tariff-constrained real-income isoquant touching $F(y_h{}^*)$ and only one other input set $F(y_i)$. The tariff has eliminated indeterminacy by specializing the economy in two (in general r) products.

The former industries will be displaced, moreover, *even if their technology is identical to that used abroad.* That is, industries which earlier on may have passed the infant-industry test and survived the elimination of their duties will now turn out to be uncompetitive thanks to the protection of the newcomer. They can be saved by a reimposition or renewal of protection, of course. Once this happens, however, there is no longer any practical way of telling which industries require tariff renewal because their entrepreneurs cannot acquire foreign technology, which ones require it because they do not fit the input vector f, and which ones require it simply because a new industry has been implanted through tariff protection or, for that matter, through any other form of subvention other than conditional protection.

This mechanism undoubtedly explains why in fact infant-industry duties never are temporary, just as it explains why countries with tariffs do not trade capital intensive products for labor intensive products in accordance with the Heckscher-Ohlin trade theory (cf. Travis[5]). Protection begets protection until only raw materials and other specialities are traded, and each protectionist country ends up with the same relative factor earnings that would appear if it were completely autarchic.

Making protection conditional upon export performance breaks the vicious circle of tariff generalization by eliminating those products which, because of a given national input vector f, would be imported *even if Morocco had the same technology in every product as its trading partners.* This cannot guarantee, in a world of technological incertitude, that wrong industries will not from time to time be granted conditional protection. It only means that they will either have to borrow abroad (thereby, without loss of economic efficiency, *changing* the input vector f) in order to export or else quit and release their resources to industries better fitting the country's input vector or better able to absorb foreign technology.

4.3. PROTECTIONISTS' OBJECTIONS TO CONDITIONAL PROTECTION

All protectionist arguments against conditional protection boil down to the assertion that in some cases no ad valorem duty rate will compensate producers for the onus of exporting any percentage of a product's apparent Moroccan consumption. That is to say, some industries, it is asserted, require pure and unconditional duties in order to survive in the Moroccan environment.

That is true, but it is also true that *all* such industries will hinder Moroccan economic growth. There is absolutely no case known to international trade theory where it is desirable to protect an industry to replace imports and not at the same time to export. This statement follows directly from the proposition that the opportunity to trade cannot be harmful even though, in particular razor-edge cases (that of two identical constant-returns economies, for example) the opportunity best remains unexploited. That case requires no duties to forestall trade, however.

It is possible nonetheless that an overvalued Moroccan exchange rate may be one of the reasons why Moroccan *net* (not total) imports of manufactures are presently too high. Unconditional protection would be the wrong way, of course, to correct that situation inasmuch as, in conjunction with the overvalued exchange rate (which is a general tax on exports of manufactures), it would simply be a supplementary tax on foreign trade. To some extent conditional protection, by drawing an implicit export subsidy from the domestic market, will compensate for an overvalued exchange rate. The best policy though is undoubtedly to aim for a neutral exchange rate (if it can be defined!) and thereby to separate the questions of protection and payment balance as much as possible.

Even though no argument to protect import-substituting industries that do not export exists, it may still be true, of course, that no Moroccan entrepreneurs will come forth to avail themselves of conditional protection. What alternative policies for implanting viable export industries exist? We have briefly touched above on subsidies to knowledge transfer. In addition one might consider explicit export subsidies, examples of which are included in the 1973–1977 Plan.

The commanding objection to selective export subsidies is that no one knows how to select the industries to encourage. The subsidies are likely to be granted therefore on grounds that have little to do with technical or economic efficiency; this has certainly been the experience in Pakistan, India, and several South American countries. A general subsidy on exports, on the other hand, is unnecessary since exactly the same effect can be achieved at much less administrative cost through devaluation. Both generalized export subsidies and especially devaluation, when they are used to subsidize industry, run the substantial risk of turning into foreign-aid programs. The Moroccan payments surplus would transfer income to foreigners. Conditional protection combined with a neutral payments balance is a much safer industrialization strategy.

The argument occasionally comes up that because the export obligation under conditional protection pertains to the *product* and not to any particular *firm* producing that product, the exports will not be forthcoming. Each firm, it is said, will be content to let the others bear the losses of exporting while it looks only to the protected, and therefore lucrative, home market.

That firm runs two risks, however, compared to any firm that decides to export. In the first place, if exports do not develop under the conditional tariff umbrella within a stated period (generally of about two years) the tariff will be eliminated. If no firm feels that it can export, then no firm will enter, just as one would want to happen.

On the other hand some of the firms may develop profitable export markets. In that case, any firm oriented exclusively towards the protected home market must fear the exporters' competition. The exporters will have two advantages: lower costs at any given output for a product of given quality and a higher level of production. For both reasons their average costs will be lower and they will have no reason to abandon the home market to firms unable to compete with them abroad. Therefore, each firm has only to worry about whether or not it can meet the export quota with respect to its own output. If it can pass that test, it and the duty will survive, regardless of what other firms may do.

In the worst possible case, then, some combination of ignorance and pusillanimity may prevent some or even all other otherwise qualified entrepreneurs from asking for and availing themselves of conditional protection. In such a situation, however, it is impossible for any other scheme to bring forth only that subset of desirable entrepreneurs without bringing forth opportunists.

Two other policies articulated at the DPDR are designed to complement conditional protection in raising through foreign trade Moroccan real wages. One is the proposal of Professor Karsten Laursen to subsidize labor employment directly (see the following chapter). That policy would not only help to train more workers on the job but would also automatically stimulate exports of the right manufactures to the extent that it lowered their prices in proportion to their labor content. The second proposal

100

is that Morocco subsidize or otherwise guarantee the construction of industrial infrastructure and facilities for rent to foreign producers agreeing to pay their wage bills, rent, and other local expenses in foreign exchange. This scheme is tantamount to the direct exportation of labor services (because foreign, not Moroccan, enterprises would engage them) and is therefore economically equivalent to emigration of workers.

These three proposals do not conflict with one another in the least; all three could advantageously be implemented simultaneously. Both the wage subsidy and the scheme for renting commercial and industrial facilities to foreign producers for foreign exchange would raise worker earnings while at the same time reducing the incentive for workers to emigrate. The enriched workers would constitute a local market for manufactures and thus increase the purchase of the conditional-protection policy. In time, of course, Moroccan enterprise would displace foreign enterprise in exporting, through products, Moroccan labor services. This would give rise to a natural process of transfering the same factory buildings and workers from employment by foreign entrepreneurs to employment by Moroccan entrepreneurs. As Moroccan industrial employment and real wages rose, the wage subsidy could be phased out.

4.4. THE TREATMENT OF INTERMEDIATE PRODUCTS

A large proportion of all manufactured products are intermediate products. Such products pose serious technical problems for any commercial policy designed to enhance economic development.

Tariff protection of an intermediate product which is not transformed in Morocco poses one obvious difficulty. Though the product is not transformed in Morocco, it may nonetheless, indirectly, be consumed there by virtue of being transformed overseas into a product eventually sold in the Moroccan market. Moroccan duties on imported products are already reduced according to their incorporation of Moroccan products. This comes very close to applying the basic idea (using duties to stimulate exports) of conditional protection to such products.

A more serious problem arises when an intermediate product is transformed locally for local use. If the intermediate product is granted conditional import protection then the industry which transforms it will require a compensatory duty, even if it receives no protection.

The transforming industry may, however, be an export industry, in which case we may assume that it enjoys conditional protection against competitive imports. Obviously it would be desirable to allow such an industry to have access to materials at world prices (even though they may

101

be locally produced) for its exports, but not for its local sales. This desire can be accommodated by allowing Moroccan producers of intermediate products to count their local sales as exports (for purposes of meeting their export obligation) provided that they are sold, at world prices, against foreign exchange. Domestic transforming industries would face the choice of purchasing at home or overseas their export-requirements of intermediate products; in either case they would pay in foreign exchange. Because such producers would have the option of purchasing duty-free intermediate products for export production, domestic producers of the same intermediate products would be forced to make their local sales to exporters at world prices as well, if they sought thereby to meet their product's export quota. Obviously they would not be obliged to sell at world prices any of their product destined in fact for incorporation in unexported products. Purchasers of intermediate products at world prices would be allowed to use for that purpose only an amount of foreign exchange proportion to their actual export sales.

While intermediate products necessarily pose practical administrative problems, their solution would not require an excessively complicated set of rules and procedures, especially when compared to the existing set of regulations. On the positive side, we might observe that the obligation to export a stated quota of protected output provides an automatic check, through published *foreign* data (on imports from Morocco), of the operation of the system. The general public could easily tell whether or not the system was achieving its stated goal of creating employment through export-oriented industrialization.

REFERENCES

1. Direction du Plan et du Développement Régional, 'Document de Service no. 454', Rabat, 1973.
2. B. Ohlin, *Interregional and International Trade*, Cambridge, Mass., 1935.
3. A.P. Lerner, 'Factor Prices and International Trade', *Economica*, 19, February 1952, pp. 1–16.
4. P.A. Samuelson, 'Prices of Factors and Goods in General Equilibrium', *Review of Economic Studies*, 21, 1953–1954, pp. 1–20.
5. W.P. Travis, 'Production, Trade and Protection when there are Many Commodities and Two Factors', *American Economic Review*, 62, March 1972, pp. 87–106.
6. S. Linder, *An Essay on Trade and Transformation*, New York, 1961.
7. R.E. Baldwin, 'The Case against Infant-Industry Tariff Protection', *Journal of Political Economy*, 77, May-June 1969, pp. 295–305.
8. J.E. Meade, *Trade and Welfare*, New York, 1955.
9. B. Sodersten, *International Economics*, New York, 1970.
10. A. Kafka, 'A New Argument for Protection?', *Quarterly Journal of Economics*, 68, February 1962, pp. 163–166.

5. Subsidize wages: a policy suggestion

K. Laursen

5.1. BACKGROUND

The background to a policy of subsidizing wages in Morocco (as in most other less developed countries) is very clear: unemployment, disguised and overt, is high, wages are low, and income distribution is skew. The ultimate goal of the policy, therefore, is to remove unemployment, to increase wages, and to improve the distribution of income.

Since a considerable part of the existing unemployment is disguised in agriculture and in urban craft sectors, the policy should cause a reduction of employment in these occupations and an increase in employment in the modern sectors of the urban economy. In this respect the objective of wage subsidy is essentially different from that of many other policies suggested to the LDC's. In fact, it is most frequently asserted that, for employment reasons, a rational development policy should encourage the agricultural and handicraft sectors, even if that means a loss in terms of growth of production. In my opinion, there is no such conflict between employment and production objectives, because the modern high productivity sectors of the urban economy are perfectly able to absorb the amount of labour necessary for unemployment, disguised and overt, to be eliminated.

But incentives need to be sufficient, and a policy to subsidize wages may turn out to be a very important instrument in this respect. In the form suggested below, it may be extended so as to solve both employment and distribution problems on its own, but it is obvious that its effect may be accelerated by appropriate policies on other fronts. In particular, I have in mind the conditional protection scheme and the monetary policy discussed in the present volume (chapters 4 and 2 respectively).

5.2. THE THEORY OF WAGE SUBSIDIES

The notion that employment may be increased through wage subsidies is

103

based, of course, on an assumption that a reduction in wage costs will induce a more labour-intensive production, i.e. on an assumption that the economy in question contains sufficient substitution possibilities between labour and the other input factors. The question of factor substitution in LDC's has long been a much debated issue in the literature, but during recent years, there seems to be a growing consensus among economists that the LDC's are not a world of fixed coefficients. Rather, substitution possibilities in all three conceivable areas of substitution, i.e. production functions for individual goods, domestic demand, and world trade, seem to have been underrated. It is not surprising, therefore, that a wage subsidy is a relatively new instrument in the packages of development policies discussed in the LDC's.

In the theoretical discussion, as well as in the discussions about its implementation in particular countries, a wage subsidy is almost always looked upon as a measure to combat overt urban unemployment. However, it may not work for that specific purpose. In fact, on certain, not unrealistic, premises it may turn out to be counter-productive[1]. This will be the case if the increase in urban employment brought about by the reduction in wage costs induces so much rural-urban migration that in the end, urban unemployment turns out to be more extensive than in the initial situation without a subsidy. It may be argued further that if this policy is then continued until the agricultural wage has risen (owing to the exodus) to the level of the urban wage, and the incentive to migrate has disappeared, the situation will not be one of optimum allocation of labour between the urban and the agricultural sector. Too much labour may then be in urban occupations and too little in agricultural occupations. This will be so if, for instance, labour is remunerated according to the value of its marginal product in both sectors of the economy. Because in that case the equilibrium position will be: agricultural wage = agricultural marginal productivity = urban wage > urban marginal productivity = urban wage − subsidy.

From a production point of view, it is not unlikely either that a wage subsidy paid to urban entrepreneurs in order to make them hire more labour may, in fact, turn out to have a negative effect. This may be the case if a sufficient number of workers are induced to leave agriculture where they had a positive although possibly very low marginal productivity, even if at the same time high productivity urban employment is somewhat expanded.

From the above considerations, it follows that a policy to subsidize wages for employment and distribution reasons should be general, in order to avoid the risk of doing more harm than good.

104

On the assumption that a wage subsidy is the only available instrument which may be used to deal with the problem, or more specifically, that the space of action is subject to the constraint that real wages may not be reduced in any sector of the economy, the following policy is implied:

a. Increase wages in the low productivity agricultural and urban craft sectors to the level in the high productivity urban modern sector. This measure, taken in isolation, will, of course, eliminate disguised unemployment, defined as a situation in which the remuneration of labour differs between occupations.* But instead it will create open unemployment.

b. Now this open unemployment may be eliminated through a wage subsidy given to all sectors by a certain percentage of the common wage rate. And now the subsidy will have none of the negative consequences discussed above.

But there are still a couple of possible objections to this policy. One is that the bargaining position of labour is probably stronger in the urban modern sector than in the other sectors. In fact, this presumably is the main reason why the initial discrepancies in wages existed. Consequently, one may fear that there is a tendency for the initial situation to re-emerge, because the increase in wages in the modern sector will reduce its employment and cause some labour either to be unemployed or to exert a downward pressure on wages in more traditional sectors in order to obtain employment there. In other words: one cannot be sure that the policy suggested above under a and b will have a lasting impact on the initial wage structure, because it is possible both that the subsidy given to the urban modern sector will in part be shifted to the employees of that sector, and that wages in the more traditional sectors are flexible downwards towards their initial relative level.

But even if this mechanism of re-establishing the initial wage structure is only weak, there is still the possibility that, as the economy moves towards full employment, money wages will start to go up. This may result merely in a rise in prices, but in a small open economy where the price level is determined exogenously to a large extent, viz. by the world-market, the increase in wages will have a contractionary impact.

The subsidy must, therefore, be combined with a control of wages,

---

* The best definition of disguised unemployment is probably a situation in which marginal labour productivities (for homogeneous labour) differ between occupations. In the present context I assume that the ratio of wage to marginal productivity is the same in all sectors. I shall abandon this assumption in a later section.

particularly in the modern sector in which the subsidy is most likely to be shifted to the employees.

A final question worth mentioning is how the subsidy may be financed. This, of course, is not a question of actually finding the money, as is frequently assumed when such policies are discussed, but rather a question of whether the saving ratio of the economy is influenced by the redistribution of income from capitalists to workers, as is involved by the subsidy. Capitalists are likely to have a higher saving propensity than workers, and in that case profits must be taxed by an amount in excess of the amount needed for the subsidy. Unless this is done resources will be channelled from investment into consumption, and ultimately this will mean that real income cannot be maintained.

5.3. A SIMPLE MODEL

A small model may illustrate further the way in which a subsidy to wages may promote employment and improve income distribution.

For simplicity I shall take only two sectors, viz. the urban, industrial sector and the rural, agricultural sector. Let sectoral outputs be given by:

$$Q_u = u \, M_u^{\alpha} \, K_u^{\beta(1-\alpha)} \, L_u^{(1-\beta)(1-\alpha)} \tag{1}$$

and:

$$Q_a = a \, M_a^{\gamma} \, K_a^{\delta(1-\gamma)} \, L_a^{(1-\delta)(1-\gamma)} \tag{2}$$

where Q, M, K, and L denote output, imports of raw and intermediate materials, capital and labour. Subscripts u and a refer to 'urban' and 'agricultural'. All units are physical.

The assumption that the production functions are of the Cobb-Douglas type is of course questionable. Most empirical evidence, although not quite convincingly, seems to indicate that the elasticity of substitution in production functions for less developed countries is slightly, but significantly below unity. However, whether it is unity or slightly less is immaterial for the main argument of this paper.

As appears, the functions in (1) and (2) apply to output rather than value-added. The value-added components may be expressed as follows:

$$Q_{u,v} = K_u^{\beta} L_u^{1-\beta} \tag{3}$$

and:

$$Q_{a,v} = K_a^{\delta} L_a^{1-\delta} \tag{4}$$

so that (1) and (2) may be rewritten to yield:

$$Q_u = u \, M_u^{\alpha} \, Q_{u,\,v}^{1-\alpha} \tag{1a}$$

and:

$$Q_a = a \, M_a^{\gamma} \, Q_{a,\,v}^{1-\gamma}. \tag{2a}$$

I assume next that remuneration rates are exogenous and that inputs of imports, capital, and labour at these rates are given by (see Appendix):

$$P_{i,\,u} = \alpha \frac{P_u}{\mu_u} \frac{Q_u}{M_u} \tag{5}$$

$$R_u = \beta (1 - \alpha) \frac{1}{\mu_u} \frac{Q_u}{K_u} \tag{6}$$

$$W_u = (1 - \beta)(1 - \alpha) \frac{P_u}{\mu_u} \frac{Q_u}{L_u} \tag{7}$$

and:

$$P_{i,\,a} = \gamma \frac{P_a}{\mu_a} \frac{Q_a}{M_a} \tag{8}$$

$$R_a = \delta (1 - \gamma) \frac{P_a}{P_u \mu_a} \frac{Q_a}{K_a} \tag{9}$$

$$W_a = (1 - \delta)(1 - \gamma) \frac{P_a}{\mu_a} \frac{Q_a}{L_a} \tag{10}$$

where P, R, W, and μ are prices, profits rates, wage rates, and monopoly coefficients, and subscript i denotes 'intermediate and raw materials'. It will be apparent that if the monopoly coefficients are equal to 1, then each factor will receive the value of its marginal product. Note also that since we have only two sectors, the industrial output good is also the capital input good.

On the basis of this model the employment situation may now be analyzed.

5.4. DISGUISED UNEMPLOYMENT

In the literature there is some confusion as to the definition of the concept of disguised unemployment. Here, I shall take it to mean simply a situation in which marginal productivities of the same quality of labour differ between economic sectors (cf. footnote on p. 105). Consequently, as appears from (7) and (10), the elimination of disguised unemployment requires that:

107

$$W_u \mu_u = W_a \mu_a. \tag{11}$$

The corresponding allocation of labour may be derived from (1), (2), (7), and (10):

$$\hat{L}_u = c^{1-(1-\beta)(1-\alpha)} \hat{L}_a^{[(1-\delta)(1-\gamma)-1]/[(1-\beta)(1-\alpha)-1]} \tag{12}$$

where:

$$c = (1-\delta)(1-\gamma) P_a a M_a^\gamma K_a^{\delta(1-\gamma)} / (1-\beta)(1-\alpha) P_u u M_u^\alpha K_u^{\beta(1-\alpha)} \tag{13}$$

and where $\wedge$ denotes 'efficient' employment.

Given that, in the present section, our concern is the elimination of disguised, but not overt unemployment, we arrive at the following:

$$\hat{L}_u + \hat{L}_a = \bar{L}_u + \bar{L}_a = L \tag{14}$$

where – denotes employment prior to the reallocation of labour.

The elimination of disguised unemployment may be illustrated in a diagram, where monopolies are ignored (Figure 1).

In this diagram $W_{a,0}$, $W_{u,0}$, $L_{a,0}$, and $L_{u,0}$ are the initial values of the variables. W_1, $L_{a,1}$, and $L_{u,1}$ are the values corresponding to an 'efficient' allocation.

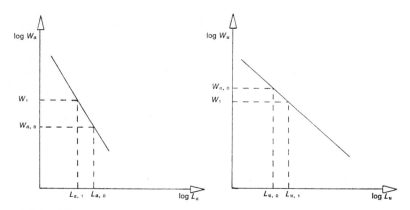

Figure 1. Elimination of disguised unemployment

However, in (11) we have derived only what might be called the short-run condition for efficient allocation. In the longer run we shall of course also require that:

$$R_u = R_a = R \qquad (15)$$

and that:

$$\mu_u = \mu_a = \mu. \qquad (16)$$

Consequently, we may, perhaps, assume that the long-run gains from re-allocating the factors of production will exceed the short-run gains. This, of course, is not necessarily so, since a differential in profit rates, for example, may be eliminated or even reversed by the short-run re-allocation of labour.

5.5. OVERT UNEMPLOYMENT

The point of departure for the analysis in this section is the 'long-run' efficient allocation as defined above. I assume, thus, that the conditions in (11), (15), and (16) are fulfilled. In addition, for convenience, I assume that imported inputs are a homogeneous product.

From the remuneration rates in (5) – (10) we may now derive the following constraints:

$$\bar{\bar{M}} \geqq \frac{\alpha\, P_u\, Q_u + \gamma\, P_a\, Q_a}{\mu\, P_i^{\$}\, E} \qquad (17)$$

$$\bar{\bar{K}} \geqq \frac{\beta\,(1 - \alpha)\, P_u\, Q_u + \delta\,(1 - \gamma)\, P_a\, Q_a}{\mu\, R\, P_u} \qquad (18)$$

$$\bar{\bar{L}} \geqq \frac{(1 - \beta)\,(1 - \alpha)\, P_u\, Q_u + (1 - \delta)\,(1 - \gamma)\, P_a\, Q_a}{\mu\, W} \qquad (19)$$

Where $P_i^{\$}$ is the import price in foreign currency, and E is the rate of exchange, so that:

$$P_{i,a} = P_{i,u} = P_i = P_i^{\$}\, E. \qquad (20)$$

These constraints may be illustrated by a diagram [2] (Figure 2).

The interpretation of the diagram is straightforward. Given the remuneration rates, the parameters, and the available quantities of the factors of production, imports are the binding constraint on production in the area ab, where capital and labour are redundant. In the area bc capital is the binding constraint, whereas labour and imports are redundant. (It is true, of course, that the capacity to import may always be fully utilized,

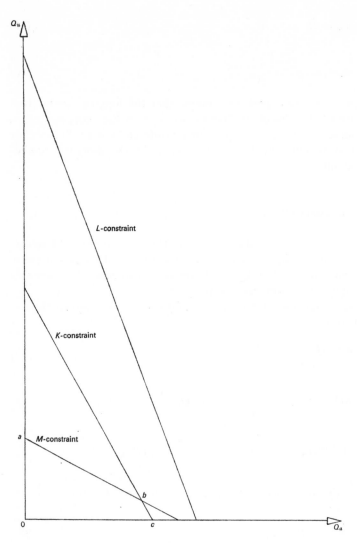

Figure 2. Constraints on production

since finished goods may be imported, but this possibility is irrelevant in the present context.)

It is obvious, however, that the three constraints may always be brought to intersect in any chosen combination of industrial and agricultural production through suitable variations in the policy instruments, viz.

110

exchange, interest, wage rates and the monopoly coefficient. Consequently, within the framework of the present model, no factor needs to remain redundant.

Conventional development models assume fixed, technical coefficients, and the three constraints appear as follows:

$$\overline{\overline{M}} \geq a\,Q_u + b\,Q_a \tag{21}$$

$$\overline{K} \geq c\,Q_u + d\,Q_a \tag{22}$$

$$\overline{L} \geq e\,Q_u + f\,Q_a. \tag{23}$$

In such models the only policy prescription is to increase the supply of the scarce factors, which are normally taken to be either imports or capital. However, it may be argued that these models, where substitution between factors cannot occur, and where consequently relative factor prices are irrelevant for the choice of technology, are unrealistic in developed as well as in less developed countries. It is true that, until a few years ago, the common view was that a symptom of underdevelopment was the lack of substitution possibilities. However, this opinion has been gradually abandoned, although the assumption of a unit elasticity of substitution implied by the present model may be considered to exaggerate the possibilities of choosing between technologies. At any rate, the only conceivable constraint on full utilization of productive resources is a possible institutional reluctance to using the available instruments, which in the circumstances include a reduction of wage costs.

5.6. POLICY CONCLUSIONS

The obvious policy conclusions which may be drawn from the above analysis are:
- elimination of existing differentials in monopoly coefficients between sectors;
- equalization of wage rates by increasing wages in one sector and decreasing them in another;
- elimination of monopolies;
- reduction of wage rates and, depending on the capital and import constraints, variations in interest and exchange rates.

However, this package will not, in general, be politically feasible. In particular, one would not want to suggest a reduction of wage rates in a

country where wages are already very low. Consequently a policy, more consistent with the general notion of social justice would be to:
- eliminate monopolies;
- increase agricultural wages to the level of industrial wages;
- subsidize this common wage to the extent of equalizing wage cost to the value of the marginal product of labour at full employment;
- control wages in order to prevent the initial distortion from reappearing.
A discussion of this policy for Morocco is the subject of section 5.7.

5.7. THE MOROCCAN ECONOMY

This section on the Moroccan employment problem is hardly more than an illustration using Moroccan data. This is mainly because the available statistics are quite insufficient, but also because the details of the suggested policy should be analysed by someone with a more profound knowledge of the Moroccan labour market than mine. Yet a refined statistical treatment is not a prerequisite for the implementation of a wage subsidy. The direction of the impact of the measure is obvious, and I see no immediate danger of doing too much.

5.7.1. *Disguised unemployment*

The point of departure for the analysis is the input-output table for 1969[3]. We shall use the following figures (Table 1).

Table 1. National income components, 1969*

	10^6 *Dirham*
Value-added, agriculture	3269
Value-added, industry	11686
Wages, agriculture	461
Wages, industry	4403
Imports, agriculture	738
Imports, industry	8079
Production, agriculture	4007
Production, industry	19765

* By industry is meant: non-agriculture.

Unfortunately, no information on the number of employed which corresponds to the wage-bills in the table is available. The census figures are

112

insufficient for two reasons: first, the census distinction between rural and urban employment does not correspond to the distinction made in the table, and second, census rural employment includes 'tenures familiales', the remuneration of which is not included in the wage-bill in the table.

To overcome this difficulty I shall make two assumptions, viz. that the minimum wage in each sector is equal to the average wage, and that the working year is 300 days. Such assumptions may, of course, be challenged, but they are sufficiently accurate for the present rough calculations. Since the minimum agricultural wage (SMAG) is 5 DH/day, and the minimum industrial wage (SMIG) is 10 DH/day, we obtain 461 millions/1500 = 307,333 workers in agriculture and 4403 millions/3000 = 1,467,666 workers in industry. This calculation is obviously not representative of the relative importance of agriculture because of the many family holdings in this sector.

We are now in a position to provide a rough estimate of the efficient allocation of labour. In the context of the short-run analysis, we can rewrite the production functions to yield:

$$Q_u = u L_u^x \qquad (24)$$

and:

$$Q_a = a L_a^y \qquad (25)$$

Furthermore, I shall ignore the possibility of monopolies since I have no way of determining the degree to which they may exist. It is fairly obvious, however, that they are more pronounced in urban sectors than in agriculture. Finally, I assume for convenience that P_u and P_a remain constant and equal to 1. Consequently we get the following wage rates:

$$W_u = x \frac{Q_u}{L_u} \qquad (26)$$

and:

$$W_a = y \frac{Q_a}{L_a} \qquad (27)$$

Thus (12) becomes:

$$\hat{L}_a = \left(\frac{xu}{ya}\right)^{1/(y-1)} \hat{L}_u^{(x-1)/(y-1)} \qquad (28)$$

noting (14), i.e. $\hat{L}_a + \hat{L}_u = L_a + L_u$.

There is no easy solution to (28), but it may be solved by iteration. The results are found in Table 2.

Table 2. National income components, disguised unemployment eliminated

	10^6 *Dirham*
Value-added, agriculture	2961
Value-added, industry	12130
Wages, agriculture	426
Wages, industry	4502
Imports, agriculture	738
Imports, industry	8079
Production, agriculture	3699
Production, industry	20209

Furthermore the wage-bills may be broken down as:

$$L_u = 1621709 \tag{29}$$

$$W_u = 9.25 \text{ DH}/\text{day} \tag{30}$$

$$L_a = 153290 \tag{31}$$

$$W_a = 9.25 \text{ DH}/\text{day}. \tag{32}$$

The main features of the short-run efficiency situation as compared with the initial situation can be summarized as follows:
- the agricultural labour force is reduced by about 50%;
- agricultural wage rates are increased very considerably, whereas industrial wage rates are only slightly reduced;
- total value-added goes up by less than 1%.

The latter result is perhaps surprising, but it is consistent with recent empirical findings[4], according to which even serious misallocations defined by differentials in remuneration rates represent only small losses to society. However, it should be kept in mind that possible differentials in monopolies have been ignored and that, as a consequence of rural-urban labour migration, other factors of production are also likely to be re-allocated. Hereby gains will be enhanced, particularly if the control of urban monopolies is successful. However, in no circumstances should one expect the impact on total production to be very dramatic.

A somewhat different question pertains to the development of relative

114

prices. By assumption they have been kept constant in the above calculation, and, given the openness of the Moroccan economy, it seems reasonable to take prices as exogenous.* True, the present degree of protection may not be the same in the two sectors.

Finally, it should be noted that a strong impact of the exodus from agriculture is a redistribution of income from urban to rural workers. In the circumstances this would seem to be a favourable effect.

5.7.2. Overt unemployment

There is no reliable information available on the extent of overt unemployment, but it seems safe to assume that employment could be increased by at least about 15%. We shall, therefore, simply assume that full employment is reached if urban employment is increased by 15%, and agricultural employment goes up correspondingly.

From (24) – (27) we may derive:

$$W_u = x u L_u^{x-1} \tag{33}$$

and:

$$W_a = y a L_a^{y-1} \tag{34}$$

so that:

$$\frac{\partial \log W_u}{\partial \log L_u} = x - 1 \tag{35}$$

and:

$$\frac{\partial \log W_a}{\partial \log L_a} = y - 1 \tag{36}$$

In order to maintain allocative efficiency we shall require that:

$$\partial \log W_u = \partial \log W_a \tag{37}$$

with:

$$(x - 1)\, \partial \log L_u = (y - 1)\, \partial \log L_a \tag{38}$$

The results of the elimination of overt unemployment are found in Table 3 on the following page.

---

* In a closed economy, agricultural prices would rise relatively to industrial prices.

Table 3. National income components, overt unemployment eliminated

	10^6 Dirham
Value-added, agriculture	3078
Value-added, industry	12797
Wages, agriculture	451
Wages, industry	4593
Imports, agriculture	738
Imports, industry	8079
Production, agriculture	3757
Production, industry	20876

Furthermore, the wage-bills may be broken down as:

$$L_u = 1864965 \tag{39}$$

$$W_u = 8.20 \text{ DH/day} \tag{40}$$

$$L_a = 173218 \tag{41}$$

$$W_a = 8.20 \text{ DH/day} \tag{42}$$

The main features of this situation as compared to the situation in which only disguised unemployment had been eliminated may be summarized as follows:
– value-added has been increased by about 5%;
– wage rates have declined by about 10%.
As appears, considerably more is to be gained from eliminating overt unemployment than from eliminating disguised unemployment. This conclusion is perhaps contrary to common belief, and admittedly it cannot be safely drawn from the above analysis.

Furthermore, it may also be somewhat surprising that the total gain from eliminating both kinds of unemployment is as modest as suggested by these calculations. However, as mentioned above, more is to be gained from the re-allocation of other factors, and in addition there is some empirical evidence that the rate of productivity increase is positively related to employment level.

5.7.3. *'Subsidize wages'*

Although by the assumption of the production functions the share of labour remains constant in each sector, and although the total share of labour goes up as a consequence of the increased importance of the industrial sector, it may easily be argued that no reduction in wage rates is acceptable (or even possible). This is the background for the wage subsidy.

The extent of this subsidy appears from the analysis in 5.7.1 and 5.7.2. Thus, a rational employment policy in Morocco implies three things:
- increase agricultural wages to 10 DH/day;
- subsidize all wages by 1.80 DH/day;
- control of wages; this control must, of course, take into account the increase in the level of productivity and be correspondingly relaxed in time (alternatively the subsidy may be gradually reduced).

It is obvious that these calculations are indeed very crude. The most important objection to the underlying model probably concerns the substitution assumption, particularly the assumption that employment in the urban sector may be increased by as much as 15% without any increase in imports of raw and intermediate products. In other words: is the effect of lower wage costs on import substitution by domestic production more or less important than the income effect on imports caused by the increase in employment? The model does not answer this question, but the implicit assumption of the above calculations is that the two effects will, in fact, cancel out.

The conventional objection, viz. that a Cobb-Douglas function overrates the possibilities of influencing capital-labour ratios through changes in rental-wage ratios is less important, to my mind. In Morocco, as in almost all LDC's, shift-work is almost non-existent. Consequently real capital may be utilized much more intensively by the introduction of two or even three shifts in many plants if relative factor prices provide a sufficient incentive.

In spite of these and other objections, there is no doubt that the calculations shown above represent the correct order of magnitude. A wage subsidy of about 20% along the foregoing lines would certainly be better than no subsidy at all.

Finally, one might challenge the assumption that labour is homogeneous, which it is not. However, I see no reason why the workers receiving only the minimum wage in rural and in urban occupations should be of a very different quality. And it is precisely these minimum wage rates that should be aligned in order to eliminate disguised unemployment. True, the calculations of the subsidy needed to eliminate open unemployment have, in fact, been based on the assumption that no worker received a remuneration above the SMIG. But this is really a minor point. In practice, it would probably be preferable to subsidize all wages by the same absolute amount. Perhaps about 2 DH/day.

APPENDIX

The remuneration rates in (7) – (12) are derived in the following manner:

For any given sector total revenue is given by:

$$R = Q(M, K, L) \cdot P(Q) \tag{i}$$

and total cost by:

$$C = WL + RP_u K + P_i M \tag{ii}$$

with profits becoming:

$$\Pi = Q(M, K, L) \cdot P(Q) - WL - RP_u K - P_i M \tag{iii}$$

Differentiating and setting equal to zero we get:

$$\frac{\partial \Pi}{\partial M} = \frac{\partial Q}{\partial M} P + Q \frac{dP}{dQ} \frac{\partial Q}{\partial M} - P_i = 0 \tag{iv}$$

$$\frac{\partial \Pi}{\partial K} = \frac{\partial Q}{\partial K} P + Q \frac{dP}{dQ} \frac{\partial Q}{\partial K} - P_u R = 0 \tag{v}$$

$$\frac{\partial \Pi}{\partial L} = \frac{\partial Q}{\partial L} P + Q \frac{dP}{dQ} \frac{\partial Q}{\partial L} - W = 0 \tag{vi}$$

from which we can derive:

$$P_i = P \left(1 + \frac{1}{\varepsilon} \right) \frac{\partial Q}{\partial M} \tag{vii}$$

$$P_u R = P \left(1 + \frac{1}{\varepsilon} \right) \frac{\partial Q}{\partial K} \tag{viii}$$

$$W = P \left(1 + \frac{1}{\varepsilon} \right) \frac{\partial Q}{\partial L} \tag{ix}$$

where we set:

$$\left(1 + \frac{1}{\varepsilon} \right) = \frac{1}{\mu} \tag{x}$$

i.e. μ is the ratio of prices to marginal cost or the 'monopoly coefficient', as it is called. With pure competition this coefficient equals 1, and remuneration rates equal marginal productivities. ε is the conventional price elasticity of demand.

REFERENCES

1. J. E. Stiglitz, 'Alternative Theories of Wage Determination and Unemployment in LDC's: the Labour Turnover Model', *Quarterly Journal of Economics*, Vol. LXXXVIII, No. 2, May 1974.

2. A somewhat similar presentation is found in: R.R. Nelson, T.P. Schultz and R.L. Slighton, *Structural Change in a Developing Economy. Colombia's Problems and Prospects*, Princeton, 1971.
3. 'Note Méthodologique sur l'Elaboration du Tableau Inter-Branches (TEI) de 1969', Rapport No. 14, Royaume du Maroc, Premier Ministre, Secrétariat d'Etat au Plan, au Développement Régional et à la Formation des Cadres, Direction de la Statistique, Rabat, November 1972.
4. Chr. Dougherty and M. Selowsky, 'Measuring the Effects of the Misallocation of Labour', *Review of Economics and Statistics*, Vol. LV, No. 3, August 1973.

Part III. Specific problems and policies

6. Earnings determinants in a mixed labour market

G. Psacharopoulos*

This paper analyses earnings differentials in Morocco utilising the results of a labour survey. Earnings functions are geared to monthly earnings and other characteristics of individual workers, with particular emphasis on schooling and nationality. The remaining nationality earnings differential (after factors like age, occupation, and years of schooling have been examined) is interpreted as a premium to differential schooling quality. Earnings analysis using individual rather than grouped data is a relatively recent activity in labour economics. Yet within the last decade or so, there have been over 100 applications of 'earnings functions'. Most of the empirical analysis refers to the United States[1]. But earnings functions have been fitted to data of other countries as well[2].

The following section presents a set of theoretical considerations of the earnings determining process. Section 6.2 gives a description of the particular sample used in this study and the overall means and variances of the variables that were constructed. Then a set of alternative specifications of an earnings function are fitted (Section 6.3) and the results interpreted in the light of the Moroccan context (Section 6.4).

6.1. WHY DO EARNINGS DIFFERENTIALS EXIST?

The theory behind the existence of personal earnings differences goes back to the foundations of economics as a discipline; and it has not changed much since. As a first step, one can think of wages as a price and thus determined by supply and demand. To add a degree of realism, one can also introduce institutional factors interfering with competitive equilibrium. For example, Adam Smith talked about *equalizing* (or *compensating*) wage

* I am indebted to my colleague Christopher Dougherty for valuable programming advice in preparing this paper and to the Center for Research on Economic Development, University of Michigan for sponsoring my visit to Morocco. The opinions expressed in this paper are entirely my own.

123

differentials. Since some occupations are more dangerous than others or involve dissatisfaction of some sort, it is natural for the employee to expect a compensating premium. Moreover, since some occupations require additional training relative to others, the extra earnings could be seen as a compensation for the costs incurred during the training period.

Cairns and Mill introduced later the concept of *non-competing* groups to explain earnings differentials. If more able people are scarcer than less able people, then the extra earnings of the more able people are due to restrictions on the supply side of labour classified into different watertight, and therefore, non-competing groups. More recently, earnings differentials have been attributed to unions, monopolistic product markets, discrimination and even differential luck[3].

Until very recently, empirical tests of the above theories were conducted mainly by means of cross-tabulations of the earnings of employees by the various explanatory variables[4]. This procedure, however, is unsatisfactory as one can never tell the statistical significance of the difference in average wages between two groups of people. The recent availability of data on earnings (Y) and other characteristics (X) of the individual (i) made it possible to fit the following earnings function:

$$Y_i = f(X_{1i}, X_{2i}, X_{3i}, \ldots) \tag{1}$$

where the X's stand for factors like ability, occupation, education and the like. Once an equation of type (1) is fitted, the relative importance and statistical significance of the variables in the right hand side in determining earnings can be assessed. Furthermore, the partial derivative of (1) with respect to any given independent variable shows the *net effect* of that variable on earnings, controlling for all the other characteristics included in the function. For example, the first derivative of an earnings function with respect to schooling shows the net effect of education on earnings, controlling for other factors like ability. Therefore, the use, par excellence, of earnings functions has been in adjusting earnings differentials for factors that render labour non-homogeneous. The particular areas of application have been the generation of theoretical (adjusted) age-earnings profiles by level of schooling for cost-benefit analysis; the study of interaction effects among the X's in determining earnings (e.g., are schooling and ability complements or substitutes in determining earnings?); the assessment of 'pure' earnings dispersion in the economics of information and job search; the testing of the 'screening hypothesis'; and the generation of idealised, forward-looking, age-earnings profiles in educational planning.

A further use of earnings functions is in the analysis of factors associated with income distribution. If the left hand side is expressed in log form, its variance gives a direct measure of income inequality. The degree of inequality can then be related to the variance and size of the arguments in the right hand side. For example, one could find out how much to increase the average level of schooling of the population in order to reduce the variance of the log of earnings by a given percentage.

Earnings functions can also be used in formulating employment creation policies in developing countries. In the first place, the employment problem can be reduced to an income distribution problem and thus studied under the latter heading. Secondly, earnings functions isolate individual worker characteristics related to low (or high) pay. Once these characteristics have been identified, a policy could be adopted for altering the relevant attributes of the lower paid segments of the labour force. For such an analysis, earnings functions should ideally be geared to observations including unemployed persons (with zero earnings) and less-than-fully-employed workers.

Before we proceed to the empirical analysis, we must warn the reader of a set of theoretical points regarding earnings functions fitting. A non-ambitious use of earnings functions is simply descriptive. A regression is fitted to observed wages and other characteristics of labour in order to make some statements on what is *associated* with what. A more ambitious use of earnings functions is in explaining what determines labour productivity.

Note that several steps exist between the foregoing two uses. In the first place, statistical association (or 'good fit') does not necessarily imply a theoretical *causation*. Secondly, one is never sure whether the fitted function refers to the demand side or the supply side. Thirdly, observed wages do not necessarily correspond to the *social* marginal product of labour. The last remark is important if earnings functions results are used in educational planning.

One particular hypothesis underlying earnings functions fitting is that different individuals possess differential human capital. The ones with higher human capital would command a higher premium in the labour market as compensation for the training costs they incurred. Human capital theory provides the rationale for the introduction of the number of years of schooling and experience (usually measured by age) in the right hand side of an earnings function. Other variables are introduced either on an *ad hoc* basis or as shifters of the entire function for a characteristic other than human capital. For example, the number of weeks worked has been introduced in the set of independent variables so to catch some of the returns that would otherwise have been attributed to schooling[5].

But this theoretical reasoning is not without problems. The 'screening hypothesis' has been suggested as a counter-argument to that of human capital: employers might offer higher wages to those with higher levels of schooling, not because the latter are more productive, but because they are probably more able than employees with less schooling. If this hypothesis is correct, the apparent social returns to education should be reduced as representing a private rather than a social gain. In other words, selection of the able could have taken place by a less expensive process than, say, 16 years of schooling[6].

Note that when an earnings function is used to formulate an employment creation policy, the assumptions of marginal productivity and absence of screening become less crucial. Depending on the planner's objective function, a trade-off might be allowed between employment creation and economic efficiency, although efficiency does not necessarily have to be foregone. My belief is that most policies aimed at employment creation are consistent with economic efficiency. It is possible, for example, that reduction of the illiteracy rate would be associated with higher productivity and employment. But of course this is a hypothesis to be tested.

6.2. SAMPLE CHARACTERISTICS

The analysis in this paper is based on a sample of 2,545 full-time employees in Morocco in 1970.* Table 1, below, shows that the sample derives mainly from the urban manufacturing sector. Males represent 80 per cent. of the observations, while 26 per cent. of the sample refers to non-Moroccans. And in this sense we shall refer to a 'mixed' labour market. The high proportion of foreign nationals (mainly French) in the Moroccan labour force also suggests a new dualistic classification of this labour market into Moroccan nationals and non-nationals.** To the extent that the two groups of employees have different work preferences, schooling or other characteristics, they would command a different salary. However, any remaining salary differential after adjusting for such characteristics, must be sought elsewhere. Later in this paper, we investigate the respects in which foreigners differ from Moroccans, and

---

* For a description of the way this sample was raised, see Appendix.
** Classic dualistic classifications of the labour market include urban-rural, traditional-modern, white-black and primary-secondary labour markets. It should be noted, however, that the dualism of the labour market is often offered as an all-embracing explanation of earnings differentials without analysing the particular attributes of workers that account for differential pay.

126

suggest alternative theories that might account for any earnings discrepancies of the type described above.

Table 1. Overall sample means

Variable	Mean or proportion in sample
Monthly salary (DH)	917
Age (years)	34.5
Schooling (years)	4.8
Experience (years)	6.8
Sex (male)	.80
Nationality (Moroccan)	.74
Occupation (white collar)	.53
Economic sector (manufacturing)	.44
Firm size (persons)	70.6
Region (cities over 1 m. population)	.80

Note: The coefficient of variation of monthly salary is equal to 1.11.

Table 1 shows that the average age of the entire sample is 35 years and the average number of years of schooling completed just under 5. Experience refers to the present employer and averages about 7 years. White collar and blue collar occupations are almost equally represented in the sample. The average firm size, where the individual is employed, is 71 persons, but this figure varies widely (coefficient of variation over 2). The average monthly salary of the entire sample is 917 DH* and the standard deviation of this variable exceeds the mean. It is, in fact, the purpose of this study to explain the variance in the observed monthly salary.

In the following, we first cross-classify salary according to the different independent variables and then proceed to multiple regression analysis. Table 2 shows monthly salary classified according to completed educational levels. Concentrating on the absolute salary level there is an almost 100 per cent. gain between illiteracy and completion of primary education. The CAP** seems to be equally satisfactory as a secondary 1st cycle, while the secondary 2nd cycle exhibits a modest gain over the 1st cycle. An engineering degree is associated with 1,000 DH extra per month relative to a non-

---

* The 1970 exchange rate was U.S.$ 1 = 4.55 DH.
** For an explanation of the different educational levels used in this study, see Appendix, Table A-8.

engineering university degree. This cross-tabulation has already reduced the variance of earnings of *educated* labour. But considerable variation in earnings remains among the illiterates.

Table 3 presents an alternative classification of education in terms of years of school completed. Once again, the general pattern is one of more stable incomes as the level of income and education increases. Table 4 gives mean earnings according to occupation. Administrators have the highest and most stable incomes, followed by technicians. It is interesting to note that sales workers do better than accountants. Blue collar workers are at the bottom of the earnings scale and exhibit the highest variability in earnings.

Earnings classified according to three dichotomous variables (sex, nationality and city size) appear in Table 5. The highest differential appears to be between Moroccans (Y = 575 DH/month) and non-Moroccans (1880 DH). We shall term this difference in earnings (1305 DH) the 'crude nationality differential'. Of course, foreigners differ in many other respects from Moroccans. For example, they might have had more years of schooling or they might work in high-pay occupations, and one should standardize for these factors.

Cross-tabulations of the kind presented above are useful in describing overall sample characteristics. But they have limitations when more than one variable is taken into account. Therefore, we turn to multiple regression analysis in order to discover the effect of individual characteristics on earnings.

Table 2. Monthly salary according to completed educational level

Educational level	Mean monthly salary (DH)	Coefficient of variation	Number of observations
None	441	1.20	1187
Primary	816	.69	240
Secondary 1st cycle	1,105	.62	187
Secondary 2nd cycle	1,259	.59	28
BAC	1,813	.74	120
University	2,451	.61	80
Engineer	3,481	.47	62
CAP	1,061	.64	286
DMT	1,312	.58	52

Note: This tabulation excludes unknown educational level and dropouts.

128

Table 3. Monthly salary according to years of schooling completed

Years of schooling	Mean monthly salary (DH)	Coefficient of variation
0	441	1.20
1–5	775	.71
6–12	1,055	.69
13	1,662	.73
14+	2,886	.57

Note: This tabulation excludes unknown educational level but includes dropouts.

Table 4. Monthly salary according to occupation

Occupation	Mean salary (DH)	Coefficient of variation	Number of observations
Administrator	3,088	.51	208
Accountant	1,015	.73	129
Office worker	885	.65	821
Sales worker	1,230	.83	182
Service worker	401	.96	152
Technician	1,733	.50	59
Skilled worker	550	1.07	579
Manual worker	311	.74	415

Table 5. Monthly salary according to dichotomous characteristics

Characteristics	Mean salary (DH)	Coefficient of variation
Sex		
Males	955	1.16
Females	765	.70
Nationality		
Moroccan	575	1.03
Foreign	1,880	.70
Region		
Over 1m. population	974	1.07
Less 1m. population	689	1.29

6.3. EARNINGS FUNCTIONS RESULTS

An almost infinite number of earnings functions specifications exist, depending on what variables are included, the form in which they are included (continuous or dummy), the expression of the dependent in log or non-log form, the inclusion of interaction terms and so on. But, of course, the specification depends (or at least should depend) upon the objectives. In the following, several specifications of an earnings function are run along with the rationale behind the particular form of the model.

The first run was exploratory and used a stepwise regression. The observations of the entire sample were used in expressing monthly earnings as a function of all nine independent variables. The independent variables were age, education, occupation, nationality, sex, firm size, region, economic sector and experience. Apart from age, firm size and experience that were in continuous form, all other variables were introduced as dummies.

The detailed results of this first run are not reported, since the regression coefficients in this case are nothing but descriptive. However, it should be noted that the nine characteristics explained 66 per cent. of the variance in monthly earnings (or 68 per cent. of the variance of the logarithm of earnings). This is an impressive R^2 from a cross-sectional sample using individual and not grouped data.* Most earnings functions report R^2's ranging between .10 to .40.

Another point that should be noted from this preliminary run is the order of entry of the independent variables in the regression, which was as follows:
- nationality (dummy for non-Moroccan);
- illiteracy;
- administrator occupation;
- sex.

The nationality dummy is the first independent variable to reduce the variance of earnings. The fact that a worker is illiterate comes second. It is interesting to note that usually the first variables to enter into a stepwise regression of this sort in the analysis of earnings are age and occupation. However, this is not the case for Morocco. The last point to note from this run is that when all nine independent variables are present, the crude nationality differential reported earlier drops to a net 666 DH

---

* E.g. Stoikov (1973) reports R^2's of the order of .9 in an earnings function in Japan. However, his 'observations' refer to grouped averages of a set of workers and, therefore, much of the individual earnings variance has been removed before the data enter in the regression.

per month. In other words, workers in Morocco who are similar in eight characteristics (age, schooling, occupation, etc.) make an extra 666 DH per month if they happen to be of another nationality.

Evidently, Moroccans and foreigners are two distinct groups in the same labour market. Therefore, the second experiment consisted of splitting the sample in two parts and running earnings functions within nationalities. Not all independent variables have been introduced in this run. Table 6 shows that only sex, age and an education dummy were included in the regression. The reason is that age and education reflect the human capital possessed by the individual and, therefore, might explain earnings differentials. Sex is included as a shifter in the function, when employers (or even employees) have different tastes or productivity beliefs, and when workers of the two sexes are employed. Note that sex does not have a straightforward marginal productivity interpretation. The education dummy in this run refers to only those who reported completion of a given educational level. Drop-outs have been excluded, as the sample did not include many observations in each drop-out category (Table A-6).

Table 6. Regression results according to nationality

Independent variable	Moroccans	Foreigners
Sex (Male = 1)	98.287	601.243
	(2.93)	(5.79)
Age (in years)	9.424	22.721
	(8.56)	(6.43)
Primary	329.839	45.464
	(8.61)	(.27)
Secondary 1st cycle	622.656	252.204
	(13.32)	(1.54)
CAP	567.646	280.417
	(14.33)	(1.87)
BAC	756.910	832.403
	(10.55)	(5.16)
University	1523.501	1120.083
	(15.71)	(6.37)
Engineer	2085.603	2459.967
	(20.12)	(12.72)
Constant term	−50.441	−37.377
R^2	.370	.446
Number of observations	1647	515

Notes: Dependent variable is monthly salary in DH.
All education variables are in dummy form ('illiterates' is the omitted category).
Numbers in parentheses are *t*-ratios.

131

Occupation was excluded as an independent variable because one of the aims of this study is to assess the gains associated with different levels of education. If occupation is controlled, education coefficients would be downward biased. This is because, by introducing the occupation variable on the right hand side, the individual's freedom to move to high pay occupations is restricted. In other words, the returns to education are realized by moving between occupations and we do not, therefore, wish to control the latter. The same reasoning applies to the economic sector, region and firm size variables, and so they are excluded from the regression. Of course, we would have liked to use experience rather than age, but it is worth noting that our 'experience' variable relates to current employment only and, therefore, understates the true on-the-job training of the worker.

On reading Table 6, it should be remembered that 'illiterates' is the excluded education dummy. Therefore, the regression coefficients show the gain associated with each level of schooling over the earnings of the illiterates, controlling for age and sex. For example, completion of primary education is associated with an extra 330 DH per month for Moroccans. An engineering degree is worth over 500 DH extra per month compared with a non-engineering university degree. Reading the table horizontally, it is interesting to note that male sex and one extra year of age are more profitable to foreigners than to Moroccans. Among foreigners, there is not such discrepancy between illiteracy and primary education completion (45 DH per month). But an engineering degree is worth relatively more among foreigners than among Moroccans.

Table 7 reports the results of splitting the sample according to sex. Foreign nationality appears now in a dummy form. The regression coefficient of this dummy shows the net nationality differential. The fact that a male worker is of foreign rather than Moroccan origin means 861 DH extra monthly earnings. Foreign females have about one third of this gain.

The nationality dummy is statistically highly significant. Note that the nationality regression coefficients reported in Table 7 control for differential schooling, age and sex. The earnings of two, equally aged and educated, male members of the Moroccan labour force differ by U.S. $ 2,271 per year, if one happens to be of foreign nationality. Before attempting to interpret this finding, let us present the results of an alternative specification of the earnings function.

We now express earnings as a function of age, age-squared, nationality, sex and education as a continuous variable equal to the number of years completed by each individual. Drop-outs are included in this run.* The

* For the length in years of each educational level, see Table A-6.

132

Table 7. Regression results according to sex

Variable	Males	Females
Age (in years)	14.31	10.361
	(9.72)	(5.45)
Nationality (foreign = 1)	861.128	290.691
	(16.95)	(6.34)
Primary	302.631	301.447
	(5.31)	(5.02)
Secondary 1st cycle	569.122	486.733
	(8.14)	(8.39)
CAP	525.666	436.002
	(8.92)	(8.20)
BAC	987.504	647.380
	(12.54)	(7.41)
University	1404.209	1296.093
	(16.04)	(7.32)
Engineer	2481.498	2199.230
	(25.97)	(7.98)
Constant term	−119.333	−14.456
R^2	.596	.511
Number of observations	1762	400

Notes: Dependent variable is monthly salary in DH.
All education variables are in dummy form ('Illiterates' is the excluded category).
Numbers in parentheses are t-ratios.

regression uses the observations from the entire sample (excluding only those of unknown educational level). The rationale for squaring age and including it as a separate variable in the regression is to meet the parabolic effect of declining age-earnings profiles after a given age. The rationale for running the function in semi-log form is to attach a particular interpretation to the years of schooling coefficient.

Following human capital theory the b regression coefficient of an earnings function of the form

$$\log Y = \text{const.} + bS$$

represents the average private rate of return to one extra year of schooling [7].

133

Table 8 shows that each year of schooling is associated with an extra 9.5 per cent. earnings. Alternatively, the private rate of return to the marginal year of schooling in Morocco is equal to 9.5 per cent. Two things should be noted regarding this regression-obtained private rate of return. Firstly, it should not be confused with a properly estimated rate of return by level of schooling. The former is an average rate of return to the marginal year of schooling (namely, averaged over all marginal years from 0 schooling to S). Secondly, it compares favourably with similar estimates for other countries (e.g. 5 per cent. in Thailand, 6 per cent. in Taiwan, 5.3 per cent. in Malaysia, 6.4 per cent. in Kenya and 5.7 per cent. in Iran)[8].

The non-log version of this model suggests that foreign nationality is associated with an extra U.S. $ 1,708 per year for workers who are similar in age, education and sex.

Table 8. Regression results: schooling as continuous variable

Independent variable	Dependent variable	
	log Y	Y
Age	.068	51.669
	(11.21)	(7.55)
Age squared	−.007	−.437
	(−9.08)	(−5.07)
Sex (male = 1)	.126	327.584
	(3.86)	(8.94)
Nationality (foreign = 1)	.646	647.554
	(18.39)	(16.39)
Schooling (in years)	.095	90.894
	(36.57)	(31.13)
Constant term	4.195	−1166.190
R^2	.59	.53
Number of observations	2,442	2,442

Note: Numbers in parentheses are t-ratios. Based on entire sample minus 103 individuals of unknown educational level.

6.4. INTERPRETATION OF THE RESULTS

The crude nationality differential in the sample is $ 3,441 per annum. When adjusted for age and education as a dummy this differential

134

drops to $ 2,271. When education enters as a continuous variable it drops further to $ 1,708. In fact, when all nine independent variables enter simultaneously in the regression (stepwise reported earlier), the differential remains about the same, i.e. equal to $ 1,795.* This means that workers of similar age, education, occupation, region, economic sector, firm size, experience and sex earn $ 1,795 more if they have a foreign nationality. This differential amounts to nearly one third of the average earnings in the entire sample.

What accounts for the remaining nationality differential?

One explanation might be that we do not have 'ability' in the set of independent variables. But this explanation must be discounted for several reasons. Firstly, I can see no reason why foreigners should have a different level of *non-acquired* ability than Moroccans. Secondly, 'ability' as usually measured by IQ and other tests has diminished in importance in explaining earnings[9]. Therefore, we have to look elsewhere for an explanation of the nationality differential.

Another possibility is that employers in Morocco (whether representing domestic or foreign enterprises) discriminate against Moroccans. In other words, they prefer foreigners, other things equal (i.e. given wage and ability) to Moroccans. Or, Moroccans are discriminated against and are forced to accept lower wages. But I would like to dismiss this explanation for two reasons. Firstly, it implies a sort of anti-nepotism; most firms are run by Moroccans and therefore the discrimination principle does not seem plausible. Secondly, foreigners might differ from Moroccans in some respects that we have not been able to standardize fully in our empirical analysis.

Another possibility is that employers in Morocco (whether they represent domestic or foreign enterprises) use nationality as a screening device. Namely, they prefer foreigners as a group, compared with Moroccans, because they believe, rightly or wrongly, that foreign nationality is associated with higher productive ability[10].

If employers were wrong in their belief, they would discover sooner or later that they did not get the value marginal product they expected from the foreigner and, therefore, they would change their hiring policy. Alternatively, they would continue to have lower profits than if they hired Moroccans of equal productive ability. It should be noted that, although this possibility cannot be fully dismissed, it is based on two crucial as-

---

* The discrepancies here are due to differences in the function specification, the exclusion of drop-outs, and treatment of the 'unknown' education category rather than the 'illiterates' as the omitted dummy to avoid matrix singularity.

sumptions. Firstly, it assumes that employers are not profit maximizers. Secondly, it assumes that foreign nationality is not associated with higher productivity.

The explanation of the nationality differential which I prefer is that it reflects returns to differential schooling quality, i.e. foreign nationals carry a premium over Moroccans because they have been educated in a better school. This explanation is consistent with marginal productivity theory and does not rely on discrimination or screening. In fact, it rationalizes the employer's tastes for and screening via nationality as it reflects an expected higher marginal product.*

The nationality differential was translated into a years-of-schooling equivalent. In other words, the hypothesized quality premium was expressed as a quantity of schooling differential. This was done by using the results of the non-log version of the earnings function in Table 8. For example, a 34 year old foreign male can achieve 1500 DH monthly earnings with 5.4 years of schooling. A Moroccan male of similar age could achieve the same earnings if he had 12.4 years of schooling. This two-point iso-wage contour suggests a 7 years of schooling equivalent to foreign nationality or, as hypothesized, differential schooling quality.

The earnings functions results were also used to derive social rates of return to schooling quantity. This was done for Moroccans only (based on Table 6, first column of figures), as foreigners must have incurred different schooling costs. Moreover, returns to foreigners would not have

Table 9. Social rates of return according to sex (percentage)

Educational levels compared	Males	Females
Primary (vs. illiteracy)	50.5	50.5
Secondary 1st cycle (vs. primary)	19.5	22.5
CAP (vs. primary)	30.0	33.5
BAC (vs. primary)	10.0	11.5
BAC (vs. second. 1st cycle)	2.5	3.0
University (vs. BAC)	13.0	14.0
Engineer (vs. BAC)	16.0	17.0

Source: Based on regression results by nationality.
Rates refer to Moroccans only.
For the direct costs used in the calculation, see Table A-7.

* Professor J. Maton, in a comment, suggests that the modern sector may have a separate production function and labour demand function. Foreigners may have a comparative advantage for working in the modern sector, whatever the quality of their education (editor's note).

any particular implication for Moroccan educational policy. The rates of return for males and females are given in Table 9 and do not exhibit any dramatic difference according to sex. Reading this table vertically, we see the typical pattern of the returns to education in countries at a similar degree of economic development[8] – primary education is more socially profitable (50.5 per cent.). This is followed by the CAP technical qualification beyond primary schooling (30 per cent. for males). The least profitable qualification is the Baccalaureat, if treated as a terminal stage. University graduation exhibits a 13 per cent. social rate of return, though engineering is not as profitable as suggested by the absolute earnings figures, because of the longer study.

6.5. POLICY IMPLICATIONS

Subject to the qualifications given earlier, the results in this paper give some hints as to the appropriate action in some policy areas. Let us classify our concluding comments under the efficiency aspect and the equity (or employment problem) aspect. The former could be divided into two parts, one referring to schooling quality and the other to schooling quantity.

To the extent that the nationality differential reflects returns to differential schooling quality, the above results raise scepticism about the current 'Moroccanisation' programme. This programme entails a gradual shift away from French schools and foreign teachers.

Ideally, we should like to have investigated the returns to Moroccans educated in Moroccan schools versus French. In the absence of this, one should investigate what attributes of foreigners can be created or maintained by the local school system. For example, if mastery in French or another subject is associated with a higher marginal product, one might wish to maintain certain aspects of the French curriculum until the country is out of the current transition period.

Turning to school quantity, the rates of return presented above suggest that priority should be given to primary education above the other levels. It should be noted here that, according to the 1971 Census, the percentage of illiterates among the Moroccans is 76 per cent. The current Moroccan development plan contemplates achievement of universal literacy by 1995, and this is certainly a move in the right direction.

Regarding the equity-employment aspect, it should be remembered that our sample consists of fully employed workers and therefore the results cannot be readily used for formulating an employment creation policy. Yet

137

it should also be noted that the income distribution within the sample is very unequal (Varlog $Y = .95$).* Furthermore, the full-time employed, but low-paid illiterates could be treated as 'unemployed' under the income definition of unemployment.

In this paper we have documented the proposition that employers in Morocco value primary education (double earnings relative to illiterates) and prefer foreigners (as the latter embody higher schooling quality). Therefore, a policy of accelerating the expansion of primary education (using the right curriculum) would not only be consistent with promoting economic efficiency, but would also contribute towards solving the country's employment problem.

APPENDIX

In March 1970 the Statistical Studies section of the Moroccan Ministry of Labour conducted a salary survey [11]. A four-page questionnaire was distributed to employers throughout the country asking details on both the establishment and its personnel. The questionnaire was divided into three parts. Part I dealt with the establishment's characteristics, part II with its permanent employees and part III with the seasonal or occasional employees.

I. Questions on *the establishment* (hereinafter called the 'firm') included:
1. the name;
2. region;
3. economic sector;
4. number of employees (distinguishing permanent from seasonal ones);
5. date of opening;
6. wage bill in March 1970.

II. Questions on each of the firm's *permanent employees* included:
1. name;
2. sex;
3. age;
4. nationality;
5. marital status;
6. occupation;
7. diploma or educational qualification;
8. seniority in the profession and in the firm;
9. hours worked;
10. salary and premium received in March 1970.

III. Questions on *seasonal and occasional employees* included:
1. the period for which they were hired;
2. the total number of these employees;
3. the total wage bill of those employees.

* As a point of reference, the corresponding statistic in the U.S. in 1969 was equal to .58 (Chiswick and Mincer [1, Table B-2]).

The Ministry of Labour sample covered 18,058 individuals employed in 737 firms in 16 regions of the country. From this total number of useful responses I have drawn a sub-sample (to be called 'the Psacharopoulos sample' or, simply, 'the sample') which included:
– all employees who reported an educational qualification of some sort, and
– one in ten of those who reported 'none' as educational qualification.
Furthermore, the sub-sample concentrated on permanent full-time employees only.
This procedure produced 2,545 observations on which all analyses in this paper are based. These observations are distributed as follows between unqualified and qualified persons:

Unqualified   1,187
Qualified   1,358

Total sub-sample 2,545 persons

Table A-1 shows the number of firms and individuals in the Ministry of Labour sample and in the Psacharopoulos sub-sample. The latter covers 507 of the 737 original firms and all 16 regions. Table A-1 shows also the city's total population. This will be used later for aggregation purposes.

In view of the scope of this study and the response to some of the questions only ten variables have been codified. These variables are:

I. *Firm*
Region
Economic sector
Size (total number of permanent employees).

II. *Individual*
Sex
Age
Nationality
Occupation
Education
Seniority within the firm
Total monthly salary and premium.

Therefore, each of the 2,545 observations in the sub-sample refers to a particular individual and lists ten characteristics. Three of these characteristics refer to the firm in which he is employed (and therefore are common to all individuals in the same firm) while the remaining seven are personal characteristics referring to each specific individual.

Definition of variables and coding

One card was punched per individual observation. Table A-2 shows the column location of each of the 11 variables. The code of the region variable ranged from 1 to 16, as in the first column of Table A-1.

The Ministry of Labour coders had produced a 3-digit economic sector code on each questionnaire. This code did not correspond to the international classification system and moreover contained gaps even within the first digit. This code was found to conform to the one used in *Résultats du Recensement du 1960*, Vol. II, Annex 2. Our sample distinguished between six sectors, according to the first digit of the Ministry of Labour coders (Table A-3).

139

Table A-1. Number of observations in the main sample and sub-sample, according to region

Code	Region	Population (1971 Census)	Number of employees		Number of firms	
			Ministry of Labour sample	Psacharopoulos sub-sample	Ministry of Labour sample	Psacharopoulos sub-sample
1	Casablanca	1,719,421	7,468	1,457	303	224
2	Rabat	641,714	830	133	39	26
3	Tangier	215,502	1,242	201	76	48
4	Nador	480,517	52	5	7	5
5	Fez	1,071,416	344	62	18	13
6	Taza	578,556	97	12	6	5
7	Tetuan	796,278	515	58	24	19
8	El Jadida	590,923	238	23	12	8
9	Khourib.-Set.	999,073*	500	28	7	7
10	Beni-Mellah	663,691	150	7	9	3
11	Oujda	633,828	417	56	28	18
12	Larach	n.a.	244	10	15	4
13	Agadir	1,168,010	2,548	228	63	47
14	Marrakesh	1,558,541	565	98	56	31
15	Mohammedhia	n.a.	874	82	34	24
16	Kenitra	1,345,975	1,974	85	40	25
	Total		18,058	2,545	737	507

* Khouribga 328,304; Settat 670,769.

Table A-2. Card location of variables

Variable number	Card columns	Variable name
1	1–2	Region
2	6	Economic sector
3	10–12	Firm size [number of employees]
4	20	Sex
5	24	Nationality
6	28–29	Age
7	33	Occupation
8	40–41	Education
9	45–46	Experience
10	50–54	Salary
11	60–63	Identification

Table A-3. Economic sector codes

Code	Sector
1	Agriculture
2	Manufacturing
3	Construction
4	(Blank)
5	Commerce
6	Banks and insurance
7	Transport and other services

Table A-4. Occupational codes

Code	Occupation
1	Comptables, chefs comptables
2	Administrateurs, directeurs
3	Employés du bureau
4	Vendeurs
5	Travailleurs dans les services (garçons, gardiens, portiers)
6	Techniciens, ingénieurs, agents techniques
7	Ouvriers qualifiés (monteurs, filateurs, contremaîtres)
8	Ouvriers qualifiés (graiseurs, électriciens, ménuisiers, soudeurs, tourneurs, ajusteurs)
9	Manoeuvres, chauffeurs, machinistes

The same procedure was followed with regard to the *occupational* classification, namely the first digit of the Ministry of Labour coder was recorded (Table A-4).

The *size* variable runs from 1 to 999 and refers to the firm's total number of permanent employees.

Sex has been coded as 1 for male and 2 for female.

141

Table A-5. Educational codes

Code	Educational category
10	Néant
21	Primary drop-out, CM 2, études primaires
22	Primary graduate, CEP, CEPM
31	Secondary 1st cycle drop-out [CO, 1e, 2e, 3e AS, niveau BEPC]
32	Sec. 1st cycle completed [CES, CESM, BE, BEPC]
47	Niveau CAP, CET
48	CAP, CET
51	Secondary 2nd cycle drop-out [4e AS, 5e AS]
52	Sec. 2nd cycle graduate [6e AS, niveau BAC]
53	BAC
67	Niveau OTM, BEI
68	DTM, BEI
71	University drop-out
82	Licencié, 1st university degree (other than engineering)
88	Ingénieur
86	Doctorat
99	Unknown

Table A-6. Years of schooling corresponding to different educational levels

Code	Educational level	Years of schooling	Number of observations
10	None	0	1187
21	Primary drop-out	2	35
22	Primary completed	5	240
31	Second. 1st c. drop-out	7	116
32	Second. 1st c. completed	9	187
47	Niveau CAP	7	12
48	CAP	8	286
51	Secondary 2nd c. drop-out	10	21
52	Secondary 2nd c. completed	12	28
53	BAC	13	120
67	DMT drop-out	12	1
68	DMT	13	52
71	University drop-out	15	10
82	University completed	17	80
88	Engineer	18	62
86	Ph.D.	20	5

Nationality has been coded as 1 for Moroccan and 2 for foreigners.

Age is in years. Unknown age has been coded 99.

The *experience* variable refers to years within the *same* firm. It does not represent seniority in the profession. Unknown length of experience has been coded as 99.

142

Owing to the particular emphasis of this study, the *education* variable has been coded in great detail. The 17 codes used are reported in Table A-5.

The *salary* variable is in monthly DH and includes premiums when applicable. It refers to full-time employees.

The card *identification* variable runs from 1 to 2545.

Table A-6 shows the assumed number of years corresponding to each educational level for the purpose of constructing the continuous education variable. The last column of this table shows the number of observations in each educational category.

The social annual costs per year for each level of education appear in Table A-7.

Finally, Table A-8 spells out in full the educational level initials used in this study.

Table A-7. Annual social direct costs according to educational level, 1970

Educational level	Costs in DH
Primary	260
Secondary	873
Higher	2,837

Source: Based on information supplied by the Ministries of Education and the Direction du Plan.

Table A-8. Educational qualifications in Morocco

Abbreviation	Educational qualification
CM	Cours Moyen
CEP	Certificat d'Etudes Primaires
CEPM	,, ,, ,, Musulman
CO	Cours Observatoire
AS	Année Secondaire
BEPC	Brevet des Etudes du Premier Cycle
CES	Certificat des Etudes Secondaires
CESM	,, ,, ,, Musulman
BE	Brevet Elémentaire
CAP	Certificat d'Aptitude Professionnelle
CET	Certificat des Etudes Techniques
BAC	Baccalauréat
DMT	Diplôme de Technicien Marocain
BEI	Brevet des Etudes Industrielles
DTC	Diplôme de Technicien Commercial
Niveau...	... Drop-out
Licencié	First university degree (non-engineering)

REFERENCES

1. For examples of such analysis, see Z. Griliches and W. M. Mason, 'Education, Income and Ability', *Journal of Political Economy*, May-June, 1972; B. Chiswick and J. Mincer, 'Time-Series Changes in Personal Income Inequality in the United States from 1939, with Projections to 1985', *Journal of Political Economy*, May-June, 1972; G. E. Johnson and F. P. Stafford, 'Social Returns to Quantity and Quality of Schooling', *Journal of Human Resources*, Spring 1973.
2. E.g. see M. Carnoy, 'Earnings and Schooling in Mexico', *Economic Development and Cultural Change*, July 1967; G. Psacharopoulos and G. Williams, 'Public Sector Earnings and Educational Planning', *International Labour Review*, July, 1973.
3. C. Jencks, *Inequality*, Basic Books, New York, 1972.
4. E.g. L. G. Reynolds and C. H. Taft, *The Evolution of Wage Structure*, Yale University Press, 1956; M. W. Reder, 'Wage Differentials', in *Aspects of Labour Economics*, National Bureau of Economic Research, New York, 1962.
5. J. Mincer, *Schooling, Experience and Earnings*, National Bureau of Economic Research, New York, 1971.
6. For an analysis of the screening hypothesis and ways of testing it, see R. Layard and G. Psacharopoulos, 'The Screening Hypothesis and Returns to Education', *Journal of Political Economy*, September-October, 1974.
7. G. Becker, 'Economic Theory', Knopf, 1971, Lecture 36.
8. For a review of rate of return studies, see G. Psacharopoulos, *Returns to Education* Elsevier, Amsterdam, 1973.
9. Z. Griliches, 'Notes on the Role of Education in Production Functions and Growth Accounting', in W. Lee Hansen (ed.), *Education, Income and Ability* (Studies in Income and Wealth), NBER, New York, 1970.
10. This kind of ability has nothing (or very little) to do with scholastic ability; see K. Arrow, 'Higher Education as a Filter', *Journal of Public Economics*, July, 1973.
11. Ministère du Travail, de l'Emploi et de la Formation Professionnelle, Service des Etudes Statistiques, *Enquête sur les Salaires*, Rabat, March, 1970.

7. Labour mobilization: the Moroccan experience

R. Andriamananjara*

7.1. INTRODUCTION

The shortage of capital has always been viewed as one of the crucial bottle-necks in the process of economic development – although recently the emphasis seems to have shifted to the shortage of skilled manpower as the critical area. Whether capital is defined to include only physical capital or also human capital (i.e., training, education, and health), capital formation still constitutes the cornerstone of the theory of, and plans for, economic development. Almost by definition, underdeveloped countries are short on capital. And the way to remedy this shortage is through capital formation.

Sub-section 7.1.1 considers how labour mobilization fits into capital formation. Sub-section 7.1.2 presents a survey of the employment situation and labour mobilization in Morocco. Sub-section 7.1.3 contains a brief outline of the work.

7.1.1. The theory of labour mobilization

It is usually assumed that only two alternative sources of capital formation exist: one is domestic savings; the other is foreign capital inflow either through direct business investment or through international loans and grants. However, a third possibility exists which Ragnar Nurkse was among the first to explore systematically in 1953 in his work on *Problems of Capital Formation in Underdeveloped Countries* (especially Chapter ii)[1]. Nurkse starts out with the observation that the underdeveloped countries – and especially, but not exclusively, those with high population density – suffer from large-scale unemployment: even with unchanged

* The material for this study was gathered during a research trip to Morocco from January to June 1970. This work was supported through a research assistantship by the Center for Research on Economic Development, University of Michigan, whose generosity is here gratefully recorded.

145

techniques of production, a large part of the population engaged in agriculture could be removed without reducing agricultural output. He goes on to note that the surplus people could be taken away from the land and be set to work on producing real capital.

Working on capital projects is only one of three possible uses of the underemployed. The other possibilities are either purely welfare support work such as leaf-raking, or the direct production of 'consumption' goods such as the digging of village wells. Actual programmes usually contain elements of all three. Furthermore, even though Nurkse's theory was formulated in terms of rural underemployment, it can be easily applied to urban unemployment and underemployment as well. If the rural underemployed can be set to work on irrigation canals, the urban unemployed can certainly be set to work on low-cost housing.

This process of unorthodox capital formation through labour mobilization is based on the assumption that labour is available for a labour mobilizing works programme. This premise, however, gives rise to problems both of definition and of measurement. On the conceptual side, what must be defined are the notions of unemployment and under-employment, since these phenomena are responsible for the existence of a labour surplus, which constitutes a labour reserve: this, in turn, represents the 'virtual' savings, or the potential labour-savings (or *épargne-travail*). No universally acceptable definitions have emerged so far despite many a conference, study and publication by numerous organisms and individuals. The definition of unemployment used in the more developed countries – whereby a person is unemployed if he or she does not currently hold a job and is looking for work – seems to be gaining international acceptance [2, p. 45]. It is the concept of underemployment which still has to be satisfactorily defined. The confusion here arises from the diversity of its manifestations, which has given rise to a multitude of terms to qualify unemployment and underemployment. The most current are visible, invisible, disguised, hidden; they are by no means the only ones. It is not our purpose here to review all of these terms or to introduce new ones. Suffice it to say that they are all intended to describe one phenomenon, namely that in underdeveloped countries available labour is not fully utilized either because the workers are idle part or all of the time, or because they are engaged in low productivity activities.*
If the concepts themselves have not yet been unequivocally defined, it is to be expected that attempts at measurement will be less than satisfactory.

---

* The latter definition was adopted in the paper by K. Laursen in this volume, see Section 5.4 (editor's note).

Myrdal's conclusion on South Asia that data-gathering efforts there have produced results that are far from satisfactory is echoed in a recent study which considered the available data for the underdeveloped countries in general[3].

For our present purpose it is not important that no generally acceptable definition and measurement scheme has yet been devised for unemployment and underemployment. What is important is that most writers agree
1. that labour in underdeveloped countries is not fully utilized, and
2. that something can/should be done not only to alleviate the employment problem,

but also to turn the apparent scourge of unemployment and underemployment into a boon as one of the means to a better future for all. Interest in labour mobilization through works programmes in the immediate post-war period stemmed from its potential contribution to capital formation. Some recent developments have given new emphasis to the whole idea. They relate to an increased awareness of the employment problem (associated with the population explosion), a recognition of the importance of agricultural development, a concern about spreading the benefits of growth more evenly, and finally the growing share of commodity aid in foreign aid.

The population problem is directly reflected in the supply side of the employment problem. From 1950 to 1965 the labour force in the less developed countries rose at an annual rate of 1.7 per cent.; this rate is expected to go up to 2.2 per cent. for the period 1965–1980 and to 2.3 per cent. for the decade 1970–1980. These represent massive increases, as can be seen by comparing them with the corresponding rates for the more developed countries: 1.1 per cent., 1 per cent. and 1 per cent., respectively [3, p. 34]. By themselves however these large increases on the supply side would not represent a very serious problem if they were offset by at least equivalent increases on the demand side. This condition has not been, and in the near future is not likely to be, satisfied in most underdeveloped countries. In particular, the non-agricultural sectors, although they have grown faster than agriculture, have not provided employment at a corresponding rate. Thus for all less developed countries, whereas output in industry rose at the rate of 7.1 per cent. in the period 1955–1965, employment in that sector increased by only 4.4 per cent.[3]. That is, while the supply of labour has grown (at an accelerating rate), the demand for it has not grown nearly as fast. The gap between the two will continue to widen unless something is done on the one hand to control the population/labour force growth rate and, on the other, to provide more jobs. Works pro-

147

grammes are directly related to the second aspect. In the short run, they provide temporary jobs at least to some of the unemployed and under-employed. In the long run, it is hoped that the work accomplished through them will create more jobs, and permanent ones.

The emphasis on the employment problem has led to some rethinking about the entire strategy of development. Formerly, most plans used to incorporate a massive effort toward industrialization. Such a strategy did not always create enough jobs, although in some cases it may have been successful in achieving the desired output target. This is why many observers have now come to the conclusion that agricultural development must play a prime role in improving employment prospects in under-developed countries.* The rediscovery of agriculture adds even more importance to works programmes.

Not only can a works programme contribute to an increase in capital formation and employment, but it can also represent a way of 'spreading' the benefits of economic growth more widely among the population. In fact, there is an increasing concern, among development theorists and policy makers alike, that the 'quality' of growth may be as important as its quantity. That is to say, the already highly skewed distribution of income should not be allowed to be accentuated further. The spreading effects of the works programme are to come partly from the wages (if any) and other incomes that it distributes directly, but mostly from the effects of these expenditures on the future productive capacity of the agricultural sector.

Finally, another factor in the renewed interest in works programmes is the growing share of commodity aid (especially food aid) in foreign aid. To take a specific example, in Morocco the average share of food aid in the total rose from 25.2 per cent. in the period 1960–1965 to 38.8 per cent. for 1966–1969. This increasing proportion of food aid may represent an unfortunate turn of events from the viewpoint of the aid recipients. They must, nevertheless, adjust to this new – and probably lasting – development by making good use of food aid. One way of doing so is through a works programme. To put things in very simple terms, a small-works programme of the type discussed above requires (at least) four distinct elements: the labourers; administrative, technical and supervisory staff; tools, materials and equipment; and food to feed the workers. The labourers are to come from the labour reserve. The staff, tools and materials will have to be provided by the government from its own resources, increased taxation, or through external assistance. As for the food, it can originate from

* For a contrary view, see the paper by W. Travis in this volume, p. 87 (editor's note).

148

three alternative sources. One is domestic procurement, which is a form of taxation. Another is commercial food imports. And the third is foreign food aid.

To summarize: the importance of a works programme stems from its (potential) contribution to capital formation and to agricultural development, the creation of present and future employment, its role in spreading the benefits of growth more widely, and the availability of food aid.

7.1.2. Labour mobilization in Morocco

Morocco represents almost a textbook example with respect to the preconditions for labour mobilization. On the basis of Plan figures, the rate of urban unemployment and rural underemployment can be computed to be 29 per cent. and 52 per cent. respectively by 1965, as shown in Table 1. The definition of labour force (or active population) recommended by the United Nations is the one used in Morocco: the active population includes all persons working or seeking work during a given period [4, p. 165]. Morocco has also adopted the standard definition of unemployment. As for underemployment the figure is obtained according to the labour surplus approach. This is one of the most widely used types of measurement. It compares the maximum labour input that the existing labour force could supply with the minimum labour input needed to achieve the present output. The difference between the two represents the labour surplus or labour reserve (expressed in man-days or man-years). This approach suffers from many shortcomings, which need not be dwelled upon here. But it is the most relevant for the theory of labour mobilization. The actual method used in Morocco assumes that an adult man can provide 250 workdays annually and an adult woman 150 workdays[5,

Table 1. The 1965 employment situation in Morocco (estimated in 1960)

Sectors	Labour force (number) (1)	Unemployed or underemployed (number) (2)	Rate of unemployment or underemployment (per cent.) (3)
Non-agriculture	1,940,000	570,000	29.38
Agriculture	3,390,000	1,750,000	51.62
Total	5,330,000	2,320,000	43.53

Sources: (1) Plan 1960–1964, p. 50.
(2) Plan 1960–1964, p. 54.
(3) Calculated: (3) = (2)/(1).

149

pp. 51–53] [6, pp. 10–13]. The number of man-days required for a unit of each agricultural activity is then computed. Given these two sets of data on the one hand, and the labour force and the levels of the various activities on the other, estimating the magnitude of underemployment becomes a matter of simple arithmetic. In 1960, rural underemployment was put at 300 million man-days, out of a total potential labour supply of 670 million. The underemployed men alone could provide 140 million [7, p. 19].

These figures must, however, be treated with extreme caution. As was previously mentioned, the concept of underemployment – let alone its measurement – cannot be easily and satisfactorily defined. One of the main sources of difficulties is that most definitions attempt to transplant Western (industrialized society) concepts into non-Western settings. In particular, it is usually assumed that a given activity constitutes employment only if it is obviously productive. And 'obviously', if people spend their time, say, just visiting each other or going from festivities to festivities, they are not productively employed. The next step in this line of logic is, therefore, that any time which is not spent on formal work (after allowing a given number of days for non-productive activities) is being wasted, and could be utilized in a more productive fashion.

In the context of the Moroccan countryside, and probably in most 'traditional' societies, such a reasoning is usually quite unrealistic. Take the case of the peasant in the Haouz plain around Marrakesh [8], an area which is quite typical of most arid and semi-arid regions of Morocco. The principal characteristic of agricultural activity in this region is that the means of production are separately owned by various people: one owns a piece of land, the other the water rights, a third one the draught animals, another the seeds, and still another the financial means, etc. What the vast majority of workers have is their labour. Each year associations for production are formed among the owners of the various means of production; and each year they are dissolved after the harvest. The formation of these associations – truly a challenge to entrepreneurial spirit – necessitates long negotiations among the various owners, lasting several weeks in September-October before the start of the ploughing season. With his very limited – if any – financial resources, the farmer usually cannot afford to buy the means of production. Whether or not he becomes a tenant or a mere labourer depends a great deal on his negotiating skills and, at least to an equal degree, on his social and personal relations with the owners who might lend him their productive factors. Cultivating these relations, especially during the period of negotiations, is therefore particularly important. Any casual observer, seeing these

150

farmers apparently idle, talking among themselves while waiting to exchange a few social amenities with landowners, might conclude that they are wasting their time, that they are 'under-employed', etc. But are they really? It is true that during this period, all the comings and goings, all the talking do not appear to be directly productive in terms of immediate output or income. Consider, however, the alternatives that confront these farmers. A farmer could go and work somewhere else, let us say on a PN worksite, and earn 4 DH per day. But if he did so, another who stayed at the village might improve his chances of getting the land. Supposing this second man does conclude the association with the landowner, then how does the first one stand? He earned 4 DH for the one day he worked on Promotion Nationale, but what he lost was a chance to have as much as half of the next harvest if he had stayed around and succeeded in becoming a tenant or sharecropper. Thus, as far as each individual farmer is concerned, the expected value of his time is not zero: it is positive and may even be quite high.

In view of these considerations, one may quarrel with any figure on underemployment in Morocco, and in any country for that matter. The official estimate of over 50 per cent. underemployment appears to be rather high. Nevertheless, hardly anybody would argue that the problem is non-existent. This is, in part, what led the Moroccan government to initiate some form of labour mobilization in the early 1960's.

Morocco is among the few underdeveloped countries with a truly *systematic* programme designed to make use of the unutilized labour force.* It has in fact several programmes. The *Entr'aide Nationale* (or National Mutual Help) includes a self-help part (building of schools, orphanages, etc.) but is mainly a welfare undertaking. It receives USPL 480 commodities through the agency of the Catholic Relief Service and the American Joint Distribution Committee. The *Community Development* programme built 6024 housing units during the 1965–1967 Plan period [9, p. 731]. The *World Food Programme* is also active: besides financing a large school lunch programme, it has participated in several rural housing projects. Under the 1968–1972 Plan, its activities will increase substantially. It will take part in constructing 90,000 rural dwelling units, mainly by providing foodstuffs as wage payments. The Moroccan government will put up 100 million DH in cash for this programme [9, p. 732]. Finally,

---

* Other recent experiences of labour mobilization include those in China, 'community development' in India, the Rural Public Works Programme in former East Pakistan, the various programmes of *animation rurale* and *service civique* in French-speaking African countries, and the successors to the 'worksites for unemployment' in North Africa. They have met with varying degrees of success.

there is the *Promotion Nationale* programme which has been in existence since 1961: the 1968–1972 Plan provides for a cash expenditure of 451.7 million DH[9, p. 174] for it. This study will concentrate exclusively on Promotion Nationale for various reasons. First, it has existed the longest. Secondly, because of the nature of work undertaken, it constitutes a works programme designed to add to capital formation, to a much higher degree than the other programmes. And, finally, it was by far the biggest programme in the 1960's, and will remain so in the future, both in terms of total expenditures and of man-days employed.

7.1.3. *Plan of work*

The present study is an attempt to review and evaluate the performance of Promotion Nationale in its ten years of existence. Section 7.2 describes the aims and the workings of Promotion Nationale, and its institutional framework.

Section 7.3 analyzes, in detail, a series of ten projects realized under the Promotion Nationale programme.

Section 7.4 examines the impact of Promotion Nationale on the population in general and on the Promotion Nationale labour force in particular: it will rely heavily – but not exclusively – on the results of a survey of Promotion Nationale workers conducted in the region of Goulmima, Province of Ksar Es Souk.

A concluding section presents an overall appraisal of Promotion Nationale.

7.2. THE AIMS AND ORGANIZATION OF PROMOTION NATIONALE

Prior to 1961, the government of Morocco had opened 'worksites for the relief of unemployment' (*chantiers de chômage*) from time to time. These worksites were designed to meet localized emergency conditions, especially in times of severe droughts or floods. The work was concentrated in urban areas or on country roads and, as a rule, had little or no economic value. In essence, these early worksites were a way of disguising charity, of channelling an income supplement to the 'worker' without making it too obvious. An effort was made to change this state of affairs at the beginning of the 1960's.

The conditions leading to the creation of Promotion Nationale, and the role and goals assigned to it are reviewed in 7.2.1. The institutional framework is described in 7.2.2. Some comments on the existing organizational structure are offered in 7.2.3.

152

7.2.1. *Role and aims*

In the early part of 1961, the country was faced with a particularly severe drought. As had been usual up to that time, 'worksites for the relief of unemployment' were opened in various parts of the country in the spring. One thing had changed, however, namely the existence of a new awareness of and concern about not only urban unemployment but also rural underemployment. When preparing the first Five-Year Plan (1960–1964) and considering the employment situation, the planners came to the conclusion that unemployment and underemployment constituted the most serious social and economic problems in Morocco[5, p. 55]. Various means could be used to improve the situation. Among other things, the planners proposed that the worksites be turned into a more productive venture. This recommendation was implemented. On July 15, 1961, a royal decree (dahir no. 1–61–205) created the *Promotion Rurale* programme which, a few months later, became *Promotion Nationale*.* The change from simply 'rural' to 'national' probably indicates that the action was to encompass the urban unemployed as well as the rural underemployed. Thus, at least in its origins, Promotion Nationale (PN) was an undertaking designed to make the best out of a bad situation: since the unemployed or underemployed received an income supplement from the government anyway, why not require from them some compensation under the form of labour contribution?

Promotion Nationale was born in the emergency drought conditions of 1961. But it had deeper *raisons d'être* than these short-term circumstances. There are at least three sets of interacting reasons: the importance of rural underemployment and urban unemployment; the poverty of the marginal regions; and the existence of possible activities which were both simple and productive. With all due reservations, it may be reiterated that the official estimates put the rate of rural underemployment at around 50 per cent. in Morocco (see Table 1). In particular in 1960, out of a potential supply of 670 million man-days, 300 million remained unused – with the men accounting for 140 million. Of these, 80 million were located in what is known as marginal regions. This brings in the second factor in the creation of Promotion Nationale, namely the

---

* Throughout this study the term 'Promotion Nationale' is used in its original French form. The reason is that no English equivalent was deemed satisfactory for conveying the intended meaning. Phrases such as 'National Development Works' translate only a part of the meaning. In this context, 'promotion' does indeed imply development; but it also includes a sense of improvement in the quality of life and an uplifting of the population's value and skills that the word 'development' usually does not carry.

153

existence of marginal regions. In Morocco, the term 'marginal regions' is used to designate the Saharan and the mountain (especially Rif) provinces. These areas are marginal in two senses: they are mostly border provinces and, more important, they are poorer than the other provinces because they have been left at the margin of the general economic development. In general, they are under-equipped in terms of infrastructure (relative to the provinces of the plains and the Atlantic) and they have the greatest number of underemployed. This disequilibrium among the various parts of the country could create serious economic, social and political problems. Promotion Nationale was partly designed to remedy this situation. Finally, before the unemployed and underemployed could be usefully put to work, it was necessary to find areas of action where this type of intervention would be appropriate. The projects would have to be technically simple, would require relatively little capital investments and a lot of unskilled labour, and they must not be completely unproductive like the worksites for the relief of unemployment. Such areas of action were/are quite numerous in Morocco: the fight against erosion on over 3 million hectares, new or improved irrigation for 3.25 million hectares, infrastructure works (roads, tracks), and equipment or community works (wells, cattle shelters, community buildings) – these are only some of the more obvious possibilities. The availability of these relatively simple and yet productive (at least for the first two groups) projects, together with the need to do something for, and in, the marginal provinces and the widespread prevalence of unemployment and underemployment, constitute the official reasons which prompted the initiation of Promotion Nationale in Morocco.

The proclaimed aims of Promotion Nationale remained essentially unchanged from 1961 to 1970. It is stated that Promotion Nationale's 'mission' is fourfold: to mobilize the rural underemployed; to associate the population to the development effort; to slow down the migration to the urban areas by improving the economic and social conditions in the countryside; and, finally, to develop the road infrastructure of the marginal regions.

The place of Promotion Nationale in Morocco's economic development can best be understood by putting it properly in its role as a part of the effort to develop the rural areas in general and the agricultural sector in particular; and also as an effort to involve the population in the development action. The former can be seen to be directly economic; but the latter, though indirect, is no less economic. So, to determine the place in national economic activity of Promotion Nationale over its ten-year existence, we must look at the priority ranking given in the successive

Plans to agriculture, the mobilization of the population, and the concern with the employment (and thereby the population) problem. Briefly stated, the first Plan (written in the late 1950's) recognizes and analyzes in some detail the conditions that made the initiation of an undertaking such as Promotion Nationale imperative. As a result Promotion Nationale was created in this Plan period, and the idea of Promotion Nationale gained increasing acceptance among technicians and administrators. The second Plan reaffirms and consolidates the existence and role of Promotion Nationale. The third continues the work, eliminates the less productive or non-productive projects and tries to expand PN activities in the more profitable areas.

7.2.2. The institutional framework: a description

Before examining the results and performance of Promotion Nationale, it is necessary to know how it works on the institutional side. The PN projects can be classified according to either of two different schemes: one is functional (in terms of the kinds of projects), the other is administrative (in terms of who administers the project). The functional classification is left for discussion at a later time. The administrative groupings are presented here first by way of an introduction to the institutional aspects of Promotion Nationale.

During the first two years, PN projects were administered directly by the provincial and local authorities, with some occasional advice from the technical services. Starting in 1963, probably in an effort to elicit a larger degree of involvement and interest in Promotion Nationale from the various technical services, the PN programme was divided into two parts. Part I projects are run by the technical services as part of their regular programmes.* The technical service pays all cash expenditures out of its own budget. These include the cash wages of skilled and unskilled workers, small equipment, supplies and transportation. Promotion Nationale provides only payment in kind. Part I is also known as Category A. Part II projects require the technical approval of the relevant technical service, which also may – but does not have to – provide some technical supervision during their execution. But they are run by the provincial and local authorities and financed directly by Promotion Nationale itself on its special budgetary account. Part II projects are divided into three different groups. For Category B, Promotion Nationale incurs all expen-

* Specifically, the Water and Forestry Service, the Direction of Land Development, and the Public Works Service.

ditures, both in cash and in kind. Under Category C, the unskilled workers receive only a payment in kind and no payment in cash; the wages of skilled workers and all other cash expenditure are paid by Promotion Nationale. For Category D, the unskilled workers receive no payment at all; Promotion Nationale pays the skilled workers and other expenditure.

When Promotion Nationale was created, two main principles governed its institutional aspects: 'maximum administrative simplification' and 'permanent links with the Provinces'. An effort was made to keep the administrative machinery to the strict minimum, because the creation of a new service would have involved an additional demand for scarce skills and further expansion of an already complex system. The PN institutions and their functions are specified in detail in the royal decree creating Promotion Nationale.

At the national level the *Conseil Supérieur de la Promotion Nationale* or CSPN – which later became the *Conseil Supérieur du Plan et de la Promotion Nationale* or CSPPN – is chaired by the King. It includes all ministers and public administrators whose departments are in any way concerned with the conception, formulation, financing and execution of Promotion Nationale programmes. This means that practically all ministers and administrators of public agencies are on the CSPN. This Council was originally scheduled to meet in May for the purpose of approving the Promotion Nationale programme for the following fiscal (or agricultural) year. Since 1964, however, the programmes are for the calendar rather than the fiscal year, and the CSPN usually meets a little earlier than May. In fact, in the last few years, the CSPN (or CSPPN later on) has met twice a year: first, late in the year to establish the PN programme for the following year; and second, early in the year to review PN's performance in the previous year.

A permanent secretariat was established to keep Promotion Nationale working during the rest of the year when the CSPN is not in session. This *Délégation Générale à la Promotion Nationale* (DGPN) is headed by a Delegate General appointed by and directly responsible to the King, whose functions are to present yearly reports, to prepare and submit annual drafts-programmes, to see that the decisions of the CSPN are duly and properly executed. This involves co-ordinating the Promotion Nationale activities of the various technical services and keeping in touch with the provinces. The Delegate General is assisted in his task by a small staff; he can also appeal to a Technical Committee, made up of representatives from the various technical services. The DGPN, as an agency, was originally on its own. Later on it was transferred, successively, to the State Secretariat for Planning (at which time CSPN became CSPPN), and to the Ministry of Agriculture and Agrarian Reform. Finally, in late 1969, it became a co-ministry in the Ministry of Promotion Nationale and Handicrafts. (Thus the old DGPN and Delegate General are formally no longer in existence.) These various changes could be interpreted as an increase in the attention devoted to Promotion Nationale and the problems underlying its existence. But in terms of staff, they have involved very little expansion, if any. As the organization stands in 1970, the Ministry consists of two separate divisions: one for Handicrafts, the other for Promotion Nationale. The Promotion Nationale Division is made up of an Accounting Section and a Planning Section; the latter, in turn, consists of the 'Planning' Office, the Study Office, and the Preparation Office.

At the provincial level,* the governor chairs the Provincial Council of Promotion Nationale, made up of administrators, representatives of the technical services, and elected representatives of the communes. He is responsible for drafting an annual PN programme for his province and for the proper execution of the approved programme. The day-to-day operations are supervised by a *caïd* who heads the PN section in the governor's office. (This role was formerly assumed by an army officer.) At the local level the *supercaïd*, in consultation with the local representatives and the technical services, draws up the programme request for Promotion Nationale and assures that the projects are properly executed.

What has just been presented may be called the backbone of PN institutions. This body has limbs, which also play vital roles. There are, first of all, the technical services which carry out Part I of the PN programme as mentioned earlier. The technical services function in a similar way to the central part. At the national level, the ministries have a PN section. Then the provincial technical service has a PN-*Bureau*. Finally, there are local 'technical service-Promotion Nationale' agents. Take, for example, the case of the *Office Régional de Mise en Valeur Agricole du Haouz* or ORMVAH in Marrakesh, which depends on the Ministry of Agriculture. (The province of Marrakesh has six *cercles*; the ORMVAH has operations in four of them.) The Promotion Nationale Bureau of the ORMVAH is headed by an *agent technique* who is a full-time civil servant. He directs all PN activities of the ORMVAH. Each *cercle* has one *adjoint technique* and one *conducteur de travaux*, both full-time civil servants. The *adjoint technique* prepares the *fiche technique* which contains a very

---

* The administrative divisions of Morocco are, from the top down, the province (headed by a governor), the *cercle* (headed by a *supercaïd*), the *caïdat* or *commandement* (headed by a *caïd*). Then come the communes, which elect municipal councils.

157

simple kind of technical feasibility study for each project and supervises the ORMVAH's PN activities in his area. In addition, another *adjoint technique* at the central ORMVAH-PN Bureau acts as a secretary-treasurer-record keeper. The *conducteur de travaux* supervises the actual day-to-day work on the projects and ensures that the work conforms to the blueprint shown in the *fiche technique*. He has usually been trained at the school for Conducteurs de Travaux in Rabat. Finally, on each project, the worksite leader or *chef de chantier* is a permanent employee of ORMVAH – although some *chefs de chantiers* are occasionally recruited from private enterprises when there are a great many worksites in operation.

Another limb to the central body of Promotion Nationale institutions is made up of the apparatus for handling payment in kind (payment in cash being handled by the central body and the technical services). Payment in kind means mostly wheat and, earlier, flour or other cereal-based foodstuffs. The unskilled worker receives five kilogrammes of wheat per day (the equivalent of 2 DH). Prior to March 1969 the totality of payment in kind came from the USPL 480 programme. Now four kilogrammes are supplied through PL 480 and one by the Moroccan government. The handling of the wheat, from dockside to project site, has been assigned to the Cereals Board or *Office Chérifien Interprofessionnel des Céréales*, with a central office in Rabat and branch offices in the provinces. This office enters into contractual agreement with the *Office National des Transports* to ensure timely deliveries of wheat to sites, and in amounts specified by the Promotion Nationale Division in Rabat. In fact, the wheat is received by, stored in and delivered from local agricultural co-operatives – the *Sociétés Coopératives Agricoles Marocaines* and the *Coopératives Marocaines Agricoles*.

This completes the description of the formal PN institutional framework.

7.2.3. *The institutional framework: comments*

The most outstanding feature of the whole organization is that, except at the very bottom, the administration of Promotion Nationale occurs mostly as an appendix to the normal activities of all departments involved, or at least as one among many responsibilities of the persons dealing with it. Although originally designed for Promotion Nationale only, the CSPPN now has an economy-wide scope and Promotion Nationale receives very little attention.* Similarly, the Ministry is shared by Promotion

---

* In fact the *Conseil Supérieur du Plan et de la Promotion Nationale* has now become an organ for reviewing the yearly execution of the Plan. Promotion Nationale does not even have a separate specialized commission of its own but has to share one. The

Nationale and Handicrafts. For the governor and *supercaïd*, Promotion Nationale is only one activity – probably a minor one so far as they are concerned – to be performed besides their primary administrative and other roles. Thus, for most offices and people involved in its administration, Promotion Nationale is a part-time activity. This basic fact has many far-reaching implications which in the end determine whether PN projects will succeed or fail.

First, as a general rule, Part I projects (run by the technical services) work better than Part II projects (run by the local authorities). This is certainly because of continued technical supervision of the former, but also because, in general, the local authorities and the *supercaïd* do not have much time to devote to the supervision of the latter.

Secondly, confusion results, even among people who are part of the PN machinery, as to the proper procedures, despite many a memorandum. The aspect that has most often given rise to confusion concerns the proper channels for, and timing of sending the 'opening notice' before a given worksite is initiated. A certain rigidity in that area results in longer and longer delays in payment in kind.* Such a situation, in general, produces a crisis and only then will it be remedied. (The effects of such delays on the specific project and on other future PN projects are quite detrimental: low productivity due to low morale, strikes, and workers' fleeing PN work – these are only a few.)

Thirdly, some duplications exist in the present institutions. One instance of duplication rests in the fact that, to effect the cash payments, the technical services and the local authorities each have their own paymasters. This is certainly a waste of scarce resources, since the paymaster of one service cannot be 'lent' to another, and paymasters are far from being in excess supply. It also produces delays in the payment in cash. Another sort of duplication rests in the fact that, at least for Type A projects, payments in cash and in kind are handled by two different offices. Surely this is wasteful, and the two ought to be put into one hand. This proposal would be opposed by each office, however. The local authorities are reluctant to turn over control of the payment in kind to the technical

*Cont. note * from foregoing page*
various commissions of CSPPN are for: 1. Promotion Nationale and Handicrafts; 2. Culture; 3. Tourism; 4. Commerce, Industry, Energy, Mines, Sea Fishing, and Merchant Marine; 5. Education and Training of Cadres, Health, Youth, Sports and Justice; 6. Infrastructure, Transportation and Housing; and 7. Telecommunications and Moroccan Radio-Television.
* It must be noted that this particular rigidity in turn derives directly from the fact that the wheat used as payment in kind comes in as foreign aid which has to be accounted for: hence the need for control, entailing lengthy and voluminous bookkeeping.

159

services because that would take away one means of political control over the workers. Similarly, the technical services would be most inimical to the idea of handing control over part of their budgetary credit to an outside authority.

Consequently, the existing institutional system has its faults. It is not devoid of merits, however. One worth mentioning is the introduction of the 'PN way' to the technical services: the technical services now think of Promotion Nationale as a way of doing things – a labour-intensive technique. This adoption and acceptance of the 'PN way' represents no small achievement: it militates against any radical re-modeling of the existing institutional framework.

Nevertheless, two questions must be asked and tentative answers provided. The first is: Can the existing system be improved? The answer is undoubtedly that it can, and even that it should in order for Promotion Nationale to continue its work with an acceptable degree of success. The second question then is: How could it be improved? There are at least two alternative answers, depending upon whether one takes a piecemeal or an integrated approach. The piecemeal approach would consist of trying – by way of localized and limited reforms – to attenuate existing rigidities, and defining more clearly the lines of responsibility and rules of procedures. The integrated approach would accomplish these aims, and others as well, by formally combining all the dispersed elements of the PN apparatus into one department. This formal step need not involve creating new jobs, recruiting new staff members, or incurring any new budgetary expenditures. The elements of this new unit, which might be called the Promotion Nationale Service, already exist. The administrator is there in the form of the provincial PN caïd. The technicians, likewise, are already present in the various technical services. The concentration of the administrative function in one unit might even result in some economy in manpower because some of the personnel now running the PN programmes of various technical services would be freed for other duties. The same applies to financial resources as to manpower. No new expenditure will be created. What will happen is simply a partial transfer of credit from some of the old technical services, at least as far as the budget is concerned. It may be noted that the first and most important step in the formation of a separate PN apparatus has already been taken. This occurred when, in late 1969, Promotion Nationale, together with Handicrafts, was made into a ministry of its own for the first time. In effect, the present proposal consists only in advocating that the logical next step be taken in formalizing the existence of Promotion Nationale.

In addition to the merits already stated, there are several beneficial effects of the integrated approach. One of the first results will be to attenuate or eliminate the major problems in the existing set-up. There will be a clearer definition of the lines of responsibility, a reduction in the friction arising from the unduly large amount of paper work as well as a reduction in unnecessary duplications of functions. Secondly, it implies that the staff will deal with, and only with, Promotion Nationale and on a full-time basis. This may reduce or entirely eliminate the existing lack of interest which is sometimes exhibited by some, either intentionally, or unintentionally, because they are already overburdened with their other responsibilities. Thirdly, the proposed set-up will lessen the load on these overburdened officials; they might then perform their other functions more efficiently.

But there are also some problems associated with the proposal. One is that Promotion Nationale would then simply become another technical service, fighting for its share of the budgetary pie like the other technical services, with no guarantee that it would not be out-competed and, as a result, that the effort devoted to the 'PN idea' would not be drastically reduced. Secondly, the formalization of Promotion Nationale as a separate entity will probably be interpreted by the other technical services to mean that they will no longer have to make an effort to use the 'PN way' as much as possible. They will then adopt capital-intensive methods and the net result, despite the existence of Promotion Nationale, might be a lower volume of employment than is achieved under the present system. Thirdly, at the local level, there may be competition between Promotion Nationale and the other technical services. Unlike at the national level, competition here will not be for financial resources but for labour, especially skilled labour. Here, too, Promotion Nationale might not come out on top; and if the present Promotion Nationale wage rate were to be kept, it would surely be the loser as it now is in many areas, where worksites of the technical services and of Promotion Nationale exist simultaneously and side by side.

Consequently, the institutional reform proposed here should not be carried out in isolation. It affects the very nature of Promotion Nationale. And so it must be envisaged in the entire context of the PN experience. A change in the institutions will be of little or no use unless accompanied by the appropriate adjustments in the various aspects of Promotion Nationale. Among these aspects one can include a clearer definition of the goal of Promotion Nationale at the national level (e.g., employment vs. productivity), a systematization and standardization of the criterion of choice among projects and of allocation of funds at the local level, and finally a revision of the remuneration system. This last aspect would

161

involve the examination of two questions, namely those relating, firstly, to the payment in kind and, secondly, to the level of wage rates (which is generally acknowledged to be too low) (see Section 7.4 below).

The problems associated with the present proposal can, by no means, be ignored. But in our opinion, they are not enough to outweigh the merits of the proposed system. The piecemeal approach will work only as a stop-gap measure, and may, for instance, be used to gain time to study and find remedies to the problems mentioned. In the end, however, the overall approach will impose itself as being both necessary and desirable for the continuation of the 'PN way' as an efficient and profitable proposition.

7.3. THE PROMOTION NATIONALE PROJECTS

The types of projects undertaken under the PN programme can be grouped under three main headings: land improvement (or *mise en valeur*), road building or infrastructure, and community works or equipment. Land improvement includes all those projects relating to the retention of soil, the extension of cultivable land and/or grazing area, and the control and use of waters. They all have an impact on the conditions of production in the agricultural sector, either directly as in the case of small and medium-scale irrigation, or indirectly as in the case of reforestation and 'defence and restoration of soils' or DRS. Under infrastructure, all those projects which involve the building or maintenance of dirt roads are grouped. Finally, equipment refers to various types of construction activities either in the urban areas (e.g., sewage systems) or in the rural areas (e.g., market-places) or in both (e.g., health centres, schools).

Ten projects will be analyzed here. All fall under the heading of land improvement. Three are of the small-scale irrigation type (Group I), four of the medium-scale irrigation type (Group II), and three are DRS projects (Group III). There are several reasons why only land improvement projects and these specific projects were chosen for detailed study. First, land improvement constitutes the economically more interesting part of Promotion Nationale: they are the PN projects which can be considered to be in the nature of directly productive investment. Secondly, the effects of land improvement projects are more readily measurable than those of infrastructure or equipment work. A third reason is simply that it was possible for me to visit these projects – and many others similar to them – and to interview the people directly concerned by their effects. Finally, one may also cite the fact that for a few of these projects the necessary data had already been presented, at least partially, in various reports, and/or could be derived from such reports[10], [11].

162

The methodology to be followed is presented in Sub-section 7.3.1. The projects and the elements of the analysis are described in Sub-section 7.3.2. Sub-section 7.3.3. presents the results, compares them with the results of other studies, and puts them in the proper perspective.

7.3.1. The methodology

The aims of this analysis are twofold. One is to evaluate each project in order to find out whether it *was* an economically worthwhile undertaking. The other is to compare the projects in the three groups considered here. These two aims do not explicitly or directly contain any attempt at choosing among the various projects. There is no longer anything to choose, since they have been completed. However, the methodology developed here can certainly be applied to future projects to establish the best combination of alternative projects.

The evaluation and comparison of different projects can be accomplished with three measures or criteria: the present value, the benefit-cost ratio, and the internal rate of return. The criteria used in the present study are the benefit-cost ratio and the internal rate of return.

The benefit-cost ratio is defined as the discounted present value of benefits over the discounted present value of costs or, in mathematical notation,

$$\frac{B}{C} = \frac{\displaystyle\sum_{t=1}^{N} \frac{B(t)}{(1+d)^t}}{\displaystyle\sum_{t=1}^{N} \frac{C(t)}{(1+d)^t}}$$

where
$B(t)$ = the benefits from the project in year t,
$C(t)$ = the costs of the project in year t,
d = the discount rate, and
N = the length (in years) of the period of analysis.

The ratio of present values is preferred to the alternative form (the ratio of annual benefits to annual costs) because of the peculiar time structure of benefits and costs for the projects under study. For all of them the costs are considerable in the first few years and become almost negligible a few years later. The benefits, on the contrary, accrue only slowly at the beginning and in large magnitudes later on. This asymmetry can be attributed to the agricultural nature of the projects (e.g., fruit trees must be x years old before they start producing, and y years old before they reach maturity output) and, in some cases, to the assumptions made regarding the time lag between a given investment and the resulting increase in production. If the ratio is greater than unity, the project can be said to be profitable or economically justifiable, in the sense that over time it generates more resources than it uses up. The benefit-cost ratio can, of course, be used to compare, i.e. to rank, various projects. However, given that the streams of benefits and costs do not necessarily have the same time paths from one project to another, the ranking will not be unique. It will vary with the discount rate being used. Projects whose costs are concentrated in the early years and benefits in later years will rank very low for high discount rates, and high for low discount rates. This makes any comparison based on the benefit-cost ratio highly unreliable in the sense that it does not provide a unique ranking among different projects. Hence the need for a criterion giving a less arbitrary ranking. This criterion is the internal rate of return.

The internal rate of return r is defined by the formula

$$\sum_{t=1}^{N} \frac{B(t) - C(t)}{(1 + r)^t} = 0$$

to be the discount rate which equates the present values of benefit and cost streams. The higher r, of course, the more profitable the project. According to Descartes' rule of sign, the definitional equation may have multiple roots if the sequence of net benefits changes sign more than once. This possibility does not create any problem in the projects considered here, however, since in all cases the flow of net benefits changes sign only once. Furthermore, it will be assumed that future opportunities will resemble current ones, so the problem of re-investibility does not arise[12, p. 439]. This assumption is entirely justified for the projects considered here because two of the conditions giving rise to Promotion Nationale are likely to persist in the foreseeable future. These are the existence of rural underemployment and the vast possibilities of, and needs for undertaking numerous projects similar to those analyzed in the present study.

In order to compute the benefit-cost ratio and the internal rate of return, certain parameters must be selected. They relate to the period of analysis, and the discount rate. The considerations which must be taken into account in this selection include, of course, the aims of the analysis, namely evaluation and comparison. In addition, they must encompass the duration of the project, the time it takes for the effects of the project to

164

be fully felt, and the availability of capital. In theory, the period of analysis should extend over the entire duration of the project. Potential project 'life' is over 30 years for Group I projects (small-scale irrigation), over 40 years for Group II (medium-scale irrigation), and over 50 years for Group III (defence and restoration of soils). To allow for risk elements, the periods of analysis have been chosen substantially shorter than the theoretical duration of the various projects: 15, 20, and 30 years, respectively. As for the proper rate of discount to be used in computing the benefit-cost ratio, ideally one would take the opportunity cost (or shadow value) of capital in the agricultural sector, since the projects studied here are all agricultural. One 'rough' estimate puts this rate at 8 per cent. in Morocco[13, p. 26], based on the institutional lending rate to agriculture adjusted for risk. However, it proves to be too low for various reasons. One is that medium or long-term Moroccan government bonds are issued at 6.5-7 per cent. Secondly, the *Banque Nationale pour le Développement Economique* makes loans at an interest rate of 7 per cent., mostly in non-agricultural sectors. Thirdly, in the late 1950's - early 1960's the return on private investment in non-agricultural enterprises (actual dividend payments) averaged 9.5-10 per cent.[14, pp. 284-85]. One must therefore assume that the shadow value of capital in the entire economy is around 7 per cent. at the lowest, and at least 9 to 10 per cent. in the non-agricultural sector. Presumably, capital is more abundant in the non-agricultural than in the agricultural sector. The shadow price of capital must therefore be higher in agriculture than in other sectors. The projects analyzed here are very small relative to total investment, so that the present study should reflect (rather than try to correct) the distortions caused by the existing relative scarcity of capital between the various sectors. Consequently, the appropriate discount rate must be at least 10 per cent. It is not clear by how much this should be adjusted for risk. Since selecting one single rate of discount rate would clearly be quite arbitrary under these circumstances, it is preferable to present the results for three different rates – 10, 15 and 20 per cent. – in the belief that the 'true' rate of discount must lie within that range. If one were really pressed to pick one rate and one only, the middle value should be chosen. In fact, there is another way of choosing one single rate, which consists of taking the average return to investment in agriculture. In this instance, it would be possible to take the average internal rate of return for all ten projects as *the* discount rate. This was not done, however, because this value (14 per cent.) falls within the range already considered.

The benefit-cost ratio, as well as the internal rate of return, are based on a comparison of benefits from and costs of the project. So the way benefits and costs are specified determines to a large extent the nature of the results. For the present study, cost is defined to include initial costs, opportunity costs (if any), and yearly maintenance costs. Initial costs include all expenditure in cash (for wages, supplies and equipment) as well as payment in kind. Opportunity costs can best be seen in the following terms. When, for instance, some crops are displaced by other crops as a result of an improvement, the total value of the latter should not be attributed to the improvement. The value of the former must be netted out since it represents what would have been produced on the given land area without the improvement. This is done by entering the value of the alternative use of the land (the opportunity costs) as an element of cost. The yearly maintenance costs are determined by the following consider-ations. For all projects it is assumed that the landowners voluntarily incur an annual cost, mostly in labour contribution, equivalent to one per cent. of the present value in year 1 of total initial costs for the upkeep of the project. In addition, the State is also assumed to contribute one per cent. for small-scale irrigation and DRS projects, and four per cent. for medium-scale irrigation projects. The State contribution may, for instance, be for repair supplies and equipment, or technical supervision. The one per cent. figures are more or less arbitrary but, on the basis of past performance, they are probably more than adequate; the four per cent. figure is based on an official estimate on how much it costs the State to maintain (large-scale) irrigation works in good repair. To summarize, the yearly maintenance costs are 2 per cent. of the present value in year 1 of initial costs for Groups I and III, and 5 per cent. for Group II.

The calculation of benefits consists in evaluating the effects of the project (say, through the availability of more water) on the output of various crops. Benefits are defined as the value of the additional output of various crops attributable to the project under consideration. In addition, the concomitant savings are included. The method for evaluating benefits can be further specified. Firstly, the prices used are those obtained by the farmers at the nearest market. Since these are agricultural crops, their prices are generally subject to wide seasonal variations. Whenever such variations are reported by the sources, no attempt is made to 'average' the various prices. Instead, in order to make the analysis as conservative as possible, a price close to the lower end of the range is chosen.*

---

* Theoretically one should use a weighted average under these circumstances, unless the projects alter the timing of output. The projects do not alter this timing. But detailed enough information on the timing of output is not available to allow the computation a weighted average.

166

Secondly, the value of the additional output is net of production costs. This is accomplished by subtracting 20 per cent. from the gross value, and by excluding outputs which are also inputs to production. In the projects considered here, they were essentially reed (used as support for the grape vine) and cattle feed (alfalfa).

Some final notes on project, benefit and cost are indispensable. Firstly, in order to avoid the type of overcounting due to attributing benefits to the project which, strictly speaking, arise from other sources, particular attention has been paid to the precise delimitation of 'the project' and of its effects in terms of both cost and benefit. This has proved especially important for medium-scale irrigation projects. They consist of three parts: the dam, the canal (*canal de tête-morte*), and the irrigation network inside the perimeter. It would obviously be erroneous to consider the project to be made up of only the first two elements and attribute all the benefits to them. The irrigation network must be included as an integral part, because without it the benefits from the dam and the canal alone would be very low, perhaps even nil. Secondly, some provision must be made for the risk element which is particularly important in Moroccan agriculture. In the areas where the present projects are located, droughts and floods can produce extreme variations in output. In this analysis the risk element is taken into account in two different ways: by choosing a low price when the price varies over a wide range, and by taking short periods of analysis. From the theoretical standpoint, it would have been more appropriate to use expected benefits and costs. The elements necessary for such an analysis are, unfortunately, not available.

7.3.2. *The projects*

The method of analysis having been specified, it is now possible to proceed with the analysis itself. The projects will be presented according to the three-group classification previously specified. For each group, one or two introductory paragraphs put the projects into the proper context. The projects themselves are then briefly described, and the elements of costs and benefits are derived. The results for all groups (in terms of benefit-cost ratios and internal rate of return) are presented in Sub-section 7.3.3.

A. *Group I: small-scale irrigation*
The three small-scale irrigation projects are located in the province of Marrakesh. This is an area classified as semi-arid. Water is a scarce and precious commodity; so scarce and precious that, like land, it belongs

to private individuals. In fact, it is often said that the three factors of production in this and other water-short areas of Morocco are land, water, and labour. Annual contracts for land and water are negotiated separately since water is a 'bachelor'. Rents for either, or both, are paid by part of the harvest. For instance, water rights can be rented at one-sixth of the crop for cereals and one-half for vegetables or alfalfa. For land, the rent may be two-fifths of the crop[15, p. 53]. Thus a man who has to rent both land and water may end up with from two-fifths to as little as one-tenth of the crop, depending upon whether he grows cereals or vegetables – assuming that he does not also have to hire additional labour besides his family's and his own. This shows that, in some cases, water (or, more precisely, the cost of water) is as important as land for purposes of agricultural production. The importance of water has long been recognized by the Moroccan farmer who, for centuries, has been bringing water to his fields from miles away either overground with dirt ditches (*seguia*) and/or underground with tunnels (*khettara*). The traditional means are, however, very inefficient. It has been estimated that, on the average, the existing system delivers only 40 per cent. of the water that could be tapped from the rivers or the sources. This overall productivity can be raised to 80 or 90 per cent. by relatively simple improvements, such as cementing or concreting the existing networks to protect them from floods and reduce infiltration. It is intuitively evident that undertaking such improvements must be 'profitable'. The following analysis in fact bears out this expectation.

Project 01, the Ain M'Kelkem source in the Cercle des Rehamna-Sud, consisted of repairing the source and the attached canal which regularly caved in every year following heavy rains. The source was cemented; concrete walls were put on the 750-metres long underground canal and the 240-metres long open-air canal. Work started in 1968 and, even though the entire project was not completed until mid-1969, its effects were already felt by the end of 1968. Project 02, the El Kouhliyne source in the Cercle des Ait Ourir, was essentially similar to Project 01. It was completed in 1968. Project 03 is the improvement of the Taddarte seguia in the Cercle de Marrakech Banlieue. It consisted of building a small (67-metres long) diversion dam on a river to feed the *seguia*, and putting concrete walls on 322 metres of underground canal and 1848 metres of *seguia*. The project was started in 1968 and completed in 1969.

All three projects were carried out as part of the Promotion Nationale programme of the *Office Régional de Mise en Valeur Agricole du Haouz* (ORMVAH), that is, as Part I projects. Their respective initial costs are presented in Table 2.

168

Table 2. Initial costs of the three small-scale irrigation projects

	Project 01 Ain M'Kelkem	Project 02 El Kouhliyne	Project 03 Taddarte
Cash initial expenditures (DH)			
1968	17,264	32,712	63,008
1969	54,804	—	23,413
Payment in kind (DH equivalent)[a]			
1968	7,854	10,414	11,152
1969	29,470	—	12,924

Source: Bureau-PN of the ORMVAH.

a. The payment in kind is obtained by multiplying the number of man-days actually used by 2 DH. This procedure introduces a slight upward error (maybe up to 10 per cent.) due to the fact that the skilled workers do not receive any payment in kind but are all paid in cash.

Strictly speaking, the improvements only have a direct effect on the waterflow. This effect is shown in Table 3. But in fact, the greater and more certain availability of water shows up in the agricultural production with a very short time lag. It is this second impact of the improvements that is of greatest interest for the economic evaluation of the projects. The impact magnitude can be determined by comparing the situation without the improvement and the situation with the improvement. The two situations in the three projects studied here can be briefly characterized as follows. First, in Projects 01 and 02 the cultivated land area increased from 101.5 to 150 hectares and from 59 to 73 hectares, respectively. In Project 03 no similar expansion of cultivated area was registered, but the number of fruit trees rose from 4650 to 6950. Secondly, some reshuffling occurred in the allocation of the land area among the various crops. Of the twenty-five crops whose areas are listed for the three projects (excluding figs.), the areas of five were reduced, eight unchanged and twelve increased. There is a highly significant tendency for yields to be lower in those crops with reduced or unchanged area than in those with increased areas.* Thirdly, no decrease in yields has been reported. This must be expected because the completion of the various projects could not possibly result in a worsening of the overall conditions of production.

It is now possible to establish the streams of costs and benefits for each project. In order to avoid cluttering the text with too many numerical

---

* The mean yields are 475.35 DH ($\sigma = 135.72$) and 2222.33 DH ($\sigma = 921.25$) respectively. The F-ratio is 42.521, which is significant at better than the 0.1 per cent. level. These figures are based on the situation without the improvement.

tables, however, the total benefits and costs, as well as the details of their derivations, are not given here. For Project 01, the benefits arise from the increase in yields and/or land areas of apricots, grapes, olives, and oranges; in addition, there are the benefits to cattle raising, and the savings in repair costs. The costs include the opportunity costs attributable to the displacement of barley, wheat, tomatoes and zucchini, the initial costs and maintenance costs. For Project 02, the benefits derive from barley, corn, wheat, carrots, turnips, tomatoes, zucchini, apricots, grapes,

Table 3. Effects of the improvements on the waterflow

	Project 01 Ain M'Kelkem	Project 02 El Kouhliyne	Project 03 Taddarte
Waterflow without the improvement:			
Maximum (litre/second)	4.34	7.71	318.54
Minimum (litre/second)[a]	1.45	3.66	119.49
Waterflow with the improvement:			
Maximum (litre/second)	15.61	13.93	429.66
Minimum (litre/second)	6.15	4.56	180.77

Source: Bureau-PN of the ORMVAH.

a. These are 'normal' summer minima. In fact, the absolute minima are zero when the diversion dam and/or *khettara*, *seguia* and source are destroyed by heavy rains.

olives, oranges, and the savings on repair costs. The opportunity costs arise from a reduction in the herd of sheep and cows; the other cost items are the same as for Project 01. For Project 03, the benefits are attributable to barley, corn, wheat, vegetables, apricots, grapes, olives, oranges and the savings on repairs. Unlike in the two previous cases there are no immediately perceivable opportunity costs; the other cost items are the same.

The last step in the computations is fairly straightforward. The processing of the data yields the final results presented in Table 8 for all projects.

B. *Group II: medium-scale irrigation*

The four medium-scale irrigation projects are located in the Cercle of Goulmima, Province of Ksar Es Souk. This area is considered to be transitional between the mountains (Atlas) and the desert (Sahara). In fact, almost all activities there, as in the desert proper, are carried out in oases or palm groves located along more or less permanent rivers and/or around wells. Water is the crucial element. Whatever was said previously about water in the province of Marrakesh applies here, only with even more emphasis. But what is more, whatever little rainwater is received falls during a very few days of the year, and on those days during only a few hours. Typically, these occasional rains result in flash floods. Among other things, two effects of this situation must be noted. First, the floods carry away good soil, crops and usually part of the physical infrastructure for irrigation. Second, most of the rainwater is lost to cultivation because only a very small part has time to infiltrate the soil. It is to remedy this unfortunate state of affairs that projects like the four studied here are undertaken. They are aimed partly at reducing the damage resulting from floods. But their main purpose is to harness the floodwater and put it to good use. For instance, in the Cercle of Goulmima alone, only 45 per cent. of the potentially cultivable area is actually cultivated at present as a result of the failure to make good use of the floodwater. There is ample room for improvement here.

Some technological limitations exist, however. The floods are as violent as they are sudden. Consequently, no attempt has yet been made to use the water when the flood is at its height. What is being done at present is to let the flood crest go by and then catch the 'flood tail' water. This is accomplished, for instance, by building dams with 'fusible' portions which are gradually carried away by the flood but which can be reconstructed rapidly, easily and inexpensively with rocks and meshed wires. The water can be used for three purposes: to increase water supply in the existing palm grove, or to expand the permanently cultivated area of the palm grove, or to bring into temporary cultivation areas that otherwise would have remained dry and sterile. In fact, it is usually a combination of all three.

The four projects studied here are typical of other projects in this area designed for the purposes previously stated. The core of the project is a medium-size low dam varying in length from under fifty metres to over two hundred metres. The dam consists of concrete foundations and sides. The central part may be concrete; but more often it consists of a few sections made up of rocks held together by meshed wire. Each section is designed to 'melt' away as the flood water reaches a certain volume. In addition to the dam, a project has a fairly large concrete canal (known as the 'dead-head' canal) to bring the water from the dam to the area of intended use, and an irrigation network of smaller canals in that area. Even where an irrigation network already exists, it is usually inefficient and very precarious. Therefore, part of the project is to install and/or improve the necessary irrigation network: this part of the project is referred to as perimeter equipment.

For the purpose of the present analysis, it is assumed that the construction of the dam starts in the first year and takes one year; the dead-head canal is started in the second year and takes two years; and the perimeter equipment is initiated in the third year and takes three years[10, pp. 33–43]. Thus the entire project should be completed in five years. This is indeed the case for Projects 05, 06, and 07. Project 04 will take seven years because a two-year gap exists between the time when the dam was completed and the time when work on the dead-head canal started. The projects to be analyzed are Tadiroust (04), Tazmout (05), Tazourmit (06), and Yfegh (07). The initial cash expenditures and payments in kind are shown in Table 4.

Table 4. Initial costs of the four medium-scale irrigation projects (dirhams or dirham equivalent)

	Project 04 Tadiroust	Project 05 Tazmout	Project 06 Tazourmit	Project 07 Yfegh
1966				
Cash expenditures	720 928	—	—	176 735
Payments in kind	95 072	—	—	45 792
1967				
Cash expenditures	0	283 932	349 850	52 500
Payments in kind	0	121 672	115 650	35 000
1968				
Cash expenditures	0	89 130	388 531	76 125
Payments in kind	0	38 390	137 208	49 176
1969				
Cash expenditures	91 001	217 405	516 806	23 625
Payments in kind	42 824	115 020	213 836	14 176
1970				
Cash expenditures	142 907	128 275	128 275	23 625
Payments in kind	73 568	76 630	76 630	14 175
1971				
Cash expenditures	51 906	128 275	128 275	—
Payments in kind	30 744	76 630	76 630	—
1972				
Cash expenditures	51 906	—	—	—
Payments in kind	30 744	—	—	—

As with the small-scale irrigation projects, the improved conditions in water availability are translated into increased yields and/or increased cultivated land area almost immediately. The existing and future cultivated areas for each perimeter are shown in Table 5. A few assumptions are

172

Table 5. Total existing and future cultivated areas in the medium-scale irrigation projects (hectares)

Project	Existing palm grove	Flood irrigated area	Extension of palm grove
Project 04: Tadiroust	240	310	50
Project 05: Tazmout	200	1300	0
Project 06: Tazourmit	200	1300	0
Project 07: Yfegh	125	150	0

necessary to derive from this table the benefits attributable to the various projects. First, the yields on the existing palm grove start increasing the year after the canal is completed and are felt in their entirety at the end of three years. Secondly, production on the flood irrigated areas starts when the dead-head canal is completed and attains the full potential after ten years. Thirdly, the extensions of the palm grove start after the perimeter has been fully equipped and reach the maximum output after eight years.

C. Group III: Defence and restoration of soil (DRS)

The erosion of land by water, and sometimes by wind, is also a problem which plagues many a tropical or equatorial country. Its most spectacular manifestations are entire hillsides scarred with deep ravines. 'Top erosion', whereby a thin slice of the topsoil is carried away year after year, is certainly less obvious but its long-run effects are no less disastrous than those of the more evident kind of erosion. The resulting losses are well known: loss of crop land, faster siltage of dams, etc. In Morocco, it is estimated that erosion takes away 60,000 hectares of good land every year. This problem, together with the existence of underemployment, was one of the official reasons cited for initiating the Promotion Nationale programme.

The fight against erosion can take various forms. The most widely used approach is reforestation, and there is some of that in Morocco. Another is known as 'defence and restoration of soils' or DRS. To some extent this is only a variant of reforestation in that it involves the planting of trees. It is indeed reforestation, but it is also more. To put it briefly, the DRS treatment attempts to keep the land from being eroded away, by planting trees on horizontally parallel *banquettes* and by building small dry rock dams. The dams and *banquettes* are designed to slow down the flow of rainwater and help it to infiltrate the soil. The distinctive feature of DRS is that it tries not simply to slow down the erosion process, but to do so in a positive way, that is, in a directly productive way. This is achieved by using mostly, or wholly, fruit trees instead of forest trees, by leaving enough room between tree rows to allow the plantation of cereals or other crops, etc. The last three Promotion Nationale projects to be studied here are DRS projects.

Project 08, the Al Hoceima DRS project, is located 5 to 7 miles outside the provincial capital of Al Hoceima. It consists of four perimeters: Ajdir I to IV. Similarly Project 09, the Imintanoute DRS project (located in Imintanoute, Province of Marrakesh), is made up of four different perimeters, themselves divided into consecutively numbered plots: Talainine II to V, Inzuma I to IV, N'Daina I to III, and Douirane I to IV. One or more plots from one or more perimeters are treated every year: 15 plots were treated in 9 years. Project 10, the Sahrij DRS project, is located in the Cercle des Sraghna Zemrane, Province of Marrakesh. The areas treated for each project and the corresponding initial costs are shown in Tables 6 and 7, respectively. It must be noted that initial costs here include the cost of planting the original trees as well as the cost of replacing the mortality victims up to five years old.

Table 6. Total areas treated in the three DRS projects (hectares)

Year	Project 08 Al Hoceima	Project 09 Imintanoute	Project 10 Sahrij
1961	—	56	—
1962	—	399	—
1963	—	100	—
1964	—	200	—
1965	672	300	—
1966	245	408	—
1967	284	149	—
1968	313	209	500
1969	0	14	1000

Sources: (08) Water and Forestry Service, Al Hoceima.
(09) Water and Forestry Service, Amizmiz and Imintanoute; Promotion Nationale Section, Province of Marrakesh.
(10) ORMVAH.

As to benefits and costs the following can be said. For the Al Hoceima project (08) the benefits derive from almond trees and forest trees. The costs include the initial costs, the opportunity costs attributable to the loss of 20 per cent. of the wheat-grown area, and the maintenance charges. For the Imintanoute project (09) the benefits stem from barley, almond trees

174

Table 7. *Initial costs of the three DRS projects (dirhams or dirham equivalent)*

Year	Project 08 Al Hoceima		Project 09 Imintanoute		Project 10 Sahrij	
	Cash expenditures	Payments in kind	Cash expenditures	Payments in kind	Cash expenditures	Payments in kind
1961	—	—	37 290	11 760	—	—
1962	—	—	164 037	87 390	—	—
1963	—	—	156 730	21 000	—	—
1964	—	—	131 546	42 000	—	—
1965	282 130	184 922	160 740	63 000	—	—
1966	105 676	89 032	282 142	85 680	—	—
1967	129 334	85 140	133 074	31 290	—	—
1968	135 845	82 762	80 502	43 890	393 656	106 344
1969	39 581	32 356	53 299	2 940	236 394	63 706
1970	28 427	22 048	—	—	73 776	18 444
1971	19 243	14 516	—	—	66 664	16 666
1972	10 866	8 196	—	—	38 616	9 654
1973	1 563	1 180	—	—	27 688	6 922

Sources: See Table 6.

and carob trees. The cost items are similar except for the fact that there was no immediately discernible opportunity cost. As for the Sahrij project (10) the benefits come from almond trees. The cost items are similar to those of Project 08, with the opportunity costs coming from the loss of 20 per cent. of the area grown in barley. The total areas treated for each project are 1514, 1835 and 1500 hectares, respectively.

7.3.3. The results

Before presenting the results, we must note that the present calculations do not, and could not, include all benefits and costs. Some of the omitted benefits or costs are potentially quantifiable, others cannot be quantified and belong to the 'intangibles'. Among the omitted costs, figures prominently the possible lowering of the water table. This is a result of the improved irrigation systems tapping more water from the sources and/or rivers in the small-scale irrigation projects. There were some fears expressed by technicians that, if these projects were carried out in large numbers, the ultimate result would be a lowering of the general level of the water table. Such a phenomenon would mean that some systems with higher tapping levels than the resulting water table level, would become

175

partially or completely deprived of water, and the yields on the fields that they irrigate would be drastically reduced. This is certainly a real cost, but it would be very hard to quantify without substantial hydrological studies. Another example of cost not accounted for can be taken from the Imintanoute DRS project (09). Prior to the beginning of DRS work there, the hillsides were used as grazing areas for sheep. With the initiation of DRS, sheep and all other farm animals have been banned from the hillsides. This is certainly a cost to the animals' owners, because they now have to find an alternative pasture area. In this case, however, this cost was deemed to be more than made up by a benefit which was not counted in the analysis either. This benefit stems from the fact that the farmers now cut the grass that grows along the DRS *banquettes* between the trees. This grass is fairly abundant and can be used to feed the sheep as well as the cattle. (Previously the grazing area was so poor that only sheep could survive on it. Now both sheep and cattle can benefit from the hillside grass.) Also in this area, one effect of the project was to produce a noticeable lowering of the temperature, especially in the summer season. This cooling-off phenomenon, probably attributable to the increased humidity of the soil, is certainly appreciated by the inhabitants; it may also, somehow, be beneficial to their crops. Unfortunately, there does not seem to be any way of taking this intangible benefit into account. Furthermore the DRS works, by reducing the amount of soil carried away and by slowing down the water flow, have many other effects which may be considered as benefits. They may raise the water table by infiltrating more water. They may reduce the rate of silting of dams situated downstream. And they can cause the *seguia* situated in the valley to be carried away by floods less often. Another type of intangible benefit is associated with small and medium-scale irrigation projects: more water means an increase not only for irrigation purposes but also for domestic uses (cooking, drinking, and washing). Finally, the increase in land value has not been included, although data were available in some cases: its inclusion would constitute double-counting.

The results are presented in Table 8 for all ten projects. Columns (1)–(3) contain the benefit-cost ratios for three alternative discount rates: 10, 15 and 20 per cent. Column (4) shows the internal rate of return. An analysis of variance performed on these results shows that the most profitable projects (the ones with the highest internal rates of return) are the small-scale irrigation projects with 23.4 per cent. ($\sigma = 5.5$). Then come the medium-scale irrigation projects with 12.9 per cent. ($\sigma = 2.4$), and the DRS projects are last at 6 per cent. ($\sigma = 1.0$). The differences between the group means are significant at better than the 5 per cent.

Table 8. Results of the benefit-cost analysis

Project or group	Benefit-cost ratio			Internal rate of return (%)
	$d = .10$ (1)	$d = .15$ (2)	$d = .20$ (3)	(4)
1. Ain M'Kelkem	1.571	1.309	1.101	23.0
2. El Kouhliyne	1.186	0.956	0.776	14.0
3. Taddarte	4.016	2.825	2.044	33.1
4. Tadiroust	0.927	0.636	0.444	9.1
5. Tazmout	0.925	0.631	0.442	9.1
6. Tazourmit	2.042	1.363	0.931	19.1
7. Yfegh	1.331	0.956	0.705	14.3
8. Al Hoceima	0.504	0.266	0.149	5.0
9. Imintanoute	0.815	0.523	0.366	8.0
10. Sahrij	0.574	0.334	0.203	5.0
I. Small-scale irrigation	2.258	1.697	1.307	23.4
II. Medium-scale irrigation	1.306	0.896	0.630	12.9
III. DRS	0.631	0.374	0.239	6.0
All projects	1.389	0.980	0.716	14.0
F-ratio	2.511	3.947	5.811	6.243
Significance level	—	0.10	0.05	0.05

level. The benefit-cost ratios also confirm the profitability ranking of the groups of projects. Although the differences among the various group mean benefit-cost ratios are not significant when the discount rate is 10 per cent., they are significant at the 10 and 5 per cent. levels when the discount rate is 15 and 20 per cent., respectively.

The results obtained here become more significant when compared with the results of other studies of similar projects. There are three groups of such studies. For PN projects, there are the IVS reports[11] and the SCET study[10]. For non-PN projects, the Stanford Research Institute has done some analyses. During the 1969–1970 period, the two IVS volunteers stationed in Al Hoceima and Ouarzazate wrote a series of brief reports. They examined various aspects and problems of Promotion Nationale in their respective regions and carried out benefit-cost analyses of several specific projects. The IVS results shown here come from these studies. The SCET is a French engineering firm which, under the French technical co-operation programme, has been involved in Morocco's Promotion Nationale since 1964. It has been active in the provinces of Beni-Mellal, Marrakesh, Tetuan, and especially Ksar-Es-Souk, where it has been closely associated with the more successful projects. Its participation covers most phases of PN projects. The SCET engineers, in co-operation with the regional *Offices de Mise en Valeur Agricole*, carry out technical feasibility studies as well as studies in adapting various methods to the 'PN way'. In addition, they supervise directly the actual work on the projects. The results used here come from a summary and an evaluation of their experience, written in late 1966. In 1966-1967 the Stanford Research Institute (SRI) undertook a series of studies on Moroccan agriculture. Among them wasan analysis of various projects in the Lower Moulouya irrigation perimeter. The aim was to find the best projects and to establish five-year programmes for carrying them out. Several of these projects have been included in the present comparison.

The results of the IVS, SCET, and SRI analyses are presented in Table 9.

Table 9. Results of other studies of agricultural projects

Project number and name	Project type (1)	Internal rate of return (%) (2)	Author(s) (3)
A. *PN Projects*			
2–01. Ternata (Zagora)	Group I	11.4	IVS
2–02. Draa Valley	,,	9.1	,,
2–03. Ktaoua (Draa)	,,	7.0	,,
2–04. Tazmout (Goulmima)	Group II	14.0	SCET
2–05. Tazourmit (Goulmima)	,,	24.5	,,
2–06. Yfegh (Goulmima)	,,	23.5	,,
2–07. Ajdir III (Al Hoceima)	Group III	4.0	IVS
2–08. Asmoud (Al Hoceima)	,,	4.0	,,
B. *Non-PN Projects*[a]			
2–09. Cereals project	Lower Moulouya	25.0	SRI
2–10. Range management project	,,	14.0	,,
2–11. Triffa Main	large-scale irrigation	20.0	,,
2–12. Sector 27	,,	8.0	,,
2–13. Sector 28	,,	9.0	,,
2–14. Triffa East	,,	6.0	,,
2–15. Triffa High Service	,,	5.0	,,
2–16. Zebra Collective	,,	5.0	,,
2–17. Zebra Remainder	,,	5.0	,,
2–18. Bou Areg Central	,,	6.0	,,
2–19. Bou Areg Remainder	,,	6.0	,,

a. Projects 2-09 through 2-19 are all part of an integrated regional development plan in the delta region of the Lower Moulouya. This plan involves large-scale irrigation as well as other schemes. The SRI study considers several alternatives. The figures presented here relate to gross output and total costs, with the assumption that 90 per cent. of potential output will be achieved and a 25 per cent. contingency mark-up on costs.

The assumptions of these various studies are not consistent with each other, nor with those of this study. The differences lie not only in the definitions of benefit and cost, but also in the choice of period of analysis. They are, however, not so great as to foreclose any comparison between these results and those of the present study, especially if the figures in Table 9 are taken to indicate no more than rough orders of magnitude. Only the internal rates of return are shown since they are more 'reliable' than the benefit-cost ratios.

The general conclusions from such a comparison are twofold. First, projects in the PN programme have a higher internal rate of return than those outside it. The mean is 13.2 per cent. for the ten projects analyzed in this study and those in Group A of Table 9, as opposed to 9.9 per cent. for non-Promotion Nationale projects in Group B of the same table. The difference is, however, not statistically significant. So the projects undertaken under Promotion Nationale are no worse than those carried out under other programmes. If anything, they are better. Secondly, water-related projects are more profitable than other types. In particular, small and medium-scale irrigation projects are more profitable than all others: 15.1 per cent. vs. 9.3 per cent. for those appearing in Table 9. And small and medium-scale irrigation are more profitable than large-scale irrigation: 16.2 per cent. vs. 7.8 per cent., the difference being significant at the 10 per cent. level.

Thus, the results of other studies do not seem to contradict the findings obtained here. Our results are somewhat higher than the others (14 vs. 10.9 per cent.), despite the fact that the assumptions made in this study are consistently and purposely on the conservative side. However, the difference is not statistically significant. One may therefore conclude that, although the projects studied here can be considered to be among the showcase projects of Promotion Nationale, they are not much more profitable than other similar projects in the agricultural sector. In particular, the difference with PN projects analyzed by other people is very small: 14 vs. 12.3 per cent.

It is important to put the results obtained here in the proper perspective. Firstly, it must be remembered that land improvement constitutes only one of the three types of PN projects (the other two being infrastructure and equipment),* and that the three sub-groups represented here do not include all land improvement. Secondly, these projects may be typical

---

* Over the period 1964–1969, land improvement constituted in each year an average of 63 per cent. of all PN worksites and 51.5 per cent. of all PN man-days (see PN Bilan, 1964 to 1969).

of similar projects in their areas but it is not known whether they are typical of similar projects in other areas. Thirdly, it is not even sure that they are representative in their areas. Consequently, the results cannot – or, at least, should not – be considered to be typical of all projects of this nature, and even less of Promotion Nationale as a whole. These projects are, more or less, showcase displays. What made them particularly successful (at least for Groups I and II) was a combination of various factors such as good design and good execution by the technical services and local authorities, popular interest and participation. What the results show is not that Promotion Nationale is, or has been, a success but that it can be, or can become, a worthwhile undertaking even in the narrow economic sense. We say 'even in the narrow economic sense' (of measurable benefit and cost) because it may be argued that Promotion Nationale has been successful in achieving certain goals which are not directly economic in their nature. Among them may be the generation of popular participation in the development effort, or the attenuation of potential sources of political problems such as un- or underemployment, or the poverty of the marginal regions.*

One last note must be added. The study, so far, has not considered the income distribution aspect of these projects. For programmes such as Promotion Nationale, it is of the utmost importance that the workers also be those who benefit from the works – or at least that some, preferably most, of them benefit. If, after their completion, the projects do not increase the means of production at the disposal of most workers, Promotion Nationale becomes no more than a channel for a temporary subsidy in the form of wage payment. It would then be no different, and no better, than the 'worksites for the relief of unemployment' upon which it is supposed to improve. The benefit-cost ratios and the internal rates of return may all be very favourable, but they reveal nothing about 'who gets what'. The question of who gets all of those benefits is at least as important as the fact that the benefits exceed the costs. This consideration must always temper any optimism in the interpretation of the statistical results. The next Section will try to determine, among other things, whether the PN workers do benefit from the projects on which they work.

7.4. PROMOTION NATIONALE AND THE PEOPLE

People are ultimately what development is all about. Its success depends

* These various aspects are considered in Sub-section 7.4.3.

on people. Its fruits – when and if they come – go to people. This is especially true of works programmes like Promotion Nationale. This Section is an attempt to establish more clearly the nature of the inter-relationships between people and the PN programme.

Ideally, we need a country-wide survey of PN workers and projects to gain insight into these questions. This, however, has not been possible owing to the material and time limitations inherent in any one-man undertaking. The next best thing is to concentrate on one specific region. A survey of PN workers was conducted in the cercle of Goulmima (Province of Ksar-Es-Souk) during the early part of June 1970.* Its results constitute the source of most of the information used in this Section. The region of Goulmima is probably not representative of all Morocco. But it is representative of most of Morocco south of the Atlas mountains and, at least in such aspects as poverty, of the Rif region as well. These two regions absorb about three fourths of the PN effort every year. Therefore, although the survey does not produce results that are 'typical' in all of Morocco, its results are acceptable as representative of the greatest part of Morocco, as far as Promotion Nationale is concerned.

The impact of Promotion Nationale – through the payment and spending of wages – is undoubtedly felt by the entire community where projects are undertaken. To that extent one might wish to survey the entire community which, for the purpose at hand, is neither necessary nor practical. It is more desirable and useful to study the people directly concerned, namely the PN workers themselves. The major characteristic of this labour force is that it is exclusively male. In all, 251 workers were interviewed at five different worksites situated within a 25-mile radius of the town of Goulmima. There were 206 unskilled labourers, 35 skilled workers (all masons), and 10 supervisory workers (*chefs de chantiers, caporaux*, and *pointeurs*).

Their age structure is shown in columns (1) and (2) of Table 10. The mean age is 34 years, with minimum and maximum of 12 and 85, respectively. Compared to the rural male labour force in the province of Ksar-Es-Souk (columns 3 and 4), the PN labour force is slightly younger: 72.1 per cent. are under 45 and 99.2 per cent. under 65, as opposed to 70.7 per cent. and 94.3 per cent., respectively, for the larger labour force. Of all 251 workers, 188 are married and 63 are not. Among the 74.9 per cent. that are married the mean number of children was 3.4, with the following distribution:

---

* A detailed description of the nature and circumstances of this survey is provided in Appendix 1. This survey will be subsequently referred to as the Goulmima survey.

181

Table 10. Age structure of the PN labour force in Goulmima and of the rural active Muslim males in Ksar-Es-Souk province

Age group (years)	PN labour force (Goulmima)		Rural active Muslim males (Ksar-Es-Souk)	
	Number (1)	Per cent. (2)	Number (3)	Per cent. (4)
Under 15	4	1.6	2 551	2.8
15–24	72	28.7	18 865	20.8
25–44	105	41.8	42 817	47.1
45–64	68	27.1	21 414	23.6
65–74	0	0.0	3 644	4.0
75 and over	2	0.8	1 489	1.6
Age not declared	—	—	42	0.1
All ages	251	100.0	90 822	100.0

Sources: Goulmima survey.
  Recensement 1960, II[4, p. 459].

0	child : 21	5–6	children: 40
1–2	children: 50	7 and more children: 16	
3–4	children: 61		

(The highest number of children reported was 11.) This implies that the mean number of persons per family (as distinct from the household) among the PN labour force is 5.4. Another survey shows the corresponding figure to be 4.3 for the rural population in the Tafilalt region[16], which includes Goulmima. Promotion Nationale would, therefore, appear to attract people with larger than average families which, as it turns out, are also poorer than average. This fact is very relevant to the question whether or not Promotion Nationale is a vehicle for income transfer, which is taken up in the next Sub-section.

This Section examines the impact of Promotion Nationale on income (7.4.1) and on employment (7.4.2). Sub-section 7.4.3 attempts to determine the level of popular participation in the selection of projects and in the enjoyment of benefits therefrom.

7.4.1. *Impact on income*

A. *The remuneration system*
The distinguishing feature of food for work programmes is that their workers are paid partially or wholly in foodstuffs. PN 'workers' can be grouped into four different categories. The unskilled workers constitute the great

majority. A second group is constituted by animals, or more precisely, workers who bring their animals, especially mules, to carry rocks, water, etc. A third group is made up of the skilled workers, who, on PN projects, are almost exclusively masons. The supervisory personnel constitute the last category. They include the supervisor *(surveillant des travaux)*, the foreman *(caporal)*, the supervisor-trainee, and the timekeeper. Their respective remunerations before 1970 and starting in 1970 are shown in Table 11. Thus under Morocco's Promotion Nationale, up to 1970 the great majority of the unskilled workers receive half their wage in cash and half in kind, while the supervisory and skilled workers are generally paid all in cash.

Table 11. Remuneration of PN workers (in dirham equivalent per day)

	Prior to 1970			1970		
Worker categories	Payment in kind (1)	Payment in cash (2)	Total (3)	Payment in kind (4)	Payment in cash (5)	Total (6)
Unskilled worker	2.00	2.00	4.00	1.60	2.40	4.00
Worker with animal	4.00	2.00	6.00	3.60	2.40	6.00
Masons	—	8.00	8.00	—	8.00	8.00
Supervisor	—	8.00	8.00	—	8.00	8.00
Foreman, supervisor-trainee, timekeeper	2.00	4.00	6.00	1.60	4.40	6.00

Sources: (1)–(3): PN au Maroc, 1964; PN Bilan, 1961 to 1969; PN: Trois Années, 1964.
(4)–(6): PN Aide-Mémoire, 1970.

On the basis of consumer theory alone, one would assume that a rational consumer would always wish to receive all cash (as opposed to part in cash and part in kind) in all circumstances since, if he needed the food-stuffs, he could go out and buy them with the cash. Thus one would expect, and many observers contend, that the PN workers would prefer to receive cash instead of the wheat part of their remuneration. Indeed, in many places, the workers do go and sell their sack of wheat on payday, some-times only a few yards from where they have just got their PN payment.

The survey findings in the Goulmima region, shown in Table 12, do not confirm this expectation.* Of 251 workers, only 48 stated that they would

* The results obtained here may, however, have been influenced by the circumstances of the survey, which was conducted either at the *supercaïd's* office and/or with the help of his aides as interpreters: see Appendix 1.

prefer to receive cash instead of the wheat: of these, 17 did not receive wheat but only cash in the first place! The great majority either favour the existing system or are indifferent. Does this mean that they value wheat as much as cash? The evidence would indicate that this is so.

Table 12. PN workers' attitude towards payment in kind

| | 'Would you prefer to receive cash instead of wheat?' | | | | | | | | | |
| | Yes | | No | | Indifferent | | Other[a] | | Total | |
Worker category	No.	%	No.	%	No.	%	No.	%	No.	%
Supervisory	4	40.0	3	30.0	2	20.1	1	10.0	10	100.0
Skilled	13	37.1	5	14.3	8	22.9	9	25.7	35	100.0
Unskilled	31	15.0	72	35.0	94	45.6	9	4.4	206	100.0
All	48	19.1	80	31.9	104	41.4	19	7.6	215	100.0

Source: Goulmima survey.

a. 'I am paid all in cash', 'It is up to the State to decide'.

Twice a month the workers are paid for their twelve days of work: for the unskilled, 24 DH in cash and a 60 kg sack of wheat worth 24 DH in theory. When asked whether they would accept a certain cash sum instead of the wheat sack only 20 (7.97 per cent.) said they would take 12 DH, 21 (8.37 per cent.) 15 DH or 18 DH, and 23 (9.16 per cent.) 21 DH. For the unskilled workers alone, the corresponding figures are 3, 3, and 4. This means that 98 per cent. of the unskilled workers value wheat at about the PN exchange rate. One may wonder why this is so. Are these workers simply behaving in an irrational fashion? This is definitely not the case, as will be seen presently, when we study their spending pattern for the cash part of their wages.

When asked what he spent his cash wages on, the average worker named three different items. Foodstuffs constitute the largest group by far (over 70 per cent.), of which wheat and flour represent more than one-fourth. In view of this, it is hardly surprising that the majority of workers see no particular advantage in being paid all in cash. Their behaviour may, in fact, be more rational than that of the hypothetical rational consumer previously referred to. Given the market conditions in this area, Promotion Nationale may, at times, represent a cheaper way of acquiring wheat than the market, when transport and other costs are taken into due account. So one may conclude that, while consumers usually prefer cash to payment in kind, there are circumstances under which they might prefer payment in

184

kind to cash. This would be the case, for instance, if payment in kind takes a form which falls nicely into their consumption pattern – as wheat apparently does in this region.

While wheat and flour are important, sugar and tea are the most popular items. This is hardly surprising in view of the fact that in Morocco extremely sweet mint tea constitutes the national drink, which is taken at any time of day. This is so true that some families would skip a meal in order to buy more sugar for the tea. In some cases, mint tea has become an addiction, not unlike alcoholic beverages in some non-Muslim societies. Together with wheat and flour, sugar and tea constitute more than half of all items mentioned. This fact may have other ramifications beyond Promotion Nationale itself.

Clothing also is very popular; it is, in fact, second only to tea and sugar. The other items are fairly minor. The most striking thing, however, is that virtually all of the cash wage is consumed. The only form of saving was debt repayment: but it was only mentioned twice in 757 times!

As was briefly mentioned above, the findings here do have further implications. One of the frequently stated reasons for initiating or continuing a works programme is that the wages paid to the workers will contribute to a widening of the domestic market, and hence to the growth of domestic industries through increased demand. It is true that all PN payments are consumed, thus expanding the domestic market. But relatively little is spent on domestically manufactured goods, mainly clothing. And so market expansion effect is rather small. A potential source of more serious problems, however, is the fact that a large share of the goods demanded are imports. Foremost among them are tea and sugar; and in some years wheat and flour may also have to be brought in from abroad in sizeable quantities.*

B. *The regional redistribution effects*

Among the four aims of Promotion Nationale, two would seem to imply an official policy of application for income transfer, if not from the rich to the poor, at least from the richer (or useful) to the poorer (or marginal) provinces of the country. One statement mentions the improvement of living and production conditions in the *disinherited areas*, and the

---

* In the years 1960 to 1968, tea and sugar accounted for 11.74 per cent. of all imports on the average, with a high of 18.65 per cent. in 1965 and a low of 7.2 per cent. in 1968. For wheat and flour, the corresponding figures are 6.08 per cent., 12.1 per cent. in 1967 and 2.55 per cent. in 1963. The four items together average 17.81 per cent. over this period. See *Annuaire Statistique*, 1960 through 1967 and *Situation Economique*, 1968.

185

social development of their inhabitants. The other says that part of Promotion Nationale's 'mission' is to develop the infrastructure (roads) of the *marginal regions*. The question then is: has Promotion Nationale, in fact, been successful as a vehicle of income transfer, for which it was, in part, designed? The answer will consist of two parts. The first will consider the regional distribution of PN activities. The next will study how important Promotion Nationale is in fact in the individual workers' livelihood.

The 'marginal' provinces include the border provinces of Oujda, Ksar-Es-Souk, Ouarzazate, Agadir, Tarfaya, and the Rif provinces of Tetuan, Tangier, Nador and Al Hoceima. The 'other' provinces include the Atlantic provinces of Casablanca (now: El Jadida, Khouribga and Settat), Kenitra, the prefectures of Casablanca and Rabat-Salé, and the central provinces: Taza, Fez, Meknes, Beni-Mellal and Marrakesh. Marginal in this case is a euphemism for poor. The marginal provinces are poorer and more crowded than the other provinces. Per capita agricultural income in the former is less than half that in the latter: 157.12 DH vs. 326.29 DH. Population density per square kilometre of arable land is almost three times as high in the former as in the latter: in 1960 they were 282 and 100; by 1968 the figures had risen to 344 and 125, respectively. A slight reduction in the ratio of the densities can be perceived between those two years, from 2.82 to 2.75. This may indicate an improvement in the relative position of the marginal provinces, which can be attributed to different causes. For instance, the population in the marginal provinces has not increased as fast as in the rest of the country either, because of a lower natural growth rate or because of domestic migration from the former region to the latter. Another possible explanation is that arable land increased relatively faster in the marginal region: this may or may not be attributable in part to Promotion Nationale. Or it could be a combination of these two phenomena. Owing to the lack of more detailed information, it is not possible to determine at this point, first, whether the decline in the ratio is significant; and, second, what is causing the decline.

Per capita agricultural income and population density on arable land (or its inverse) both provide a good measurement of poverty, at least in Morocco. The two are inversely correlated. In regressing arable land density on per capita agricultural income, the following equations are obtained:

$$Y = 348.83 - 0.573 \, X_1 \qquad R^2 = 0.4560$$
$$(41.71) \ (0.174)$$

$$Y = 352.81 - 0.483 \, X_2 \qquad R^2 = 0.4546$$
$$(42.80) \ (0.147)$$

where
Y = per capita agricultural income,
X_1 = inhabitants per sq. km. of arable land in 1960,
X_2 = inhabitants per sq. km. of arable land in 1968.

The regression coefficients are significant at a better level than 1 per cent. This correlation is important for the following discussion to the extent that, even though data on agricultural income must be treated with caution due to the existence of *auto-consommation* or subsistence consumption, data on population and arable area (and hence on arable land density) are usually more reliable. The following discussion is, therefore, in terms of both income and density.

When we compare the PN effort in the various provinces, it is obvious that we cannot take the raw number of man-days employed in each year. Clearly, if we assume that the rate of underemployment is uniform all over the country, a province with a large population will be able to absorb or produce a greater number of PN man-days than one with a smaller population – other things being the same. The number of man-days must, therefore, be adjusted for differences in population size. One possible deflator would be the rural population. The resulting criterion could be called 'PN per capita'. It would be expressed in terms of PN man-days for every rural inhabitant. One unit of 'PN per capita' would have the following interpretation: each and every inhabitant of the province could have worked on a PN project for one day during the year, if he had so wished. For institutional reasons, however, only males can work on PN worksites. Thus, a more appropriate deflator proves to be the rural active male labour force. This is indeed what we have done here: the 1960 'rural active males' is the deflator. The resulting unit will still be loosely called 'PN per capita' for lack of a better term. Only the words 'active male' need be inserted in front of 'inhabitant' in the definition given above.

The results of analyses of variance performed on agricultural income, arable land density and PN per capita over nine years are reproduced in Table 13. From 1961 to 1969, the PN per capita in the marginal provinces averaged more than 2.5 times that in the other provinces. In every year, except 1965, the differences are significant; for four out of the nine years they are highly significant. Available data are therefore consistent with the proposition that Promotion Nationale has indeed been a vehicle for income transfer from the richer to the poorer provinces. This hypothesis assumes, of course, that the rate of taxation is no higher in the poorer provinces than in the rest of the country. (Strictly speaking, it is only necessary that this rate should not be more than 2.5 times higher.) There

Table 13. Analysis of the regional distribution of PN activities

	Marginal provinces	Other provinces	All provinces	F- statistic	Signif- icance level
1960 per capita agricultural income (DH/Year)	157.12	326.29	236.07	2.812	0.10
1960 arable land density (inhab./sq. km. arable land)	281.75	99.86	196.87	25.148	0.01
1968 arable land density (inhab./sq. km. arable land)	343.50	125.43	241.73	29.278	0.01
Promotion Nationale per capita (man-days per rural active male/year)					
1961	9.416	2.657	6.262	79.362	0.01
1962	16.281	5.826	11.402	33.511	0.01
1963	11.506	5.348	8.632	7.638	0.02
1964	14.130	6.583	10.608	6.460	0.02
1965	11.200	6.171	8.853	1.695	—
1966	20.214	8.305	14.656	6.112	0.01
1967	18.131	8.028	13.416	2.909	0.10
1968	20.201	7.731	14.382	6.221	0.02
1969	22.667	6.427	15.088	12.086	0.01
Mean	15.972	6.342	11.478		

Source: See Appendix 2, Tables A2.1 and A2.2.

is every evidence that this is the case, in view of the fact that the peasants in especially poor provinces like Ksar-Es-Souk and Ouarzazate pay insubstantial amounts of direct taxes; in some cases none at all.

C. The effects on individual income

The other aspect of the question is to ascertain the importance of PN wages in the workers' incomes. The results of the Goulmima survey show that Promotion Nationale plays an extremely large role in providing a supplement to the workers' incomes, especially their cash incomes. Only 6 out of 251 workers said that they had any other source of cash incomes besides Promotion Nationale. The average cash wage received on Promotion Nationale is 210.16 DH per year, with the supervisory worker getting 1556 DH, the skilled worker 281.77 DH and the unskilled worker 132.66 DH. These figures must be interpreted in terms of the general economic situation of the worker.

The overwhelming majority of the PN workers interviewed are peasants. Their livelihood depends directly on whether they own any land, and if so,

188

how much. Table 14 shows the pattern of landownership and income for the PN workers. Significantly fewer supervisory workers than other workers own land because many of them are full-time civil servants or permanent employees of the technical services. (The average size of their holdings is, however, twice that of the other groups). Fewer skilled than unskilled workers own land, probably because they have to spend more time off the land practising their trade. However, they may originally have had to acquire these skills just because they did not own enough (or any) land.

Table 14. PN cash wages and landownership among PN workers

Worker category	Own no land % (1)	Own some land % (2)	Mean size of land-holding moud[a] (3)	Value of corre-sponding output[b] DH (4)	Mean cash income from PN(DH) (5)	Mean total income DH (6) = (4)+(5)	Share of PN in total income % (7) = (5)/(6)
Supervisory	40.0	60.0	3.300	333.48	1556.00	1889.48	82.35
Skilled	31.2	68.6	1.657	167.45	281.77	449.22	62.72
Unskilled	17.5	82.5	1.563	157.95	132.66	290.61	45.65
All	20.3	79.7	1.647	166.24	210.16	376.40	55.83
F-ratio	—	3.083	5.815	—	83.704	—	—
Level of significance	—	0.05	0.01	—	0.01	—	—

Source: Goulmima survey.

a. Strictly speaking, a *moud* is a measure of volume for grains used to indicate the '*decalitre*' (or 10 litres) which is equivalent to 0.35 cubic feet. It is also used as a measure of area: it then designates the area which can be sown with a 'decalitre' or *moud* of wheat. Clearly this area is not fixed, and varies with the fertility of the soil and with how densely the grains are sown. But, on the average, the *moud* in the southern Moroccan palm groves is about 0.1 ha or 0.2471 acre.
b. Valued at 1010.55 DH per hectare (see Table A2.3 in Appendix 2).

The small holding-size shows that it is the poorer inhabitants who tend to work on PN projects. If we assume that each PN worker is the head of a household (close to three-fourths are married; of these 79.8 per cent. own land), the average PN worker household proves to own about one-fifth of the average household's landholding in the region: 1.645 vs. 8.7 *mouds*.*

* This figure is derived from data on four neighbouring palm groves, presented in Appendix 2, Table A2.3.

189

Very detailed agricultural engineering studies of this area show that the crop patterns and the yields do not vary too widely from one village or palm grove to the next. The average total yield has been estimated to be 1010.55 DH per hectare. Applying this value to the landholdings and assuming that Promotion Nationale and land are the sole sources of income for the workers, the proportion of income derived from Promotion Nationale proves to be inversely related to the size of the landholding as shown in Table 14. However, if the PN payments in kind to the unskilled workers are included (by multiplying their cash income by 2) the difference between skilled and unskilled workers is almost nil: 62.724 per cent. vs. 62.683 per cent.! The important point to be made here is not, however, that supervisory and skilled workers derive a greater proportion of their incomes from Promotion Nationale than do unskilled workers. Rather, it is that Promotion Nationale contributes a very sizeable share of the incomes of all PN workers: 55.9 per cent. if only cash is considered, and 63.5 per cent. if payment in kind is also included. It is not known what proportion of all households have one or more of their members working every year on Promotion Nationale: but for those that do, Promotion Nationale can in no way be considered to be a marginal factor.

7.4.2. Effect on employment

In 1960, agricultural income per capita in the province of Ksar-Es-Souk was 165 DH per year[9]. This would work out to 874 DH for the typical PN family of 5.3 persons, and 709 DH for the general average family of 4.3 persons. Assuming an increase of one per cent. for agricultural per capita income, the corresponding figures for 1970 are 965.99 DH and 783.73 DH, respectively.* The average income from land and Promotion Nationale estimated here (376.40 DH) is, however, less than half the lower figure. The findings, therefore, have two possible implications. First, the PN workers are much poorer than average: this is the more likely alternative. Or, secondly, the households of the workers included in this survey must have other sources of income besides their land and Promotion Nationale. Such possibilities would include occasional and temporary work off the fields for the skilled workers, and farm labouring work, either locally or in more distant places, for the unskilled labourers. This

---

* It is interesting to note that the output corresponding to the average landholding in the cercle of Goulmima (8.7 *mouds*) falls almost exactly halfway between these two figures. The halfway point is 876.86 DH, while the output from 0.87 ha is 879.18 DH. In this respect the region of Goulmima is quite representative of at least the whole province.

brings us to the question of employment and underemployment, which is the very crux of the matter.

Attempts to measure the level of underemployment, for instance when the availability of labour to Promotion Nationale is estimated, use a group as the unit. Ultimately, however, underemployment can make sense only at the level of the individual worker. The survey conducted in Goulmima partially investigated this question. The main characteristic of the Goulmima survey is the fact that the sample was made up exclusively of PN workers. For the study of such a large question as underemployment, however, a more appropriate sample would have included members of the rural labour force at large, or at least of the male labour force. Despite this severe limitation the survey nonetheless yields some interesting results, which may provide clues to the answers to the larger problem.

Almost by definition, a worker's presence on a PN worksite is proof that he is underemployed or at least that he felt he would earn more there than elsewhere. Therefore, it is relevant to find out whether the workers have looked for work elsewhere before coming to the PN worksite, and what other activities they would have engaged in had there been no PN worksite.

The results concerning these questions, as well as the length of time spent on Promotion Nationale, are produced in the next three tables. The proportion of those who looked for work before coming to the PN work-

Table 15. Search for employment and length of time spent on PN

	Looked for work elsewhere before coming to PN (%)	Number of years on PN (years)	Number of 2-week periods per year on PN (2-week periods)
By worker category			
Supervisory	50.0	6.30	17.400
Skilled	57.1	5.60	6.514
Unskilled	45.6	3.32	4.966
All	47.4	3.76	5.677
F-ratio	0.8046	9.7516	37.9727
Level of significance	—	0.01	0.01
By employment search category			
Did not look for work	—	3.27	5.06
Looked for work	—	4.29	6.36
F-ratio		5.4354	4.1816
Level of significance		0.025	0.05

Source: Goulmima survey.

191

site is unexpectedly low: 47.4 per cent. It could be attributed to the socio-economic tasks mentioned by Pascon[8]. This is quite unlikely, however, since the survey took place in early June, a time of harvesting and not yet of negotiations or festivities. Two other alternative explanatory hypotheses relate to the nature of the labour market in this area. First, given the type of work available, these workers may have felt that Promotion Nationale represented the optimum solution in their effort-minimizing/income-maximizing calculations. To illustrate: the average product per available man-day spent in agriculture in this area has been estimated to be 3.66 DH.* This is less than the total PN earnings of an unskilled worker (2 DH in cash, 2 DH in kind), and certainly much less than those of a skilled worker (8 DH in cash). Secondly, there may have been a manifestation of the 'discouraged worker' phenomenon: a worker may not have gone out to look for work because he somehow 'knew' that the labour market was saturated. In fact, the labour market accessible to these workers is very limited. Out of 251 workers, 4 came to work on motorized bicycle (3 of whom were supervisors), 59 on bicycle and all the remaining 188 had to come on foot. The furthest distance travelled by these workers – in this case, a mason – from home to work was 30 km (about 19 miles) on bicycle. However, the largest employer – and probably one of the very few for masons and unskilled workers in this area – was the Ziz dam construction situated near Ksar-Es-Souk at a distance of over 50 miles. Clearly, short of moving there these workers could not have access to that employment. Thus, a hypothesis combining the discouraged worker phenomenon and the attraction of PN money appears to be the one most consistent with the data in explaining the relatively low number of workers who looked for work elsewhere. In addition, there is the possibility of a voluntary element. Promotion Nationale may be what the worker wants, certainly because of the wages but also because the flexibility of the two-week PN employment period fits conveniently into the timing of his other occupations. In fact, to the question 'Have you looked for work somewhere else before coming to this worksite?', two or three workers answered that they looked for work elsewhere *only when no PN worksite was in operation in their area*.

In order to appreciate the value of PN money, the workers presumably must have had prior experience on PN worksites. This is, indeed, the case. Although there were about 50 beginners, the great majority had previously worked on PN worksites for periods of up to 10 years – that is, ever since Promotion Nationale was officially instituted. (Three of the supervisors and two of the masons reported periods in excess of 10 years,

---

* See Appendix 2, Table A2.3.

192

Table 16. Frequency distribution of length of work per year on Promotion Nationale

Number of two-week periods	Supervisory workers	Skilled workers	Unskilled workers	All workers
2 or less	1	5	60	66
3–5	0	16	92	108
6–9	1	10	42	53
10–19	1	2	8	11
20 and over	7	2	4	13
Mean (number of periods)	17.400	6.514	4.966	5.677

Source: Goulmima survey.

probably because they were confusing working for the technical services with working for Promotion Nationale. For them, perhaps, both are 'the government'.) The average period of work on Promotion Nationale is 3.76 years, with the supervisory and skilled workers indicating significantly longer periods. This does not mean that for all those years they have worked continuously and on a full-time basis on PN worksites. One year, a man may decide to work because his crops failed. The next, he may be more fortunate and not feel as pressing a need. And, even if some do work every year, only very few do so on a year-round basis.

The mean working period on Promotion Nationale works out to about 5.7 two-week periods (almost three months) a year. Again the supervisory and skilled workers work for much longer periods (see Tables 15 and 16). The unskilled worker apparently spends 10 weeks a year on Promotion Nationale – about two and a half months. Can it be concluded that the 'rate of underemployment' is about 20 per cent.? This is possible. However, it may be an under-estimate due to the fact that in this area, and probably in other areas, PN employment is still rationed. With very few exceptions, workers, especially unskilled ones, are not permitted to work two successive periods, in order that as many workers as possible can be reached by Promotion Nationale. Thus, the 5 periods must not be compared to the theoretical 24, but rather to 12. The effect is to double the rate of underemployment to 40 per cent. This, however, can constitute no more than a very rough estimate.

One feature which appears in the findings shown in Table 15 is that those who do look for employment elsewhere work for Promotion Nationale more weeks per year than those who do not. This is probably evidence that, even though workers are not fully satisfied with what Promotion Nationale

193

Table 17. Alternative activities of PN workers

	'Nothing' (1)	Work in fields (2)	Work at home (3)	Trade (4)	Seasonal emigration (5)	Long-term emigration (6)	All activities (7)
By worker category							
Supervisory							
– Frequency	2	3	0	2	3	0	10
– Percentage	20.0	30.0	0.0	20.0	30.0	0.0	100.0
Skilled							
– Frequency	10	7	2	0	16	0	35
– Percentage	28.6	20.0	5.7	0.0	45.7	0.0	100.0
Unskilled							
– Frequency	43	112	5	1	42	3	206
– Percentage	20.9	54.4	2.4	0.5	20.4	1.4	100.0
All							
– Frequency	55	122	7	3	61	3	251
– Percentage	21.9	48.6	2.8	1.2	24.3	1.2	100.0
By landownership status							
Own no land							
– Frequency	16	17	1	0	17	0	51
– Percentage	31.4	33.3	2.0	0.0	33.3	0.0	100.0
Own some land							
– Frequency	39	105	6	3	44	3	200
– Percentage	19.5	52.5	3.0	1.5	22.0	1.5	100.0

Source: Goulmima survey.

has to offer, it still represents the best source of income for them – second only to the land.

What, indeed, are the alternatives to Promotion Nationale? The findings are shown in Table 17, classified according to worker category and to landownership status. The importance of 'work in the fields' is to be expected. The very fact that almost half mention it, is proof that there is excess labour in agriculture. For, at the moment the survey is taken, they are working on Promotion Nationale and not in the fields; thus they probably feel that their presence on the fields would not add to the output of the other members of the family. It is interesting to note that almost all those who would have worked in the fields (105 out of 122) own land. As previously mentioned, the survey took place during harvest time. Therefore, this could mean that they hired outside labour to do their harvesting while they worked on Promotion Nationale – a very unlikely proposition in view of the small sizes of their landholdings and of the fact that PN wages are almost always lower than the wages harvesters would have to be paid. Or it could mean that other members of the family do the harvest and/or they themselves come back after work to do it or help do it. This last alternative is indeed quite possible – and even probable – for many workers. In this area, work on PN worksites starts around 6:30–7:00 o'clock in the morning and is usually over by 3:00 o'clock in the afternoon. This leaves them enough daylight to do work in their own fields if they so wish.

Seasonal emigration is the next alternative to PN work, with 'nothing' coming a close third. Might the proportion of those who would do 'nothing' if they were not on Promotion Nationale not provide an indication of the level of open unemployment? Trading and working at home barely need to be mentioned. However, the low frequency of 'long-term emigration' – probably to the cities, very rarely abroad – makes one wonder where the rural exodus, so frequently referred to, is coming from. Since PN workers are generally among the less well-off, could this mean that those who are fairly well-to-do are leaving the countryside? Or, alternatively, those who work on Promotion Nationale are less inclined to migrate to the cities? This last aspect, if it exists, would be one of the more promising aspects of Promotion Nationale and could bear more detailed studies.*

7.4.3. *Popular participation*

The general impression that one gets in studying the findings presented so far is that Promotion Nationale must certainly be very important for the community, and especially for the workers' families. This, however, does not constitute the whole picture. One can distinguish between three stages at which Promotion Nationale affects the people and their feelings towards the whole programme. The first one is at the preparatory stage when project selection takes place. Then comes the execution of the programme itself. Lastly, and probably of greatest importance, is the final stage: what effects does it all have on the worker's livelihood? Virtually everything that has been discussed so far is directly related to the execution stage. I now propose to examine the interactions at the other two stages; for they, too, determine how the worker perceives Promotion Nationale, and consequently, the extent to which he will co-operate in the whole exercise.

---

* It must be remembered that the Goulmima survey sample does not include those (if any) who have already emigrated.

A. *The peasant in the preparatory phase*
During the preparatory phase, in theory the peasant is to participate in the selection of projects collectively and indirectly through the village or communal council. He can, and in many instances does, present a list of projects he would most like to see undertaken in his area in the following year. But in the end, he has very little influence on the final selection. This is due to the form of local administration in Morocco, which is a somewhat uneasy mixture of centralization and decentralization.

On the one hand, the elected communal council and its president in theory possess certain important prerogatives. Very generally speaking, the communal council settles, by its deliberations, the affairs of the commune. In practice, however, things do not usually work out that way. For, on the other hand, there are the local authorities, the *caïd*, the *sheikh* and the *moqqadem*, who are the representatives of the Ministry of the Interior. A certain rivalry seems to exist in many areas of the country between the two parts of this two-headed executive, the council president and the local authority. By the sheer power of the State, the local authorities always come out on top in the solution of any actual or potential conflict[17].

This situation – which may be described by saying that in Morocco, the farmers are still minors in the legal sense – is recognized by the official use of the words *autorité de tutelle* (tutelage authority or guardian) to designate the State and its representatives. This minor's status of the local collectivities manifests itself in the selection of PN projects where in the end it is the local authorities who, for budgetary or other reasons, decide how many and which projects are to be undertaken. Some people contend that such a system tends to produce – and in some cases has produced – the selection of projects which benefit only a few, especially the retired agents of the State. It would, therefore, be interesting to find out how many of the PN workers benefit from their work, and how much they benefit.

B. *The distribution of benefits*
In the Goulmima survey, one way to try to approach this question is by studying land ownership, land distance, and whether or not the land benefits from the work. As in all traditional societies, family ties in Goulmima are very strong. Consequently, questions were asked relating not only to the workers themselves but also to their relatives. The projects were all related to irrigation. Therefore, the questions and the answers were fairly straightforward. The findings appear in Table 18.

Over 60 per cent. of all workers feel that their lands benefit directly from the projects they are working on. And, more important, a greater

Table 18. Landownership and the distribution of benefits among PN workers and their relatives

	Distance from worksite to village	Self				Relatives			
		Land owner (%)	Land area (moud)	Land distance (km)	Land benefiting (%)	Land owner (%)	Land area (moud)	Land distance (km)	Land benefiting (%)
By worker category									
Supervisory	5.700	60.0	3.300	3.250	40.0	90.0	6.300	4.700	60.0
Skilled	4.723	68.6	1.657	2.914	45.7	57.1	1.914	2.700	37.1
Unskilled	3.912	82.5	1.563	3.527	70.0	69.9	2.233	3.207	56.8
All	4.096	79.7	1.645	3.431	62.9	68.9	2.351	3.196	54.2
F-ratio	2.302	3.083	5.815	0.584	4.165	2.300	8.958	1.184	2.416
Significance	—	0.05	0.01	—	0.05	—	0.01	—	0.10
By landownership status									
No land	4.837	0.0	0.0	0.00	0.0	31.4	1.265	1.882	23.5
Some land	3.908	100.0	2.065	4.306	79.0	78.5	2.628	3.530	62.0
All	4.096	79.7	1.645	3.431	62.9	68.9	2.351	3.196	54.2
F-ratio	3.480	0.0	91.971	109.395	190.328	50.237	7.894	8.603	26.601
Significance	0.10	—	0.01	0.01	0.01	0.01	0.01	0.01	0.01

Source: Goulmima survey.

proportion of the unskilled than of the other workers feel that way. Furthermore, over half report that their relatives benefit. These facts may be significant in explaining their participation on the worksites. If one adds the proportion of those who benefit directly (62.9 per cent.) to the proportion among those who do not benefit but whose relatives do (16.1 per cent.), an impressive total of 79 per cent. does benefit in one way or another, directly or indirectly. (These results must be interpreted with caution, however, for the survey included PN workers only and not the entire population.) At least in the Goulmima region, people work on Promotion Nationale partly because they or their relatives benefit from the PN projects.

When the results are broken down according to landownership status, certain characteristics of the rural society emerge. To put it very simply, if land be taken as an index of wealth, the poor have poor relatives and the rich have rich relatives. More precisely, those who themselves have land tend very significantly to have relatives who own land; and further-more, these relatives have more land than the relatives of those who do not own land. It is this significant correlation which explains why, of those who own land, almost three times as many as of those who do not own land feel that their relatives benefit.

C. *The training function*
Benefits to the land constitute only one aspect of PN effects on the workers. There are others which may equally affect how the workers view Promotion Nationale. Among them, one can cite the social overheads, such as better roads, better public buildings, etc. Another aspect relates to training or skill-acquisition.

The term 'promotion nationale' means national development, national improvement, national uplifting not only in terms of aggregate physical output of goods and services but also in terms of individual life and inner quality. Thus, by definition, 'promotion' in this sense implies that the programme is to carry out some training function so that the worker has a better chance to improve his lot. On the type of projects undertaken in the Goulmima region, the only kind of skills that can be taught and acquired are those of masons. When asked whether or not they had learned any skills on PN worksites, only 20 out of the 251 workers (or less than 8 per cent.) answered affirmatively. Such a figure is quite low. This is definitely one area where much can be done to improve the performance of Promotion Nationale.

198

7.5. CONCLUSION

In the course of its ten-year existence, Promotion Nationale has been, and remains, the object of a heated controversy. Its achievements[18] have been celebrated almost as many times and with as much conviction as its failures[19] have been publicized. The present study does not claim to resolve this controversy. But it sheds some light on the points of contention and on other aspects as well.

The importance of schemes for capital formation through labour mobilization stems from several sources. Foremost among them are the contribution to capital formation and agricultural development, the creation of present and future employment, and the role in spreading the benefits of growth more widely – or, more generally, of imparting to the masses a sense of participation in the national development effort. In the case of Morocco's Promotion Nationale programme, the analysis carried out in the previous chapters permits the evaluation of its performance in each of these aspects during the ten years of its existence.

Sub-section 7.5.1 reviews the achievements of Promotion Nationale. Sub-section 7.5.2 considers its shortcomings, and some facets of foreign aid. The general conclusions emerging from the study of the Moroccan experience in labour mobilization are briefly restated in Sub-section 7.5.3.

7.5.1. *The achievements of Promotion Nationale*

The achievements of Promotion Nationale lie in three different areas. It has helped to spread the benefits of economic growth and to alleviate the immediate employment problem. It has also made a limited contribution to capital formation and agricultural development.

A. *Spreading the benefits of economic growth*
Promotion Nationale's role in spreading the benefits of economic growth has taken two different forms. Firstly, it has been an effective vehicle of income transfer from the richer provinces to the poorer ones. For the period from 1961 to 1969, on the average, it has provided annually 6 days of work to each rural active male inhabitant in the former region, as opposed to 16 days of work in the latter.

Secondly, within the poorer provinces Promotion Nationale plays an important role for the more destitute segments of the population. The survey of PN workers conducted in the region of Goulmima, Province of Ksar Es Souk shows that PN workers have larger than average families (5.4 vs. 4.3 persons), and are poorer than average: their average landholdings amount to less than one-fifth of the regional mean holding. PN wages constitute a very sizeable part of their incomes, perhaps as much as one-half. In addition, over three-quarters of the workers felt that they, or their relatives, benefited directly – in terms of improved irrigation of land – from the PN projects on which they were employed.

This part of our findings contradicts frequent criticism of Promotion Nationale. According to some observers, the existing system of re-muneration is a very bad one. On the one hand, they say, it represents a very low upper limit to any extension of Promotion Nationale as an in-strument for solving the employment problem. At the existing wage rate, for instance, it would take more than the government's entire investment budget to employ the available or surplus 300 million man-days. (Let us grant for a moment that this figure is in some sense meaningful.) On the other hand, the 4 DH a day is not sufficient to attract workers. The solution offered for these two problems is very simple: Promotion Natio-nale should be tied to land reform. Workers would not be paid wages; instead they would receive land for the work. As a result, they would have higher productivity since they would be working on their land. And the government would no longer have to spend on PN wages: it could limit its contribution to providing supplies and small equipment for the various improvements.

The reasoning is not entirely convincing. To begin with, even if the figure on underemployment had been correctly measured, it is inappro-priate because it includes both men and women. The more relevant figure for Promotion Nationale would be 140 million man-days. If voluntary and/or short seasonal underemployment is excluded, the final figure may be as little as half that amount. It has, by now, become clear that the first part of the argument has very shaky foundations indeed. As for the sec-ond aspect, the Goulmima survey findings do not support the contention that PN wages are unattractive to the peasants. Thus, while land reform may be desirable from many points of view, it is an entirely futile exercise to try to make it into a necessary and sufficient condition for a labour mo-bilizing works programme. And in any case, those who try to relate these two problems do not offer any realistic answer to the question: What shall be done about employment while waiting for land reform? (We realize that the easy, but unrealistic, answer is: Let us have land reform now!)

B. *Employment*

For those peasants who do work on PN projects, Promotion Nationale represents the only alternative to doing nothing or working in the fields at very low productivity. The Goulmima survey revealed that, on the average,

200

the workers interviewed spend three months of full time work on PN worksites every year. These results indicate that Promotion Nationale has a favourable effect on the immediate employment problem.

At the national level, it provided 20 million man-days annually in the period 1966–1969. This is certainly a minute proportion of the under-employed if compared to 300 million. As previously mentioned, however, this figure is rather high for PN discussion. If the lower and more relevant figure of 140 million, or even less, is used (with great reservation) the PN performance in this area begins to look respectable. In any case, it cannot be termed negligible.

As for the effects of Promotion Nationale in providing future employment, no direct evidence is available. This depends mainly on how much of the work undertaken is of a productive nature.

C. *Capital formation and agricultural development*

The share of purely 'make-work' or equipment projects in the PN programme fell from 17 per cent. in 1961 to 7.2 per cent. in 1969, that of infrastructure from 52.2 per cent. to 35.9 per cent., while *mise en valeur* projects rose from 30.7 per cent. to 56.9 per cent. over the same period.*

Clearly, the proportion of useful or productive projects – whether defined to include the last two as we have done here, or only the last one – has been increasing, and with it the contribution of Promotion Nationale to capital formation.

At the micro level, an analysis of ten PN *mise en valeur* projects located in the provinces of Al Hoceima, Ksar Es Souk, and Marrakesh yields a mean internal rate of return of 14 per cent. This shows that Promotion Nationale does undertake projects which compare favourably with similar projects realized in other parts of the economy. It does not, however, mean that all PN projects are equally profitable. Through these projects, Promotion Nationale makes some important contribution to agricultural development. The present finding weakens somewhat the criticism that, due to the passivity and laziness of workers, Promotion Nationale is characterized by extremely low productivity.

At the aggregate level, a linear programming model enables the PN contribution to capital formation to be estimated, and hence to agricultural development since the bulk of PN projects lie in the agricultural sector. Directly, as much as 4.6 per cent. of total net investment in Morocco could have originated from the investable part of PN output in the period 1962–1969, if Promotion Nationale had been at the optimum levels

* See Appendix 3.

201

prescribed by the model. This estimate is based on reasonable assumptions concerning the quality of work accomplished on Promotion Nationale. More conservative assumptions would lead to figures ranging from a minimum of 2 to 4.6 per cent.

Promotion Nationale also contributes to capital formation in a second way, through the government budget. More PN output means more investable PN output, which means more investment and more output of goods and services. This, in turn, implies increased government resources, making possible a rise in PN output, and so on. This indirect contribution is probably fairly small, but it cannot be ignored.

The proportion of productive projects in the total PN programme and the quality of work accomplished on PN worksites constitute the two crucial elements in determining the magnitude of PN's contribution to capital formation. They are the instruments with which PN performance in this area can be further improved.

7.5.2. Other aspects of Promotion Nationale

A. *The shortcomings of Promotion Nationale*
While Promotion Nationale's performance on the material side has been far from disastrous, it has not been devoid of shortcomings, especially in the human aspects of the undertaking.

The first one arises on the institutional side. Except at the very bottom, the administration of Promotion Nationale occurs mostly as an appendix to the normal activities of all departments involved or, at least, as one among many responsibilities of the persons dealing with it. This gives rise to endless confusion and unnecessary duplication of functions which greatly reduce the efficiency of the system and result in some waste. However, its contribution to increasing adoption and acceptance of the 'PN way' (i.e. labour-intensive methods) by the technical services militates against any radical remodelling of the existing PN institutional framework.

Secondly, Promotion Nationale seems to have accomplished very little in the direction of imparting to the masses a sense of active participation in the national development effort. The whole exercise remains a highly centralized programme, with very little room for local initiative. This situation may or may not have given rise to corruption in hiring, as some critics contend. The evidence on that aspect is not clear. Although it is rather extreme to hold that Promotion Nationale has become the undertaking *par excellence* which kills the democratic spirit in the management of the Nation's affairs, it is a fact that the effective (as opposed to formal) participation of the peasants in the decision-making process remains low.

202

This is probably the case in most things and not just with Promotion Nationale, however, so that it may not be justified to consider this as one of PN's failures.

Finally, Promotion Nationale has not performed adequately in 'promoting' the worker to an improved status, as its name indicates that it should have. Very few workers acquire skills of any kind on PN worksites. Of the 251 PN workers interviewed in Goulmima, only 20 reported that they had learned a trade while working on PN projects. Thus, Promotion Nationale has very little effect on the worker's access to another, more remunerative occupation.

B. *Some facets of foreign aid*

Some characteristics of foreign aid and general features of works programmes emerged during this study of Morocco's Promotion Nationale programme. They relate to food aid and the role of a works programme in expanding the domestic market.

In an economy with a works programme, where foreign aid is received as food aid and cash aid, and where a portion of the former is used as part of the payments to the works programme labourers – in such an economy, foreign aid has the following characteristics. Firstly, in terms of contribution to the social welfare function, food aid is less productive than cash aid. This is because commodity aid represents the extreme form of aid tying, and aid tying always reduces the effective (as opposed to nominal) value of aid to the recipient. Secondly, the difference in productivity of cash aid and food aid stems from the fact that the former, through the government budget, contributes to the output of the works programme – as well as directly to consumption. More precisely, food aid has a lower value to the extent that using or purchasing one additional unit of foodstuffs above the available food aid reduces cash aid correspondingly, which, in turn, occasions a decline in the output of the works programme and the investable part of that output. Thirdly, in terms of the linear programming model there may be cases when food aid is counter-productive: it has a negative shadow price. Under such circumstances, the intended recipient country would be willing to pay the donor country – in the form of a reduction in the total volume of aid – in order to reduce food aid, or at least not to force any more of it into the recipient country.

Finally, some of the findings of this study suggest that the works programme cannot be expected to provide, indirectly, a stimulus to the development of domestic industries. The labourers are among the poorest of the inhabitants. They spend the overwhelming proportion of their works programme wages on agricultural products, mostly foodstuffs. Therefore, expenditure on the works programme will contribute very little to the expansion of the market for domestically manufactured goods.

7.5.3. *Some facts on labour mobilization*

From the economic standpoint, Morocco's Promotion Nationale represents a moderate success. Although an attempt to transplant any type of experience into different settings is always an exercise fraught with danger, the general conclusions from the Moroccan experience should prove of great interest to those underdeveloped countries which, like Morocco, are trying to find at least a partial solution to the employment problem.

A labour mobilization works programme is an effective vehicle for income transfer. Its impact on immediate employment is favourable – though the longer run effects remain uncertain. It contributes in a limited way to capital formation and agricultural development: this contribution increases with the proportion of productive projects included in the programme and the quality of work on those projects.

The effectiveness and usefulness of the entire undertaking may, however, be severely circumscribed unless great care is taken to avoid unnecessary duplication and confusion in establishing the institutional apparatus, and to generate popular participation at all stages.

EDITOR'S POSTSCRIPT

Dr. Andriamananjara's paper was completed in 1971, and therefore does not cover recent developments in the area of Promotion Nationale. An important change was introduced in 1972, with the elimination of payment in kind, and a cash payment which was tied to the agricultural minimum wage (SMAG). In the 1973–1977 development plan, the programme is maintained at approximately the same level as before (100,000 workers employed per year). Half the programme will be devoted to land improvement projects, 20 per cent. to road infrastructure, and the rest to community works and equipment. The financing is to be provided entirely from domestic sources, half on the budgets of the different ministries, and half on a special PN account. If the present trend continues, the PN programme will gradually lose its specific identity and will become indistinguishable from the regular operations of the different technical departments.

APPENDIX 1. THE GOULMIMA SURVEY OF PN WORKERS

From June 5th to June 8th, 1970, a survey of PN workers was conducted in the Cercle of Goulmima, Province of Ksar-Es-Souk. A total of 251 workers on five different worksites were interviewed. The worksite names, the types of project, the date of the survey and the number of workers interviewed are as follows:

1. Ouakka   : *seguia* or irrigation canal;
                June 5th, 1970; 39 workers.
2. Ait Yahia : *seguia* or irrigation canal;
                June 5th, 1970; 28 workers.
3. Touroug   : *seguia* or irrigation canal;
                June 6th, 1970; 78 workers.
4. Mazlaghate: medium-scale dam;
                June 8th, 1970; 77 workers.
5. Tiliouine : *khettara* or underground irrigation canal;
                June 8th, 1970; 30 workers.

The workers for the first two projects came to the *cercle's* administrative building at the end of their work day for the interviews. The remainder were interviewed on the worksites themselves.

The interviewing was done through interpreters: five during the first day, and two for the other days. All interpreters spoke both Arabic and Berber, as well as French. Some of the workers spoke (and were interviewed in) Arabic; some spoke (and were interviewed in) Berber. Very few – usually the supervisory workers – knew French; none were interviewed in that language.

The survey questionnaire was discussed with the *supercaïd*, who made helpful suggestions with regard to its content as well as in the phrasing of some questions. The interpreters were also provided through his office. We are grateful for his help and co-operation, without which the survey would not have been possible.

The original questionnaire was formulated in French. An English translation is attached.

Questionnaire: Promotion Nationale Labour Force

Name of the worksite:
Location of the worksite:
Number of workers on the worksite:
Date of the interview:

1. Are you
   a. a worksite leader;
   b. a timekeeper;
   c. a foreman;
   d. a skilled worker;
   e. an unskilled worker?
2. How old are you?
3. Are you married?
4. How many children do you have?
5. A. In which village or *ksar* do you live?
   B. How far from the worksite is your village? (km)
6. How do you come to the worksite?
   a. on foot;
   b. on bicycle;
   c. other means (specify).

7. How long ago did you work on a Promotion Nationale worksite for the first time? (number of years)
8. How much time per year do you work on Promotion Nationale worksites? (number of two-week periods)
9. Have you looked for work somewhere else before coming to the present worksite?
   a. Yes. b. No.
10. What would you be doing now if the worksite did not exist?
    a. nothing;
    b. work in the fields;
    c. work at home;
    d. trade;
    e. seasonal emigration;
    f. long-term emigration.
11. Do you have any land?
    a. Yes. b. No.
12. If yes, how many *mouds*?
13. How far from the present worksite is your land? (km)
14. Does your land benefit directly from the work on this worksite?
    a. Yes. b. No.
15. Do you have any relatives who own land?
    a. Yes. b. No.
16. If so, how many *mouds*?
17. How far from the present worksite is the land of your relatives? (km)
18. Does your relatives' land benefit directly from the work on this worksite?
    a. Yes. b. No.
19. How much money per year do you receive on the worksites of Promotion Nationale? (dirhams)
20. What do you buy with the money that you receive from Promotion Nationale?
21. Do you have any other sources of income?
    a. Yes. b. No.
22. Would you like the payment in wheat to be replaced by cash?
    a. Yes. b. No.
23. If yes [to 22], instead of the 60-kg sack of wheat, would you accept 12 DH?
    a. Yes. b. No.
24. If yes [to 22], instead of the 60-kg sack of wheat, would you accept 15 DH?
    a. Yes. b. No.
25. If yes [to 22], instead of the 60-kg sack of wheat, would you accept 18 DH?
    a. Yes. b. No.
26. If yes [to 22], instead of the 60-kg sack of wheat, would you accept 21 DH?
    a. Yes. b. No.
27. Have you learnt a trade on the worksites of Promotion Nationale?
    a. Yes. b. No.
28. If so, what is that trade?

APPENDIX 2. DATA FOR 'PROMOTION NATIONALE AND THE PEOPLE'

This appendix contains the data used in the analysis of the regional distribution of Promotion Nationale activity (Sub-section 7.4.1-B), and a summary of data on four palm groves situated in the region of Goulmima, Province of Ksar Es Souk.

Province or prefecture	1961ᵃ	1962ᵃ	1963ᵃ	1964	1965	1966	1967	1968	1969
Agadir	406 175	690 302	475 522	621 877	593 551	582 985	692 091	379 069	552 031
Al Hoceima	246 810	531 737	523 452	376 325	520 440	1 067 355	1 054 890	541 642	1 079 728
Beni Mellal	327 068	694 784	484 147	711 320	546 320	833 016	671 705	813 753	467 040
Casablancaᵇ	251 388	528 569	670 042	546 343	432 273	780 795	829 518	596 138	644 860
Fez	765 038	1 495 912	1 185 050	1 355 932	1 390 122	2 203 518	1 625 422	2 039 059	1 343 472
Kenitra	496 108	993 014	721 876	721 435	665 026	1 041 916	1 102 602	1 152 310	1 138 572
Ksar-Es-Souk	503 173	847 813	477 012	758 424	1 442 772	3 759 448	2 822 753	3 198 785	2 937 819
Marrakesh-Safiᶜ	670 988	1 413 234	1 296 776	1 560 321	1 275 929	1 801 795	1 568 963	1 095 858	841 657
Meknes	276 044	739 379	942 577	1 141 524	1 052 377	859 440	1 439 779	1 382 917	1 039 368
Nador	198 047	408 758	457 194	439 147	244 645	567 626	863 629	852 227	1 137 576
Ouarzazate	517 186	850 274	426 538	2 933 913	1 608 924	1 995 005	1 571 075	2 809 786	3 786 357
Oujda	408 863	950 079	951 058	896 221	714 904	900 409	1 138 682	729 194	374 000
Tangier	267 944	381 531	188 527	172 182	78 861	194 760	134 003	265 434	247 764
Tarfaya	0	39 354	60 646	36 000	111 641	215 931	224 172	227 021	154 383
Taza	290 732	697 124	627 144	950 952	1 029 188	1 566 491	1 235 723	809 959	1 162 268
Tetuan	664 407	1 731 388	1 710 204	1 317 534	1 364 111	1 775 259	1 573 481	1 719 943	2 026 839
Casablanca Pre.	534 306	574 881	255 813	315 000	354 159	877 446	612 621	675 705	143 798
Rabat-Salé Pre.	101 000	123 450	152 549	99 681	287 150	359 650	452 627	457 840	283 000
Total	6 934 278	13 691 591	11 606 131	14 954 132	13 812 393	21 392 845	19 613 736	19 746 640	19 360 532

Sources: PN Bilan, 1961 to 1969; PN au Maroc, 1964; PN: Trois Années, 1964.

a. Promotion Nationale data for the years 1961 to 1963 are published on an agricultural year basis (July to June). They were adjusted to the calendar year in order to make them comparable to the data for later years. The formulas used in the conversion are:

$$1961 = \frac{\text{original } 1961}{2}, \quad 1962 = \frac{\text{original } 1961 + \text{original } 1962}{2}, \quad 1963 = \frac{\text{original } 1962 + \text{original } 1963}{2}.$$

b. In 1966, the province of Casablanca was divided into three separate provinces: El Jadida, Khouribga, and Settat. For the sake of continuity the data for these three provinces starting in 1967 were added up and entered under the single province of Casablanca (which, officially, no longer exists).

c. In 1965 the province of Marrakesh was also split between Marrakesh and Safi. Similarly data for these two provinces for the later years have been combined into a single entry.

These notes apply to all Promotion Nationale data cited in the text.

207

Table A2.2. Rural population and agricultural income, according to province

Province	Rural active men 1960 (1)	Rural population 1968 (2)	Density on arable land (rural inhab./sq. km.) 1960 (3)	1968 (4)	Per capita agricultural income (DH) 1960 (5)
Agadir	192 938	890 000	189	212	139
Al Hoceima	40 495	215 000	350	430	114
Beni Mellal	109 354	500 000	105	130	438
Casablanca	292 187	1 415 000	61	87	418
Fez	146 219	690 000	100	123	246
Kenitra	229 528	1 110 000	84	109	448
Ksar Es Souk	90 822	425 000	435	522	165
Marrakesh-Safi	426 767	1 970 000	93	114	243
Meknes	87 854	430 000	97	123	307
Nador	67 426	415 000	231	291	91
Ouarzazate	90 324	495 000	526	625	101
Oujda	54 052	320 000	86	110	289
Tangier	6 732	30 000	143	192	159
Tarfaya	5 196	20 000	—	—	—
Taza	110 070	490 000	159	192	184
Tetuan	119 596	555 000	294	366	199

Sources: The following sources are arranged by column:
1. *Recensement 1960*, II, Table 31, pp. 447–481.
2. *Plan 1968–1972*, Vol. III, p. 8.
3. *Plan 1968–1972*, Vol. III, p. 9.
4. *Plan 1968–1972*, Vol. III, p. 9.
5. *Plan 1968–1972*, Vol. III, p. 20.

Table A2.3. Land, labour, and output in four palm groves of the Goulmima region

	Goulmima	Tinejdad	Yfegh	Tadiroust	Mean
1. Land per household (ha)	0.80	0.71	0.98	0.99	0.87
2. Area (ha)	2 000.00	1 310.00	155.00	580.00	—
3. Output (DH)	—	1 310 400.00	171 970.00	534 675.00	—
4. Available labour force[a] (man-days)	930 150.00	320 000.00	47 250.00	165 530.00	—
5. Productive labour force[b] (man-days)	502 800.00	232 000.00	30 500.00	102 812.00	—
6. Output/land (DH/ha)	—	1 000.31	1 109.48	921.85	1 010.55
7. Output/available labour (DH/md)	—	4.10	3.64	3.23	3.66
8. Output/productive labour (DH/md)	—	5.65	5.64	5.20	5.50
9. Rate of under-employment[c] (%)	27.5	35.5	37.9	36.7	34.4

Sources: Lines 1 to 5 are taken from SCET, 1968 and SCET, 1969. Lines 6 to 9 as well as the means are computed from these data.

a. The available labour force is computed in the sources by assuming that on a yearly basis an adult male provides 250 days of work in agriculture, an adult female 60 days and a child between the age of 10 and 20 years also 60 days.
b. The productive labour force is computed – also in the sources – on the basis of man-days per year required by a unit of the different activities: cereals, fruit trees, animal raising, etc.
c. It goes without saying that the rates of underemployment derived in this table should only be taken to indicate orders of magnitude.

209

Table A3.1. Distribution of Promotion Nationale man-days according to project types and categories, 1961–1969

	Man-days					
Year	*'Mise en valeur'*	*Infra-structure*	*Equipment*	*Part I*	*Part II*	*Total*
1961	2 130 485	3 621 267	1 182 527	—	—	6 934 278
1962	4 705 025	7 208 801	1 777 764	—	—	13 691 591
1963	4 491 733	5 302 608	1 816 090	2 102 854	9 503 275	11 606 131
1964	7 991 654	4 623 455	2 339 023	5 267 993	9 686 139	14 954 192
1965	7 162 031	4 622 491	2 027 871	5 334 399	8 477 994	13 812 393
1966	9 013 473	7 766 846	4 612 525	8 814 821	12 578 024	21 392 845
1967	9 072 865	7 350 440	3 190 431	6 394 642	13 219 094	19 613 736
1968	11 523 794	5 536 708	2 686 138	6 203 093	13 543 547	19 746 640
1969	11 025 373	6 944 721	1 390 438	5 719 767	13 640 765	19 360 532
	Percentage					
1961	30.7	52.2	17.0	—	—	100.0
1962	34.3	52.6	13.0	—	—	100.0
1963	38.7	45.7	15.6	18.1	81.9	100.0
1964	53.4	30.9	15.6	35.2	64.8	100.0
1965	51.9	33.5	14.6	38.6	61.4	100.0
1966	42.1	36.3	21.6	41.2	58.8	100.0
1967	46.2	37.3	16.3	32.6	67.4	100.0
1968	58.4	28.0	13.6	31.4	68.6	100.0
1969	56.9	35.9	7.2	29.5	70.5	100.0

Sources: Same as Table A2.1.

REFERENCES

1. R. Nurkse, *Problems of Capital Formation in Underdeveloped Countries*, New York, 1953.
2. International Labour Office, *The International Standardisation of Labour Statistics*, Geneva, 1959.
3. D. Turnham, *The Employment Problem in Less Developed Countries: A Review of Evidence*, OECD Development Center, Paris, 1970.
4. Service Central des Statistiques, *Résultats du Recensement de 1960*, Vol. II: 'Population Active', Rabat, 1965.
5. Division de la Coordination Economique et du Plan, *Plan Quinquennal 1960–64*, Rabat, 1960.

6. A. Tiano, *La Politique Economique et Financière du Maroc Indépendant*, Presses Universitaires de France, Paris, 1963.
7. Promotion Nationale, *La Promotion Nationale au Maroc*, Rabat, 1964.
8. P. Pascon, 'La Main-d'Oeuvre et l'Emploi dans le Secteur Traditionnel', *Bulletin Economique et Social du Maroc*, Vol. xxviii, Nos. 100, 101–102, pp. 99–132 and pp. 123–135.
9. Division de la Coordination Economique et du Plan, *Plan Quinquennal 1968–72*, 4 Vols., Rabat, 1968.
10. Y. Lancelot, *Trois Années d'Aide Technique à la Promotion Nationale*, SCET-Coopération, Rabat, 1966.
11. J. Chitty, 'Cost-Benefit Evaluations of DERRO Fruit Tree Plantings in Al Hoceima Province', International Voluntary Service Report, June 1969 (mimeographed).
12. J.A. Seagraves, 'More on the Social Rate of Discount', *Quarterly Journal of Economics*, Vol. 84, No. 3, August 1970, pp. 430–450.
13. R.C. Brown, E.G. Altouney, E.A. Podesta and E. Thor, *Analysis of Selected Programs for Moroccan Agricultural Development*, Stanford Research Institute, 1967.
14. A.A. Belal, *L'Investissement au Maroc (1912–1964) et ses Enseignements au Matière de Développement Economique*, Paris, 1968.
15. Ministère de l'Agriculture et de la Réforme Agraire, *Les Potentialités Naturelles et la Mise en Valeur Actuelle de la Plaine du Haouz*, Marrakesh, 1968.
16. E. Mennesson, 'Ksour du Tafilalt', *Revue de Géographie du Maroc*, No. 8, 1965, pp. 87–91.
17. S. Ben Bachir, *L'Administration Locale du Maroc*, Casablanca, 1969.
18. G. Ardant, 'A Plan for Full Employment in the Developing Countries', *International Labour Review*, Vol. 88, No. 1, July 1963, pp. 15–51.
   J.P. Arles, 'Manpower Mobilization and Economic Growth: An Assessment of Moroccan and Tunisian Experience', *International Labour Review*, Vol. 94, No. 1, July 1966, pp. 1–25.
19. F. Oualalou, *L'Assistance Etrangère Face au Développement Economique du Maroc*, Casablanca, 1969.

211